Ancient Roots and Modern Meanings

ANCIENT ROOTS

and

MODERN

MEANINGS:

A Contemporary

Reader in Jewish

Identity

Jerry V. Diller

Bloch Publishing Company, New York

Library of Congress Catalog Number: 77-99196
ISBN 0-8197-0457-1

Manufactured in the United States of America

Contents

ACKNOWLEDGEMENTS

The editor gratefully acknowledges the following permissions to reprint material:

The Inner World of the Polish Jew by Abraham J. Heschel: Reprinted by permission of Sylvia Heschel and Schocken Books Inc. from *Polish Jews* by Roman Vishniac. Introductory Essay by Abraham Joshua Heschel. Copyright 1947 by Schocken Books Inc. Copyright renewed 1975 by Sylvia Heschel and H. Susannah Heschel.

Brooklyn's Hasidim by Jerome R. Mintz: Reprinted by permission, from *Natural History* Magazine, January, 1977. Copyright The American Museum of Natural History, 1977.

The Mystical Element in Judaism by Abraham J. Heschel: In *The Jews: Their History, Culture, and Religion,* 4th Edition edited by Louis Finkelstein. Copyright 1949, 1955, 1960, 1971 by Louis Finkelstein. By permission of Harper & Row, Publishers, Inc.

Judaism and Personal Growth by Dov Peretz Elkins: Reprinted by permission of the Author. Copyright 1977 by Dov Peretz Elkins.

Judaism and History: Historical Events and Religious Change by

Irving Greenberg: Reprinted by permission of Spertus College Press, Chicago, Illinois, from the *Solomon Goldman Lectures: Perspectives in Judaica.*

The Sabbath by Erich Fromm: From *You Shall Be As Gods* by Erich Fromm. Copyright 1966 by Erich Fromm. Reprinted by permission of Holt, Rinehard and Winston, Publishers.

Symposium on Jewish Belief by Richard L. Rubenstein: Reprinted from *Commentary,* by permission; copyright 1966 by the American Jewish Committee.

The Making of a Jewish Politics by Arthur I. Waskow: Reprinted by permission of the Author. Copyright 1977 by Arthur I. Waskow.

On Being a Religious Jewish Woman by Rita M. Gross: Reprinted by special arrangement with the publisher of *Anima,* Chambersburg, Pennsylvania. Copyright 1974 by Conococheague Associates, Inc.

Special acknowledgement is made to those authors who wrote articles especially for the present volume and who generously granted permission for reprinting. A final thanks must be extended to Betsy Jay, Gilbert Davis and Edward Diller for helpful suggestions and editorial work.

*For Carole, my wife, who has been
so supportive and understanding;
And for Rebecca, our daughter,
who will hopefully grow up with
an awareness of and pride in
her heritage.*

A PERSONAL PREFACE

This book is the reflection and outgrowth of a personal search. For me it symbolizes the culmination of a long and at times painful re-discovery, the re-discovery of a part of me too long hidden and too often denied—my own Jewishness. Initially it was conceived as a text on Jewish identity, intended both to stimulate those interested in developing a more complete understanding of what it means to be a Jew in America today and to provide a model for relating to Jewishness with greater awareness, creativity and personal relevancy. Upon completion, however, it became clear that it had potential relevancy to other minorities and, indeed, anyone concerned with the task of finding answers to personal identity problems.

The re-discovery of my own Jewishness and the realization of its impact upon my life has served a very important psychological function within me. It has acted as an organizing principle, as a mechanism for integrating the various threads and diverse elements of my personality and experience. In the process of re-discovering this side of my being, in pulling together the morass of Jewish-related images and experiences from my childhood, adolescence and adulthood, I have also found a sense of comfort, belonging and identity. These experiences have been fundamental to my own evolution. By sharing them here I can, I hope, further illuminate the understanding of this self-discovery process and how it affects the Jew.

The need to know and understand was kindled early in me. As a result, the identity questions of—Who am I? Where do I belong? How shall I live my life? What shall I do with it?—came to loom particularly large within my consciousness, especially during adolescence and early adulthood. More accurately, they were an obsession, an all-consuming passion which demanded both answers and my full attention. I could never rid myself of these thoughts and concerns. Every project I undertook, every idea I pursued, had to bear some relationship to my search or it was dropped quickly. As soon as I realized some endeavor no longer held promise as a potential answer, I lost interest, became bored, and went on to something new. In short, I spent much of my youth flailing about for answers, a prisoner of a drive towards meaning which I did not understand at the time.

Only later did I realize that this fervor for seeking a place in the world was not merely a personal peculiarity, but rather something intimately bound up with the eventual end-point of my search. The intensity, I later discovered, was a psychological legacy of my Jewish past, a product of the high value placed on intellectual curiosity within Judaism, as well as the personality penchant for survival which has infused the Jewish lifestyle for thousands of years. Without these characteristics, the Jew could not have sustained his incessant need to wander homeward. As a descendent of that heritage, I too was driven by them. The repeated dissatisfaction and restlessness stemmed from an intuitive sense emanating from deep within me. Perhaps a part of me knew where the answers were to be found and would not allow me to rest until I had reached that source. The signs were clear, but I did not recognize their meaning for many years.

The rejection of my Jewish past seemed almost a natural consequence of growing up. In spite of the fact that my early years were spent in a moderately religious and culturally-infused home, I slowly slipped away from my Jewish roots. The reason was not so much the content of those early experiences, but rather the quality. My memories of that world are mainly joyless and uneventful, an endless succession of unexplained rules, illogical demands, and invocations of the wrath of the "All Mighty" in order to get me to behave properly. The cultural remnants I retained from it were few —a smattering of Yiddish and the fragmented memories of being chased out of a dilapidated and rundown Galitzianer "shul" by grisled old men, and a few years later fighting a schoolmate who called me a "dirty Jew." All resulted in an indifference to a world which I did not understand and which no one took the time to explain.

My turning away was not met with hysterical protests or emotional scenes as is so often the case; it just happened. The silence of those around me reflected neither a lack of caring for me nor a de-valuing of those things Jewish, but rather a belief in the inevitability of assimilation. For my part, I experienced a sense of relief and freedom, as if a millstone, an impediment to my open experiencing of the world, had been removed. The superstition, blind faith and dogma with which I equated Judaism had no place in my adolescent understanding of how one should relate to the world. As was typical of my generation, I traded family and cultural ties for independence, and religion and faith for intellectual concerns and rationality. Having stripped away the past, I felt ready to commence the journey toward self-definition. Self-discovery, I believed, could only begin anew, having washed away the old.

In the years that followed I pursued many avenues as potential sources of fulfillment. I earned a Ph.D. in psychology; became a college teacher; involved myself in psychotherapy and encounter group work; became a social activist; experimented with drugs and the Hippy lifestyle; and studied and practiced various forms of Eastern disciplines. Although I learned much from each, none by itself held any lasting satisfaction or fulfillment. Each seemed slightly hollow and incomplete, incapable of totally satisfying my identity needs. And never, during that entire period, did I give even the slightest thought to my own cultural heritage as a potential end-point to my search. Later the reasons for this became painfully clear.

The impetus to re-explore and re-discover my Jewishness came while visiting a favorite uncle. During my visit, I learned that he had of late become exceedingly interested in his own Jewish past. As a result, he had joined a synagogue and begun to read various interpreters of the Jewish tradition, men like Martin Buber and Elie Wiesel. I was shocked. My uncle was a college professor, an intellectual, a scholar. He had always stood apart in my mind, had always been different from my other relatives. He too, I felt, had transcended a limiting past and had spent his life openly and rationally interacting with his world. Why would such a man suddenly turn to Judaism or to any religion for that matter?

We talked, and he told me of his growing concern about how to raise his children. He had realized how unfair it would be to cut them off from a birthright which they might find valuable later in life. The decision to reject their Jewishness should be theirs, not his. By not exposing them to the Jewish experience early in life, he was indirectly making the choice for them. More personally, as he grew older he realized more and more that something was missing from his life, that some dimension was lacking. He found himself thinking of the world of his childhood with greater frequency, of the teeming and bustling world of the Jewish ghetto with its pushcarts, animated Yiddish and close sense of family and neighborhood. In these nostalgic memories he sensed the presence of something meaningful, something which filled the void in his present world. For these reasons, he was seeking to re-establish contact with his Jewish past.

The shock and confusion which my uncle's disclosure set off in me remained long after our visit had ended. I found myself thinking of it repeatedly, trying to make sense out of the great dissonance which existed for me between my old image of him and his new-found interest. Finally, several months later I decided to pick up a few of the books he had suggested and see for myself what he found in them. With this, the process of re-discovery began.

The ensuing years of exploration brought forth within me a flood of insights, discoveries, self-realizations and strong emotional reactions. These experiences led the way to a new appreciation of what it meant for me to be a Jew. They helped me to bring out, accentuate and truly value that side of my being.

The sense of shock I had experienced with my uncle was to become a frequent visitor as I sought to learn more about my Jewish past. I was surprised to meet rabbis who did not fit into old stereotypes, and men and women who could verbalize their beliefs in terms I could understand, people who made the Jewish lifestyle and experience come alive for me. I was surprised to discover the breadth and richness of Jewish culture and how much was available within my own heritage.

I was struck by the modern relevancy of so many Jewish ideas, thinkers and movements, some hundreds and thousands of years old. Each seemed to address itself to one of the issues which concern us today. The parallels between these and the various avenues I had earlier explored were striking. In Martin Buber I found a thinker whose concerns for the quality of human relationships and the need for community clearly pre-dated today's Human Potential Movement in psychology and the youth counter-culture of the late 1960's. In Hasidic Judaism I discovered a style of life which closely resembled that stressed and valued in Eastern philosophy. Its here-and-now focus, its oral tradition of folklore and parable, its sanctification of the simple life and its non-judgmental character were strikingly reminiscent of Zen Buddhism. And within the Kaballah, the Jewish mystical text, I found a system of occult and esoteric knowledge as rich and complex as any developed throughout the history of man.

Approximately a year into my exploration, a single event occurred which brought to awareness a previously unsuspected reaction to my own Jewishness, unconscious feelings which for many years had been actively at work within me. One morning, while walking across campus, I looked down at the bundle of books I was carrying and saw on top a book entitled *The American Jew.* Unconsciously, I reached down with the other hand and turned it over so that the word "Jew" could not be seen. Seconds later I realized what I had done. Was I really that ashamed of being a Jew? Slowly my confusion turned into anger: anger at myself for hiding and being ashamed of what I was, and anger at a society which would allow, and even encourage, this to happen. For a moment I truly experienced the hatred and resentment which was so much a part of the lives of my Black and Chicano friends. For the first time, I understood the fascination and attraction their liberation movements had always held for me.

From this event, a new gestalt of understanding emerged. I had learned to feel ashamed of, to degrade and discount my own heritage. As a result of this awareness many of my past reactions began to make sense: why I had repeatedly been surprised and shocked at the richness of the Jewish experience; why I had never considered Judaism as a potential source of answers to my existential searchings; and why I had been so repelled when my uncle showed an interest in his Jewish past. This experience was one of the most powerful in my life.

In the fiction of Phillip Roth, an author often maligned by his own Jewish community for some of his honest and human portraits of the American Jew, I discovered yet another little-realized aspect of my Jewishness—a conflicting allegiance to two different cultures and ways of life. I felt particularly touched and at one with the hero of his short story "Eli the Fanatic." Eli is a lawyer who is given the task of modernizing several Old World Jews recently relocated in his suburban community. It is feared that their immigrant appearance and actions will offend the Gentile community and disrupt the hard-won positive relationship between the Jews and their neighbors. After Eli succeeds in getting one of the old Jews to trade his dirty and worn gabardines for a more modern business suit, something snaps within the lawyer. He becomes obsessed with the old clothes and eventually feels compelled to put them on. So dressed, he wanders about suburbia dazed and confused, ending up at the maternity ward of the local hospital, where he gazes at his new-born child through the glass of the nursery. In Eli's conflict I saw many of my own symbolically echoed: the value I place on group identity, exclusiveness and pride versus that of universal humanism; my deep feelings of sympathy for the State of Israel and my revulsion at its militancy; my desire to remain open and learn from those different from me versus my periodic need to surround myself with fellow Jews.

As I explored the long history of the Jews, I found my very sense of personal existence and place in time being radically altered. I discovered an old and fascinating world which took hold of me and transported me back into time. I became aware of the history of inhumane persecution, of the rich folklore and culture of the Eastern European shtetl and its Yiddish language and literature, of the mysterious religious cults, of the zealous Zionists and of the peculiar, but strong, temperament of a people who remained together and survived thousands of years of homeless wandering. Seeing myself symbolically extended so far back into time and becoming a part of such a wide array of movements, experiences and events were both sources of great comfort and of disorientation. I had never before thought of my roots extending further back in time than two generations, beyond grandparents and great-grandparents I barely remembered.

While I was travelling in Europe, this sense of timelessness and oneness with my past became a permanent part of me. I sat in the oldest synagogue in Europe on Yom Kippur eve and watched hundreds of candles project strange and eerie shadows on an ancient pulpit and congregation. Leaving the sanctuary and the walled courtyard which protected it, I could not help but shudder when I thought of the purpose of those gates and walls. I grew nervous and edgy whenever I rode trains through Germany. I could not relax until we crossed the border into Denmark, where I somehow sensed a friendliness and safety. I experienced a strange pride and expansiveness as I entered an art museum in Nice dedicated solely to the work of a single Jew—Marc Chagall. And I visited Dachau and was suffocated by its restored barracks, barbed-wire, manicured landscape and smell of ashes. As I watched a group of Italian tourists descend upon it like Disneyland, littering and posing for pictures in front of the ovens, I knew deep within me that it could all happen again. It was then I experienced my Jewishness with an intensity and certainty I had never known before.

The most difficulty I encountered in my search was in the religious and spiritual side of my Jewishness. It was not an easy task to put aside long-held intellectual and rational prejudices and allow myself to openly experience the wonder and mystery of the various rituals and practices. My reaction to participating in such religious experiences was embarrassment. What could be more irrational than attending services I did not understand or observing rituals and holidays I did not believe in? I was reminded of old memories from childhood and adolescent years, memories of being expected to go through the motions of prayer and observance without understanding why.

With the discovery of a new and more satisfying understanding and perspective on the Jewish religious experience, this discomfort was relieved and I found it easier to put my doubting into neutral. The source of this re-interpretation was my work as a psychologist and my interest in methods of promoting mental health. To me, this means discovering experiences and practices which help individuals meet their many psychological needs, live more fulfilling lives and grow towards their potential. I put aside my suspicion and began to look at the religious practices in light of these mental health dimensions. What I found was a great psychological wisdom and function inherent in the various aspects of Jewish ritual and religious practice. In the practices revolving around death, I discovered a sophisticated and complex method of facilitating and bringing to completion the grieving process; in the celebration of the Sabbath a weekly opportunity for turning inward, contemplation, re-establishing contact with one's inner existence and rejuvenating the self; and in the different holidays and celebrations various existential issues and concerns which must be periodically focused upon and remembered. It was as if they had been intentionally designed to promote the existential satisfaction and mental health of those who would follow them.

I came away from this realization humbled. I had been presumptuous enough to doubt a tradition thousands of years old, and in response it had answered me in terms relevant to my own experiences and values. I could not help but wonder how many others over countless centuries had stood in a similar spot and expressed similar doubts. Did they too receive an equally personal and relevant message, tailored to their own understanding and interpretation of the world?

The experiences I have related here are very personal and obviously cannot be taken as a model for another's search. They are offered rather as a stimulus, as an example that meaningful re-interpretation and re-discovery of one's past is a possibility. My own search took me back to my Jewishness. The final destination at which others will find themselves depends solely on their own unique roots and experiences.

It is my growing sense that many individuals, including other Jews, having found little in the way of substantive psychological satisfaction outside of their own heritages, are ready to take a new look at them. I find this dissatisfaction among students flocking to my courses on Jewish identity and other topics of self-discovery, and among those who seek out the privacy of my office to ask help in dealing with personal confusion and aimlessness. Also I find this sense of dissatisfaction among my colleagues, who like myself long ago rejected their own heritages. Such individuals are standing on the brink of initiating their own searches. All that is lacking in an impetus, a justification and means of beginning. It is in the hope of providing that push that this book is written.

Jewish Identity: Its Psychology, Re-Discovery and Modern Meaning

Harken to Me, ye that
follow after righteousness,
Ye that seek the Lord;
(And ye that seek yourselves;)
Look unto the rock whence
ye were hewn,
And to the hole of the pit
whence ye were digged.

(Isaiah LI, 1)

Jewish Identity—Its Psychology

Identity is both an experience and a process of discovery. As an experience it entails a sense of inner stability, harmony, meaningfulness, and certainty in one's own beliefs and actions. Allen Wheelis describes this aspect of identity as follows:

> Identity is a coherent sense of self. It depends upon the awareness that one's endeavors and one's life make sense, that they are meaningful in the context in which life is lived. It depends also upon stable values, and upon the conviction that one's actions and values are harmoniously related: It is a sense of wholeness, of integration, of knowing what is right and what is wrong and of being able to choose. (p. 19)

When this sense exists within the person, it serves as a stable and comforting base from which to reach out and relate to the external world.

Experientially, Jewish identity is the sense of pride, belonging, and personal meaning a Jew derives from the fact of his own Jewishness. It provides him with a valuable source of self-definition, a referent or anchor point for beginning a systematic understanding of his own psychology and that of his times. Historically, it has functioned as a glue, cementing together a cultural group repeatedly challenged to survive in the face of great adversity. Without a strong sense of identity as a source of strength and vitality, the Jewish people could not have survived the thousands of years of persecution and wandering which make up its history.

While the experience of identity is similar for all people, the process by which it is reached is not. It is, in fact, uniquely individual. Self-discovery or discovering one's identity is a process of creating meaning, of finding a personal relevancy and meaningfulness in the experiences of one's life. As such, it requires the person to draw upon his own individual sources. Each person has his own unique background, experiences, valuing process, and style of understanding and relating to the world. It is out of these that a sense of identity evolves.

The necessity of looking inward for one's identity is particularly well captured by Martin Buber in one of his Hasidic Tales.

Rabbi Bunam used to tell young men who came to him for the first time the story of Rabbi Eizik, son of Rabbi Yekel of Krakow. After many years of great poverty which had never shaken his faith in God, he dreamed someone bade him look for a treasure in Prague, under the bridge which leads to the king's palace. When the dream recurred a third time, Rabbi Eizik prepared for a journey and set out for Prague. But the bridge was guarded day and night and he did not dare to start digging. Nevertheless, he went to the bridge every morning and kept walking around it until evening. Finally the captain of the guards, who had been watching him, asked in a kindly way whether he was looking for something or waiting for somebody. Rabbi Eizik told him of the dream which had brought him here from a faraway country. The captain laughed: "And so to please the dream, you poor fellow wore out your shoes to come here! As for having faith in dreams, if I had had it, I should have had to get going when a dream told me to go to Krakow and dig for treasure under the stove in the room of a Jew—Eizik, son of Yekel, that was the name! Eizik, son of Yekel! I can just imagine what it would be like, how I should have to try every house over there, where one half of the Jews are named Eizik and the other Yekel!" And he laughed again. Rabbi Eizik bowed, traveled home, dug up the treasure from under the stove, and built the House of Prayer which is called "Reb Eizik Reb Yekel's Shul."

"Take this story to heart," Rabbi Bunam used to add," and make what it says your own: There is something you cannot find anywhere in the world, not even at the zaddik's, and there is, nevertheless, a place where you can find it."

For the Jew the identity search, the search for existential treasure, must begin with his own Jewishness. He must at some point in his quest come to grips with his cultural past. He must discover what it means for him to be a Jew and the impact that his Jewishness has had upon him.

It is important to realize that a strong sense of Jewish identity is not the automatic consequence of being born into a Jewish home and community. It is not the guaranteed birthright of every Jew. Rather, it must develop within the child, or perhaps later in life, as a result of fulfilling and positive experiences with the Jewish tradition.

Finding meaning in one's Jewishness is a very personal and individual process. For some it occurs easily and naturally. For others it is a difficult and long-term struggle. And for a few, it never occurs, with their Jewishness remaining a source of agitation and frustration throughout life.

*

To truly understand the Jew and his search for identity, one must become aware of a number of interlocking psychological factors, each in itself capable of shaping, directing, and, in some cases, distorting his quest. One must understand the chaotic nature of our times and the particular problems that they pose for anyone seeking self-discovery, Jew and non-Jew alike. One must understand the unique psychology of the minority group member growing up in a majority culture and how he may unconsciously internalize its values, learn to despise himself and his heritage, and, as a consequence, turn away from his own beginnings. One must understand the kind of Judaism which is offered to many Jews today, a diluted and compromised life-style which is unable to satisfy their idealistic and critical demands. And one must understand, finally, the drive towards worldliness and rationality which is so often a critical aspect of the Jew's psychological make-up. Only through an appreciation of these factors can one begin to discern and discover the direction that must be taken in order for the Jew to find a satisfying, meaningful, and fulfilling identity within his own heritage.

*

The young person growing up in America today finds himself confronted with a psychologically troubled and unstable world. Everything is changing. Everything is in flux, even the most basic dimensions of our culture. The affluent lifestyle which has characterized American society for the past two decades is threatened by the prediction of economic doom. The integrity of our entire political system and leaders, that of the entire established order, is being called into question. Even technology and its underlying consciousness of rationality—the ethic in whose name so many turned their backs on religion, the family, and tradition—is under suspicion.

Alvin Toffler believes modern man suffers from a malady which he calls "future shock."

Future shock is a dizzying disorientation brought on by the premature arrival of the future. It may well be the most important disease of tomorrow . . . Unless intelligent steps are taken to combat it, millions of human beings will find themselves increasingly disoriented, progressively in-competent to deal rationally with their environments. The malaise, mass neurosis, irrationality, and free-floating vio-lence already apparent in contemporary life are merely a foretaste of what may lie ahead unless we come to under-stand and treat this disease.

Future shock is a time phenomenon, a product of greatly accelerated rate of change in society. It arises from the superimposition of a new culture on an old one. It is cul-ture shock in one's own society.

Take an individual out of his own culture and set him down suddenly in an environment sharply different from his own, with a different set of cues to react to ... then cut him off from any hope of retreat to a more familiar social landscape ... If this new culture is itself in constant tur-moil, and if, even worse, its values are incessantly chang-ing, the sense of disorientation will be still further intensified.

This is the prospect that man now faces. Change is ava-lanching upon our heads and most people are grotesquely unprepared to cope with it. (pp. 11-12)

In the midst of this changing and chaotic world the young person must search for his identity. The unstable social cli-mate makes the task doubly difficult. First, there is a particu-larly urgent and pressing need to find one's self in such times. Without a sense of identity and the inner stability and peace it affords, the young person may find it difficult to adequately deal with and survive in his world. Sensing this urgency, he may not be selective enough in choosing an appropriate source to explore, wasting valuable time and energy trying to relate to ones which fit neither his needs nor tempera-ment. Or he may be drawn to those avenues which promise instant and immediate results but little permanence, to drugs or one of the many false gurus and movements which seem to arise in troubled times to prey on the hopes of young

xxxii   Ancient Roots and Modern Meanings

people. In either case, the results may be greater confusion rather than less.

Second, such times are typified by a limiting of the potential identity sources available. Old ways, methods and institutions rapidly lose their meaning and become hollow and grotesque caricatures of what they once were. In a culture not experiencing an identity crisis itself, where laws and traditions are held sacred and diligently followed, the child develops a sense of identity through day-to-day contact with a stable and harmonious social environment. He is continually made aware of the meaningfulness of the cultural symbols which surround him, and learns to value them and to experience them as his own. On the other hand, in a "future shocked" world the young person cannot depend upon a socialization process to provide him with a sense of identity. All that remain are starting points and vague glimpses of roots which once provided other generations with meaning.

In such a world the identity quest must be an individual one. The young person may look in many directions for answers: to other times, to other places, to other philosophical systems and lifestyles. But in the end, it is up to him alone to contruct a meaningful understanding of himself and his world. He must choose those cultural remnants which may be of value to him; he must infuse them with a personal relevancy; and he must shape them into a coherent whole which can provide the stability and direction he craves.

*

Against this background, the Jew finds himself in a particularly unique, although paradoxical, position. He has at his disposal a valuable source of potential answers in the form of his own Jewishness, but is, at the same time, pushed away from it by additional forces which themselves are bound up with that heritage.

Three psychological processes are of primary importance

in understanding the tendency of the Jew to turn away from his heritage. The first is the potential self-hatred which is the legacy of every member of a minority group, the Jew included. The second is the quality and nature of Judaism as it is practiced in much of America today. The third is the Jew's quest for worldliness and a rational understanding of the world around him. Together these factors profoundly affect the direction of the Jewish youth's search for identity, pushing him away from his own roots and traditions.

Every member of a minority group living within a majority culture is potentially susceptible to the psychological dynamics of self-hatred. Social psychologist Kurt Lewin has explored and shed considerable light upon this process. According to Lewin "negative chauvinism," a term used to denote an individual's turning against his own ethnicity, can best be understood as a consequence of conflicting group loyalties. The American Jew, the subject of Lewin's extensive analysis, is born into the midst of two competing cultures: that of his own Jewish heritage and that of the majority gentile community. Since the two typically prescribe different and frequently opposed modes of behavior and value systems, the child from early in life is placed in a conflict situation. He is repeatedly forced to choose one over the other. This pressure comes from both sides: his parents and Jewish community demanding allegiance in exchange for acceptance, belonging and nurturance; the gentile world offering escape from a limited lifestyle, greater freedom and opportunity and the status and rewards of society's most highly privileged group.

In a totally free-access situation the individual will be drawn toward that group which offers the most potential reward, the highest probability of meeting personal needs. According to Lewin:

> Under "free" conditions . . . a group will contain only those members for whom the positive forces are stronger than the negative . . . However . . . the forces towards and away

xxxiv Ancient Roots and Modern Meanings

from the group are not always an expression of the person's own needs. They may be imposed upon the individual by some external power . . . An individual may be forced against his will to stay inside a group he would like to leave, or he may be kept outside a group he would like to join. (p. 191)

Many Jews, young and old alike, find themselves in this position, preferring to leave behind their Jewish past and to assimilate into the Gentile world. Often, however, the majority group will block an individual's entrance into the mainstream culture, labelling him as different and therefore unacceptable. The result of such conflicting situations on the individual is typically marginality, frustration and eventually negative chauvinism and self-hatred. As Lewin points out:

A person for whom the balance is negative will move as far away from the center of Jewish life as the outside majority permits. He will stay on this barrier and be in a constant state of frustration . . . Such frustration leads to an all-around state of high tension with a generalized tendency to aggression. The aggression should, logically, be directed against the majority, which is what hinders the minority member from leaving his group. However, the majority has . . . higher status . . . [and] is much too powerful to be attacked . . . Under these conditions, aggression is likely to be turned against one's own group or against one's self. (p. 191)

This hatred of oneself and one's Jewishness is further reinforced by a second psychological dynamic. It is a frequent psychological occurrence that the upwardly mobile individual will identify with and internalize the values and ideas of the majority culture. Lewin goes on:

In the case of the underprivileged group it means that their opinions about themselves are greatly influenced by the low esteem the majority has for them. This . . . heightens the tendency of the Jew with a negative balance to cut himself loose from things Jewish. The more typically Jew-

ish people are, or the more typically Jewish a cultural
symbol or behavior pattern is, the more distasteful they
will appear to this person. Being unable to cut himself
entirely loose from his Jewish connections and his Jewish
past, the hatred turns upon himself. (p. 194)

It would be inaccurate to say that this self-hatred and negative chauvinism is present in the psychological make-up of
every Jew. There are those who are born into a world so
totally traditional and isolated from the American mainstream that conflicting lifestyles never become an issue.
However, such individuals are more the exception than the
rule. Most American Jews, raised in a bi-cultural environment, possess some modicum of these two traits. Because of
their self-destructive nature, they usually operate unconsciously. He is most often unaware of their presence and
their subtle manifestations: the discomfort and shame for
things Jewish; the devaluing of and looking past Jewish
mores, history and values; and the strong preference for ways
and lifestyles which are distinctly non-Jewish. Even in their
most innocuous forms, these motives are capable of affecting
behavior, of pushing the Jew to acts and attitudes which deny
and negate a basic and immutable part of himself.

Negative chauvinism and self-hatred develop early in life,
when the child first looks beyond his own familiar world,
desiring to understand, relate to and become a part of all he
sees. His curiosity does not differentiate between Jewish and
non-Jewish; everything is open to inquiry and exploration.
That he is barred from and denied access to some of what he
finds makes little sense to his young mind. He can understand neither the attitude of his parents nor that of the outside world. The only way that he can possibly interpret these
rebuffs is personally, that something about him is responsible. Slowly, he will discover that it is his Jewishness and,
subconsciously, retain this awareness throughout life. For the
Jewish adolescent this memory and awareness may serve to
steer him away from his own Jewishness as a potential source
of answers.

*

If the young Jew is not diverted from his Jewishness by the presence of negative chauvinism, he may be turned away by the very nature of the Judaism which he finds offered to him in many communities in America today. Taking this watered-down and assimilated brand of Judaism as the sum total of what his heritage has to offer him, he may well turn away and look elsewhere, never again to give his own roots and ancestry a second thought.

The beginnings of the failure of much of American Judaism can be traced back to the immigrant Jew and his desires to both leave behind the vehement anti-Semitism of the *shtetls* and towns of Eastern and Central Europe and to become a "good citizen" in the new land which held so much promise for him and his family. Although these desires were certainly understandable and laudable, his attempts to satisfy them were to have significant consequences for himself and his heirs. To fulfill these hopes, he would radically re-shape and diminish the rich Judaism of his ancestors, trading it for a modernized version based on the affluence and material comfort of his new land. He put his faith in two beliefs which turned out in retrospect to be only unfulfilled myths.

The first was that the anti-Semitism of which he had been so aware in the "Old Country" could be avoided if only he would "Americanize," would take on the outward trappings of the majority culture and become far less recognizable as a distinct minority. If he could not be identified, he would not be persecuted. And in this hope he began the task of modernizing himself, his religion, his community and his culture.

Meir Kahane, founder of the Jewish Defense League, accurately, although rhetorically, describes this occurrence:

From his insecurity and fears, from his obsession with those who hated him and his frantic need to escape that hate, the Jew grew to build for himself a brave new world standing on all the above-named foundations. [The Melting Pot, Education, Liberalism, Equality, Democracy, Secularism, Materialism, Love, Public Relations, Respectability and Internationalism] He begat leaders who took an oath to these principles. He chose rabbis who would swear fealty to them. And as the years passed, a Jewish Establishment grew up, strong, fat, and entrenched, that worshipped hourly at the alter of Melt and that led its flock into green pastures. Yea, though we walked through the Valley of Exile, we had no need of fear, for our Establishment assured us that all was well. If only we melted and if only our Judaism was properly modified and if only our Jewishness was properly muted we would be safe and secure and would dwell in the House of America forevermore. (p. 72)

The second myth revolved around the belief that by assimilating he would only be trading one vital culture for another. He did not, at the time, realize the bankruptcy and chaos of the American culture itself, that he was exchanging a total culture and lifestyle for a behavioral ethic, affluence, which had little that was uniquely cultural to back it up.

As the Jew became more and more "modernized" and "Americanized" his Jewishness slowly changed character. According to James A. Sleeper, it eventually lost its "driving moral force" and its status as the "source of a way of life," becoming instead "an increasingly dispensable appendage of middle class culture."

This change occurred slowly and imperceptibly. But the specifics did not really matter, for the Jew was too busy enjoying the bounties of his new land to notice. Sleeper goes on:

There was no time to evaluate and criticize a society which promised physical security and material success to anyone, regardless of his religion. Every day in every way the world was getting better; as American-born Jewish children were socialized into the general culture through the public schools and the business world, the ghetto community quietly dissolved. (p. 13)

Remaining ever true to the two myths described above, the assimilating Jew continued on with his work, sincerely trying to integrate what he saw as the best of two worlds.

Jewish suburbanites promptly and masterfully tailored an almost forgotten religion to the norms and aesthetics of middle class culture. Houses of worship were made bigger and more modern than everyone else's. "Americanized" rabbis were to be hired by highly discriminating synagogue boards to bless their congregants' achievements, to consecrate the new way of life, to give time-honored meaning and legitimacy to puttering, large lawns, and automobiles, and to present Judaism "properly" to benevolent ministers and curious neighbors (p. 14)

In the name of a better and less persecuted life, many Jews traded in the Jewishness of their past and replaced it with a diluted and less vital, although more acceptable, successor. One legacy of this exchange was the alienation of their children. The new lifestyle and the type of Jewish experience it embodied offered little in the way of substance to the young. To them, this Judaism appeared as just another instance of the decaying American lifestyle of which they were becoming more and more critical. There was little in it to satisfy their idealistic and demanding identity needs. And so they turned away.

*

A third and final force pushing the Jew toward assimilation is his frequent desire for worldliness. The strange world existing outside of his own environment and social group has for centuries attracted his attention and piqued his curiosity. In it he sees ideas and practices which point up the limited nature of his own culture. If he desires to escape the restric-

tive demands and in-groupness of his Jewish family and community, he may well project his hopes for a more fulfilling
lifestyle upon this external screen. In this world of the unfamiliar he sees a salvation which he believes will make him
more complete and provide a more satisfying way of life.
Escape into worldliness does give the individual an immediate sense of relief and freedom, an opening up of new possibilities and opportunities. The consequences are not
one-sided, however, for worldliness extracts an equally negative toll of its own, demanding ultimately that the person
reject his own past. Socialization into this new world requires
the Jew to internalize a perspective that will make him question and eventually deny and negate his Jewishness.

Paradoxically enough, the very cultural and religious
mechanisms which have evolved to insure survival of the
Jewish group contain the potential seeds of their own destruction. Over the past five thousand years Judaism has developed out of necessity an all-encompassing complex of
beliefs, rituals and practices aimed at promoting group survival. One function of these mechanisms is to keep the individual within the group. Thus, the mutual dependency
between parent and child fostered within the family, the
strict rules of observance such as *Kashrut* and the powerful
taboo against intermarriage, can be seen as examples of
methods of retaining the individual Jew within the group and
insuring his loyalty and its survival.

Although these psychological elements are effective in
perpetuating the life of the group, they often have an unin-
tended and detrimental effect upon the individual. The person may experience these various practices and, as a result,
his Jewishness as suffocating, stifling and limiting, and desire
to escape from it. When one combines this sense of psychological constriction with the high value Jewish culture places
on learning and seeking truth, the lure of "forbidden fruit"
becomes doubly powerful. It is out of this interplay that the
attraction of worldliness is born.

In the past hundred years worldliness for the Jew has been synonymous with scientific rationalism. What he found in the intellectual circles beyond the ghetto was a glorification of the scientific process and its rational approach to understanding the world. The Jew was particularly taken with the social movements which grew out of this perspective. In Socialism, Communism, Zionism, psychology and democracy and equalitarianism he found movements worthy of his allegiance and dedication. Each promised both an end to his immediate suffering and the widespread institution of a social order which would embody the high ethical standards valued within Jewish tradition. Bernard C. Rosen describes the evolution of scientific rationalism as follows:

> In the ghetto or shtetl, the Jew had been relatively isolated from the influence of scientific rationalism. The Jewish school, which was for most East European Jews the only kind of school they attended, was primarily an institution for the transmittal of traditional religious learning and values; science played no role in the curriculum. Not until the Jew was permitted to move freely in the general society—in Western Europe as early as the eighteenth century, but not until the twentieth century for Eastern Europe—did he feel the full impact of scientific rationalism. This influence has been especially strong in American society, where the virtues of modern science are daily extolled in the schools and in the mass media of communication. (pp. 340-341)

Underlying all expressions of scientific rationalism is the valuing of a single epistemology and the belief that man can meaningfully relate to his existence and experience only through logical-rational understanding. To truly know his world the person must find underlying causes and purposes within it, must be able to break it down into more basic substances and patterns, and must—in the case of human behavior—project logical motives and intentions into individual acts. The rationalist is, as a consequence, highly suspect of emotion, intuition and spiritualism—the non-rational modes of relating to reality. They are in his view invalid and inferior ways of experiencing, akin to superstition and blind stupidity.

Religion and religious practices, being based primarily on faith and custom rather than logical analysis, have received a majority of the brunt of the scientist's intolerance for non-rational ways of understanding. In their widespread popularity over time, he sees the source of all major world problems, be they personal, interpersonal or societal. His solution would include both a widespread adoption of rationality among decision-makers and lay people alike and the demise of all non-rational institutions, especially that of religion.

In adopting the rational perspective, it becomes incumbent upon the Jew to question the ritual and practices of his own past, to demand that he be shown their rational bases and purposes. As rationality becomes a dominant theme in the life of the individual, he finds it more and more difficult to behave in ways or to adopt practices which lack an obvious rational purpose.

In the ghettos of Europe and America the Jew's demand for a rational explanation was met with only shrugs, for those he challenged had never before been asked to justify their religion. Their belief was and always had been based on faith and tradition, not logical argument. They could only stand before him mute, aware of his distress but unable to even grasp the meaning of his question. The worldly Jew read this silence as a confirmation of his suspicions and found it easy to generalize his contempt for ritual to all aspects of Judaism.

In today's world the picture is even more one-sided. Scientific rationalism is the dominant worldview, and religion is and has been significantly on the decline. Where Judaism has thrived, it has been most typically as a social and cultural phenomenon, not a religious one. In these spheres questions regarding the purpose of Jewish religious practices are seldom even asked.

Jewish Identity—Its Re-discovery

The Jew will not return home until the effects of these three forces—this negative chauvinism, this diluted brand of Judaism and this penchant for worldliness and rationality—are overcome. As long as he believes that he can deny his own Jewishness by simply ignoring it and disassociating himself from anything Jewish, he will never turn to it for answers. As long as he sees it as only a vapid and non-fulfilling lifestyle, a mere extension of middle-class America, he will have no reason to delve into it further. And as long as he views it and its practices as irrational, he will not attempt to discover a personal relevancy within it.

Three realizations are necessary in order to bring about a redirection in the Jew's perception of his past. The first is an awareness of the impact that his Jewishness has had upon him. He must realize that he cannot possibly understand himself without first understanding his Jewishness. The second is the discovery that Judaism has throughout its history taken on a multiplicity of forms, many far different and infinitely richer than that of the American suburb. With such an awareness he can begin to acknowledge the possibility of Judaism as the source of a rich and fulfilling life experience. The third is the realization that Jewish observance and practices are not merely irrational and emotional acts but can also serve rational and purposeful ends, that they can provide a valuable source for answering one's identity questions.

*

To the Jew in conflict over his own heritage, escape may appear the easiest means of resolution. By avoiding all things Jewish, by actively trying to assimilate, he hopes to rid himself of the stigma he sees in his own Jewishness. But it is difficult to eradicate one's past. First, one's cultural upbringing leaves an indelible and irreversible imprint upon the human psyche, a legacy which cannot be escaped. Second, one's ethnicity is not defined solely from within but also, and to a large degree, from outside.

The impact of one's culture and socialization is all-pervasive. It profoundly shapes every aspect of the individual, leaving upon him an indelible mark for life. An intact and vital culture has the potential of radically affecting the person's core personality, thought patterns, emotional style, modes of behavior, beliefs about oneself and the world, and values and ethics. From birth the child is at the mercy of cultural forces which shape and channel him along certain pre-determined dimensions. The result is a psychological consistency shared by members of the same culture.

To be born a Jew has a similar impact, an impact which is difficult to change no matter what the desire. Within the American Jewish family, the child develops and incorporates a unique set of personality traits, modes of thinking and acting, beliefs and attitudes and values and ethics. These qualities are shared in varying degrees by most American Jews and form the basis for easier communication, predictability and trust within the group. Such personal attributes make one a Jew just as much as the outward appearances and practices.

James Yaffe speaks of a:

... Jewish cast of mind, a characteristic attitude toward life, an instinctive strategy for dealing with the world, which has arisen unconsciously out of four thousand years of common experience. When the East European immigrants came to America, this attitude was as much a part of them as the peasant clothes they wore. Sooner or later they burned the clothes, but they carried their peculiar cast of mind uptown with them, and passed it on to their children, who passed it on to their grandchildren in the 1960's. Today it gives a special color and flavor to Jewish life in America. It may even explain certain things about that life. (p. 20)

Yaffe's description of the American Jewish personality includes the following characteristics: an idealism mixed with pragmatism, a tough-mindedness softened by sentiment, a passion for argument and ideas, a basic suspicion of leaders and movements, a contempt for greatness, an optimistic pessimism, a sensitivity to injustice and a fear of anti-Semitism. Taken together these traits shape and determine the way the Jew will interpret and react to the world. He will be similarly affected by the values and ethics he internalizes, the style of living and interpersonal dynamics he experiences and the tempo, rhythm and pace of living he is exposed to in the Jewish home and community. All of these forces create and define him, make him what he is. To totally escape their impact is next to impossible.

It is not a difficult task to find a physical and material place for oneself in the non-Jewish world. Whether such a re-rooting will yield a sense of belonging and psychological comfort and ease is a very different question. The limits for successful cultural adaptation are set early in life and are intimately bound up with the socialization process. In general, a person will experience the greatest comfort and sense of belonging in an environment similar to that of his youth. The rhythm, pace and quality of life in such a world are familiar, not foreign, to him. By sharing basic personality characteristics with others within that world, he will feel at ease, knowing how to behave and what to expect. If a person chooses to reside in an environment too different and distant from that of his own cultural roots, he will be plagued forever by feelings of being an outsider, of not belonging emotionally and psychologically. The endless wanderings of the Jewish people in Diaspora can, perhaps, find an individual counterpart in the life of the Jew attempting to find a niche and comfortable place in the non-Jewish world.

A second source of the inevitability of one's Jewishness

comes from the fact that group belonging is defined interactively, by both the individual himself and by forces beyond him. Although the individual may wish to repudiate his own Jewishness, others, both individuals and groups, may not allow him this luxury. The assimilated Jews of Germany were made painfully aware of this fact during the Holocaust, when they, people who were more German than Jewish in outward trappings, attitudes and allegiances, were interred and murdered alongside of devout and traditional Jews. The long history of the Jewish people has been a chronicle of repeated periods of movement towards assimilation in various majority cultures followed inevitably by cruel and sadistic reminders of their differences, their Jewishness. In a sense this is one of the more ironic meanings of the biblical title for the Jews, "The Chosen People."

To truly understand his belonging to the Jewish group, the adolescent, according to Kurt Lewin, must realize that his membership is based not on "similarity or dissimilarity" but rather on "interdependence of fate." Although at times he may feel more kinship with gentile friends than with particular Jews, this fact does not negate his Jewishness. All groups, especially cultural ones, are typified by diversity and variety within their membership. The criteria for belonging to an ethnic group must, rather, be based upon social interaction and interdependence, on the realities of external pressures.

In Lewin's view, a realistic sociological awareness of interdependence:

... will help him [the adolescent] to see that his belonging or not belonging to the Jewish group is not a matter mainly of similarity or dissimilarity, nor even one of like or dislike. He will understand that regardless of whether the Jewish group is a racial, religious, national, or cultural one, the fact that it is classified by the majority as a distinct group is what counts. He will be ready to accept the variety of opinions and beliefs or other dissimilarities within the Jewish group as something quite natural as in any other group. He will see that the main criterion of belonging is interdependence of fate. Young American Jews may abhor Jewish national mysticism; they may not be willing to suffer for cultural or religious values which they do not fully understand, or perhaps even dislike; but they must be sufficiently fact-minded to see clearly their interdependence of fate with the rest of the American Jews and indeed with the Jews all over the world. (p. 184)

*

Accepting the inevitability and impact of one's ethnic past is the first step on the road to discovering one's unique identity. Only with this realization will the Jew begin a sustained exploration of his cultural heritage and fairly evaluate what it has to offer.

His exploration will require two very different efforts. The first is an intense survey of Jewish history, ideas, cultural artifacts and religious practices. Only by discovering and becoming aware of the variety of forms and expressions that Judaism has taken from Biblical times to the present can the individual begin to understand his past and the forces which have to a large extent shaped his present being. In the process he will find examples of Judaism as an alive and vibrant experience and realize that it can take forms other than that of the American Jewish suburb. This survey will also provide the building blocks necessary for the second task, that of finding a modern and personal relevancy within his Jewishness.

*

As stated earlier, the identity seeker in today's society must fashion his own meaning. Out of the cultural artifacts available to him, he must create a framework for better understanding himself and his times. He must begin with what is of value to him and somehow connect this valuing process to the behavior, experiences and symbols of his own life. In so doing he infuses his life with a purpose and personal relevancy necessary for living a joyful and fulfilling existence. In so doing he creates for himself a personal identity.

Although at some points in history it was sufficient for such a framework to be based upon faith and religious doctrine, modern man demands rational understanding. This is especially true for the Jew. His unique set of personality characteristics coupled with the social forces at work upon him demand that he question, challenge and critically analyze all ideas and beliefs, especially those offered by his own heritage. He cannot rest and feel at peace until he has found a truly satisfying reason for believing. According to Hayim Halevy Donin:

> There were periods in Jewish life, particularly when Jews lived in ghettos, removed from contact with competing influences, when the mass of Jews did not find it necessary to understand *why* and were satisfied with knowing *how*. That time is gone. Today, as during other times in the history of our people when Jews were in contact with other cultures and confronted with competing ideologies and movements, it is vital for Jews to develop an understanding and appreciation of the reasons, some grasp of the *why*. This is important not only to strengthen the convictions of the observant Jew himself, but also to provide him with the wherewithal to rebut those who may mock or question his practices. It is also necessary to be able to present Judaism to the Jew and non-Jew alike as a dynamic creed, as a living faith, as a relevant philosophy and way of life capable of challenging the various "isms" and spiritual fads that from time to time sweep across our society. (p. 34)

The second task of the Jew in exploring his cultural past is, thus, to find a satisfying rational meaning in his Jewishness. He must discover what his heritage can offer him in his present world, how it can meaningfully function within his own life's activity. Put in a slightly different manner, he must discover how to infuse ancient symbols and rituals with contemporary meanings, so that they might meaningfully function within his own world. If he can accomplish this feat, he will probably feel comfortable enough with Jewish ideas, ritual and practices to begin to relate to them in a more intuitive, emotional and spiritual way. In so doing, he may in time learn to give up his over-dependency on strictly intellectual ways of relating to the world and strike a more harmonious balance between rationality and spirit and faith.

*

Each Jew will relate differently to what he discovers in his search. Some may choose Orthodoxy, finding a deep satisfaction in the practice of ancient rituals. Others may try to create newer rituals and find more modern meanings in old ones. A few will be content simply with an awareness of how their Jewish past has affected them. And there are those, no doubt, who will come away dissatisfied and look elsewhere for a more satisfying source of identity. Such a decision, no matter what its outcome, cannot be rationally made, however, without a realization of the impact of a cultural past, a knowledge of what that past includes and a sincere effort to discover what modern meaning it might hold.

Jewish Identity—Its Modern Meaning

The Jew can, perhaps, best understand his own Jewishness and the modern relevance it can hold for him in relation to the sense of identity it can provide, in relation to the questions about life and living it can potentially answer.

Identity is a time-related concept and experience, one which connects the individual to a past, a present and a future. It roots him in time and gives him a meaningful point of contact with what has gone on before him, with what is presently occurring and with what will be in the future.

Many of man's most profound ills are linked to his limited

perception of time. Morris Adler speaks of today's estrangement from a past:

> In the absence of a tradition modern man stands denuded before the immediate. Without a past he is the captive of each solitary moment or day or year. Uprooted he sways with every impulse and fugitive whim. His existence disintegrates into episodic and disparate clots, and his life is an improvised series of unrelated variations. He is uncertain and apprehensive because the pin-point in time which he occupies is isolated and solitary. . . .

> Contemporary man is at sea because he has lost his sense of history as well as his relatedness to it. He tends to forget that while human history may seem to take a new turn, man never really starts over. In reacting against the encrustments, irrelevancies, and follies of the past, he turns his back upon its entirety and has thus cut himself off from a vital resource of strength, continuity and wisdom. (p. *xi*)

A major factor in the experiences of isolation, aloneness and anomie is the lack of connection with a past. Having nothing or no one of substance behind him, modern man senses himself alone. Many people today experience themselves in this way, isolated and free-floating, unattached to either an historic past or meaningful future. Their approach to living is existential and here-and-now, an attempt to deal with and make sense out of their isolation. Such feelings are relatively unknown in traditional societies. They are a modern psychological phenomenon which developed as strong historical identity and rich cultural ties diminished.

The experiences of purposelessness, meaninglessness and lack of fulfillment and direction are also symptoms of an incomplete sense of timeliness. They speak of the individual's inability to relate to his present world and to that of the future. Each denotes a lack of knowledge of how one is to behave: an inability to choose between different acts or behaviors in the present and an inability to direct behavior toward a consistent future goal.

The lack of a past almost insures an inability to relate to the present and the future. The ability to make meaningful contact with one's present and future depends largely on a viable sense of valuing; without it, it is impossible to make coherent, consistent and satisfying decisions about one's immediate behavior and one's future enterprises. And it is almost impossible to establish a sound basis for valuing within a single lifetime. A mature set of values and ethics evolves slowly over time and requires the wisdom and seasoning of many generations of use and development.

Salvation for the contemporary person lies in re-establishing a meaningful connection with time. Morris Adler describes the process as follows:

> Modern man can find a way toward wholeness by examining the abundant bequests of the past reverently but critically and with mature independence. He can suffuse his life with its echoes without losing his own voice in the process. It cannot be either-or, either the past or the present. It must be both in behalf of the future. (p. *xi*)

A true sense of identity provides the individual with a meaningful experience of his own timeliness. It allows him to become a part of an historic past, thereby escaping the feelings of aloneness and isolation. It affords him a purposefulness and direction, a prescription for present living and future action.

It is within this context that the identity-potential of one's own Jewishness becomes obvious. By looking to his own traditions and ancestry, the Jew can discover a meaningful connection to time. Within it, he can find roots: a connection to timeless generations, a rich cultural heritage and an intellectual tradition which has shaped Western thought. Within it, he can discover valuable lessons for living in the present, a prescription for living a psychologically healthful and fulfilling life. And within it, he can also find a direction and purpose: a reason for being, a goal, hope or fantasy worthy of his lifelong endeavors.

*

The essays which follow provide various glimpses into these time spheres. Each represents a unique aspect of Judaism. Taken together they provide a sense of the breadth and richness available within this ancient tradition. They are not meant in any way to be exhaustive or to summarize Jewish history, thought, belief, practice or experience. Exploring such a wealth of material would take a lifetime, or perhaps many lifetimes. These selections are offered instead as stimuli, stimuli for greater understanding, awareness and appreciation.

The essays are presented in four different sections, according to the time sphere to which they speak. The first two are oriented toward the past, sampling the rich legacy that is the heritage and roots of every Jew. The first focuses on the cultural past, providing a glimpse into the vibrant and alive lifestyles which were once synonymous with the Jewish experience. The second looks into the world of Jewish ideas, stressing intellectual roots which have profoundly affected Western thought. In the third section the time orientation is switched to the present. In these articles the reader is offered examples of the psychological wisdom inherent in Jewish rituals and practices and shown how to find within them a valuable prescription for day-to-day living. The final section talks to the future, to the issue of finding meaning and purpose within one's existence. Each article offers a different means of accomplishing this end.

A number of unique and interesting individuals have been kind enough to contribute to this collection. They bring to their articles very different knowledge, understandings and perspectives on Judaism. It was felt that such variety would broaden the scope of this work. Together these contributors capture the great diversity which is a vital characteristic of the Jewish world. This diversity is an important part of the potential value Judaism can hold for so many different Jews, irrespective of their unique past experiences and individual psychological needs.

References

Adler, Morris (ed.). *Jewish Heritage Reader.* New York: Taplinger, 1965.

Buber, Martin. *The Way of Man According to the Teachings of Hasidism.* London: Routledge and Kegan Paul, 1950.

Donin, Hayim Halevy. *To Be A Jew.* New York: Basic, 1972.

Kahane, Meir. *Never Again.* New York: Nash, 1971.

Lewin, Kurt. *Resolving Social Conflicts.* New York: Harper and Row, 1948.

Rosen, Bernard C. Minority group in transition: a study of adolescent religious conviction and conduct. In Sklare, M. (ed.). *The Jews.* New York: Free Press, 1958.

Sleeper, James A. and Mintz, Alan L. (eds.). *The New Jews.* New York: Random House, 1971.

Toffler, Alvin. *Future Shock.* New York: Random House, 1970.

Wheelis, Allen. *Quest for Identity.* New York: Norton, 1958.

Yaffee, James. *The American Jews.* New York: Random House, 1968.

PART I

Cultural Roots

Introduction

Historians look back not merely to discover what was, but more importantly, to better understand what is and what will be. The same is true of the self-discovery process. Only by looking back to their roots and sources can individuals truly understand who and where they are today and, as a consequence, where they wish to go in the future.

The cultural roots of most Jews stretch back to Eastern and Central Europe, to the world of the *shtetl.* Life in the *shtetl,* or market town, possessed two very different aspects. In relation to the non-Jewish world it was precarious and oppressive. For most Jews mere subsistence was the rule. For the few who were fortunate enough to become agents and landlords for the wealthy nobility, the unbridled hatred of the peasants who were dependent upon them more than made up for their improved financial status. For all Jews anti-semitism and pogroms were daily possibilities and, too often, realities. Politically, the Jews were disenfranchised, barred from any rights of citizenship, heavily taxed and a prime candidate for military service. At best they were merely tolerated by their Gentile neighbors who geographically surrounded them.

Within the *shtetl,* life had a far different character, however, and acted as a barrier to this hostile world. The tempo was warm, intense, supportive. Its inhabitants visited, gossiped, bartered, argued and, in all ways, shared their common plight. Various helping societies grew up to look after the needs of the poor and the unfortunate. The external realities of life were blotted out by study, Torah and the coming of the Sabbath. Jewish ritual and observance dominated and structured the lifestyle of the market town. In the first article of this section, "The Inner World of the Polish Jew," Abraham Heschel, in characteristically poetic and moving terms, captures the sense of spirituality and community which was the essence of *shtetl* existence and is so lacking in contemporary society.

The *shtetl,* and the Jews who inhabited it are no more, victims of Nazi insanity and the most evil crime ever witnessed in human history. Memories of this lost world are fragmentary and fading. Only a single living remnant remains: the Hasidim. Hasidism, an extremely Orthodox sect of Judaism, grew up in Eastern Europe two centuries ago. Its mysticism, joyfulness and folk-appeal served to revitalize a segment of the Jewish people severely alienated by the religious elite, and particularly hard hit by economic depression, rampant anti-semitism and the quick succession of two false messiahs. The fact that Hasidism remains intact today very much as it did two hundred years ago, essentially unchanged by either the Holocaust or the modern world, attests to the vitality of its lifestyle. More than ever before in American Jewish history, young Jews are being drawn to and fascinated by the Hasidic world. While these Old World Jews remain an embarrassment to many of their parents, the young see within the Hasidic lifestyle a paradigm for true religious community: vitality, integrity and spirituality. Jerome Mintz, in his article "Brooklyn's Hasidim," describes the life, practices and problems of this unusual and transplanted people as they struggle to retain their unique identity and way of life in contemporary America.

The transition from the Old World to the New was a painful and disorienting one. For those who chose to forsake their old homes and set off for America, the prospect of better times helped soften the blow somewhat. The result was still chaos and disorganization, however. Irving Howe, in his epic undertaking *World of Our Fathers,* examines this process in detail and with sensitivity. For those who made no such choice, but were nevertheless violently uprooted and against their wills ushered into the contemporary world, the experience was catastrophic and psychologically overwhelming. Many of these refugees are still, three and one-half decades later, trying to piece together their lives and make sense of the experience. Their literary spokesman has become Elie Wiesel. As he wrote of his own life, he wrote of theirs as well. In a sense this transition is the legacy of every contemporary Jew, challenging him or her to find meaning in a heritage and identity nurtured in a world that no longer exists. Thus, Elie Wiesel's struggle has come to symbolize a like process in all Jews. In "Jewish Identity in the Works of Elie Wiesel," noted-scholar Maurice Friedman traces Wiesel's confrontation with his Jewishness through his literature and, in the process, highlights the issues, emotions and inner dynamics facing the Jew today.

In the final article of Part I the focus switches from what was to what will be. The problem of transplanting Judaism into the cultural milieu of America has brought forth different responses on the part of contemporary Jews. One has been to summarily reject the entire heritage as no longer relevant. Another has been to retain the Jewish lifestyle of the past intact and unchanged, and to somehow grapple with the many and complex problems that such a choice inevitably creates. A third alternative has been to change Judaism in order to better adapt it to its new environment. This last solution, the tact taken by most Jews today, is fraught with potential danger, however. It is too easy to lose the essence and vitality of what was in the process of creating a new cultural form. Much of modern Judaism has been criticized on just this point, for having internalized the worst aspects of contemporary society, while losing touch with what was once Judaism's most vital concerns. In order to avoid such a situation and, at the same time, create a faithful continuation, one must remain highly sensitive to the cultural roots of the past and build directly upon these. Though forms may change, the essence cannot. A new sapling severed from its roots will quickly wither and die; so too a culture. In "New Age Judaism" Philip Mandelkorn describes the process whereby he and others are working to develop a radically new Jewish lifestyle, one in keeping with traditional roots of the past.

The Inner World of the Polish Jew

Abraham J. Heschel

The culture of the Sephardic Jews of the Iberian peninsula marked a brilliant epoch in Jewish history, distinguished not only by monumental scientific achievements but also by the universality of its spirit.

In Eastern Europe, the spiritual life of the Jews was lived in solitude. Growing out of its own ancient roots and developed in its indigenous environment, their life remained independent of the trends and conventions of the surrounding world. Unique were their cultural patterns in thinking and writing, unique their communal and individual ways of life. Tenaciously adhering to their own traditions, they were bent upon the cultivation of what was most their own, to the utter disregard of the outside world. Literature for them was writing by Jews and for Jews. They did not apologize to anyone, nor did they compare themselves with anyone else.

In Eastern Europe the Jewish people had come into its own. It did not live like a guest in somebody else's house, who must constantly keep in mind the ways and customs of his host. The Jews lived in their own way, without reservation and without disguise, outside their homes no less than within them. When they said in their commentaries on the Talmud that "the world asks," they did not refer to a problem raised by Aristotle or a medieval philosopher. The "world" to them was the students of the Torah.

Among the Spanish Jews there were numerous men who

possessed high learning. Their achievements in medicine, mathematics, and astronomy contributed greatly to the development and progress of European civilization. Through their translations of scientific and philosophical works from Arabic into Latin they made available to the European nations the treasures of culture and science then in the custody of the Arab world. Many Sephardic authors wrote largely in Arabic; even works dealing with questions of Jewish ritual, homilies on the Bible, and commentaries on the Talmud were often written in Arabic.

To an East-European author it would seem inconceivable to write in a foreign tongue. Unlike the aristocratic society of the Sephardic world, whose poets wrote in a Hebrew so complicated and involved that only erudites could enjoy it, Jewish society in Poland had an intimate, organic character. The healthy earthiness of the villagers, the warmth of plain people, and the spiritual simplicity of the Maggidim penetrated into the house of study and prayer. Laborers, peasants, porters, artisans, they were all partners in the Torah.

The amalgamation of Torah and Israel was here accomplished. Ideals became folkways; the people itself was the source of Judaism, a source of spirit. The most distant became very intimate, very dear. Spontaneously, without external cause, the people improvised customs of religious significance.

Classical books were not written in Eastern Europe. *The Talmud,* the *Mishneh Torah,* the *Book of Splendor,* the *Guide of the Perplexed,* and the *Tree of Life* were produced in other countries. East-European Jewry lacked the ambition to create consummate, definitive, perfect expressions. Their books were so rooted in a self-contained world that they are less accessible to moderns than the books of the Sephardic authors. They are not literature, they read like notes of discussions with pupils. They did not write books that stand like separate buildings with foundations of their own; all their works lean upon older books, are commentaries on classical works of ancient time, modestly hug the monumental walls of old citadels of learning.

In their lives everything was fixed according to a certain pattern, nothing was casual, nothing was left to chance. But they also had sufficient vitality constantly to modify the accepted pattern. New customs were continually added to, and the old customs enriched with fresh nuances. The forms and ceremonies were passed on from generation to generation, but the meaning which was attached to them did not remain the same. A perennial source gave renewed life to tradition.

There was profound sadness in their joy. The "moralistic" melodies that the wedding players intoned before the veiling ceremony would almost rend the soul of the bride. Under the canopy, mother and grandmother would sob, and even a man who heard a piece of good news would usually burst into tears.

But the Jews all sang: a student over the Talmud, the tailor while sewing a pair of trousers, the cobbler while mending a pair of shoes, and the preacher while delivering a sermon. A unique form of musical expression evolved.

The dishes to be served on certain days, the manner of putting on or removing one's shoes, the position of one's head when walking in the street—everything was keyed to a certain style. Every part of the liturgy, every prayer, every hymn had its own tune. Every detail possessed its own physiognomy, each object its own individual stamp. Even the landscape became Jewish. In the month of Elul (September), during the penitential season, the fish in the streams trembled; on Lag b'Omer, the scholar's festival in the spring, all the trees rejoiced. When a holiday came, even horses and dogs felt it. And a crow perched on a branch looked from a distance "as though it were wearing a white prayer shawl, with dark blue stripes in front: and it sways and bends as it prays, and lowers its head in intense supplication."

In almost every Jewish home, even in the humblest and

poorest, stood a bookcase full of volumes; proud and stately folio-tomes together with shy small-sized books. Books were neither an asylum for the frustrated nor a means for occasional edification. They were furnaces of living strength, time-proof receptacles for the eternally valid coins of spirit. Almost every Jew gave of his time to learning, either in private study, or by joining one of the societies established for the purpose of studying the Talmud or some other branch of rabbinic literature. To some people it was impossible to pray without first having been refreshed by spending some time in the sublime atmosphere of Torah. Others, after the morning prayer, would spend an hour with their books, before starting to work. At nightfall, almost everyone would leave the tumult and bustle of everyday life to study in the Bet ha-Midrash. The Jews did not feel themselves to be the "People of the Book." They did not feel that they possessed the book, just as one does not feel that one possesses life. The book, the Torah, was their essence, just as they, the Jews, were the essence of the Torah.

A Jewish township in Lithuania and in many other parts of Eastern Europe was, in the words of Mendele, "a place where Torah has been studied from time immemorial; where practically all the inhabitants are scholars; where the synagogue or the house of study is full of people of all classes busily engaged in studies, townsfolk as well as young men from afar; where at dusk, between twilight and evening prayers, artisans and other simple folk gather around the tables to listen to a discourse on the great books of Law, to interpretations of Scripture, to readings from theological and ethical writings . . . where on the Sabbath and the holidays, near the Holy Ark, at the reading stand, fiery sermons are spoken that kindle the hearts of the Jewish people with love for the Divine Presence, sermons that are seasoned with words of comfort from the prophets, with the wise parables and keen aphorisms of the sages, in a voice that heartens one's soul, that melts all limbs, that penetrates the whole being."

To be sure, in the life of the East-European Jews there was not only light but also shadow—one-sidedness of learning, neglect of manners, provincialism. In the crowded conditions in which they lived—persecuted and tormented by ruthless laws, intimidated by drunken landowners, despised by newly-enriched city-dwellers, trampled by police boots, chosen as scapegoats by political demagogues—the rope of self-discipline sometimes snapped. In addition, naked misery and frightful poverty deafened the demands and admonitions of religious enthusiasm. The regions of piety were at times too lofty for plain mortals. Not all Jews could devote themselves to the Torah and service to God, not all the old men had the faces of prophets; there were not only Hasidim and Kabbalists, but also yokels, shnorrers, and tramps.

There were many who lived in appalling poverty, many who were pinched by never-ending worries, and there were plenty of taverns with strong spirits. But drunkards were never seen among Jews. When night came and a man wanted to while away his time, he did not hurry to take a drink; he went rather to his books, or joined a group that, either with or without a teacher, gave itself over to the pure enjoyment of study. Physically worn out by their day's toil, they sat over open volumes and intoned the austere music of the Talmud.

Poor Jews, whose children knew only the taste (as one of their songs has it) of "potatoes on Sunday, potatoes on Monday, potatoes on Tuesday," sat there like intellectual princes. They possessed whole treasuries of thought—the knowledge, ideas, and sayings of many ages. When a problem came up, there was immediately a crowd of people to offer opinions, proofs, quotations. One raised a question on a difficult passage in Maimonides' work, and many vied in attempts to explain it, outdoing one another in the subtlety of dialectic distinctions. The stomachs were empty, the homes overcrowded—but the minds were replete with the riches of the Torah.

A story is told of a simple, uneducated Jew who on the

Feast of the Rejoicing of the Torah danced so passionately with the scrolls as if there were no limit to his joy. "Why are you so happy?" someone asked him. "It is natural that scholars who all year round do nothing but search in the Torah should rejoice on this day, but why are you so jubilant?" Answered he: "When my relative celebrates a wedding, do not I have a good time at his feast?"

The state did not have to compel the Jews to send their children to school. Their most popular lullaby proclaimed: "The Torah is the highest good," and mothers at the cradle crooned: "My little child, close your eyes; if God will, you'll be a rabbi." At the birth of a baby, the school children would come and chant the Shema Yisrael in unison around the cradle. When taken for the first time to the Heder, the child was wrapped, like a scroll, in a prayershawl. Schoolboys were referred to as "the holy flock," and a mother's tenderest pet name for a boy was "my little zaddik," my little saint. Parents were ready to sell the pillow from under their heads to pay tuition for their children; a poorly tutored father wanted at least his children to be scholars. Women toiled day and night to enable their husbands to devote themselves to study. Those who could not devote themselves to the Torah because of economic exigencies tried at least to support the students. They shared their scanty food with wandering students. And when the melancholy, sweet chanting of a talmudic study coming from the Bet ha-Midrash penetrated the neighboring streets, exhausted Jews on their cots felt sweet delight at the thought that by their acts of support they had a share in that learning. The ambition of every Jew was to have a scholar as a son-in-law, and a man versed in the Torah could easily marry a well-to-do girl and obtain *kest,* board, for a few years, or even permanently, which meant he was able to devote his time to study.

A blazing passion permeated all intellectual activities. It is an untold, perhaps incommunicable story of how mind and heart could merge into one. Immersed in complicated legal discussions, they could at the same time feel the anguish of the Divine Presence that abides in exile. In endeavoring to unravel some perplexity raised by a seventeenth-century commentary on a commentary on the Talmud, they were able in the same breath to throb with sympathy for Israel and all afflicted people. Study was a technique for sublimating feeling into thought, for transposing dreams into syllogisms, for expressing grief in difficult theoretical formulations, and joy by finding a solution to a difficult passage in Maimonides. Tension of the soul found an outlet in contriving clever, almost insolvable, riddles. In inventing new logical devices to explain the word of God, they thrilled with yearning after the Holy. To contrive an answer to gnawing doubts was the highest joy. Indeed, there was a whole world of subdued gayety and sober frolic in the playful subtleties of their *pilpul.*

Their conscious aim, of course, was not to indulge in self-expression—they were far from being intent upon exploiting the Torah—but humbly to partake of spiritual beauty. Carried away by the mellow, melting chant of Talmud-reading, one's mind soared high in the pure realm of thought, away from this world of facts and worries, away from the boundaries of here and now, to a region where the Divine Presence listens to what Jews create in the study of His word. There was holiness in their acumen, the cry. "My soul thirsteth for God, the living God," sounded in their wrestling with the Law.

Their learning was essentially non-utilitarian, generally free of direct and practical designs, an esthetic experience. They delved into those parts of the lore that had no relevance to daily life no less eagerly than into those that had a direct bearing on it. They grappled with problems absent from our mundane reality, remote from the banalities of the normal course of living. He who studied for the purpose of becoming a rabbi was the object of ridicule. In the eyes of these people, knowledge was not a means for achieving power but a way of arriving at the source of all reality.

The *pilpul* was a continuation of the ways of study pursued at the ancient academies in Babylonia in the first centuries of the present era. The goal was not to acquire information about the Law but rather to examine its implications and presuppositions. The method of study was not just to absorb and to remember, but to discuss and to expand. All later doctrines were considered tributaries of the ancient, never-failing stream of tradition. One could debate with the great sages of bygone days. There was no barrier between the past and the present. If disagreement was discovered between a view held by Rabbi Akiba Eiger of Posen, who lived in the nineteenth century, and Rabbi Yizhak Alfassi of Morocco, who lived in the eleventh century, a Warsaw scholar of the twentieth century would intervene to prove that the views were consistent after all, and so the unity of the tradition was maintained.

Just as their thinking was distinguished by a reaching out for the most subtle, so their mode of expression, particularly that of those engaged in mystic lore, was marked by a tendency toward terseness. Their sayings are pointed, aiming at reaching an idea in one bound, instead of approaching it gradually and slowly. They offered the conclusion and omitted the premises. They spoke briefly, sharply, quickly, and directly; they understood each other in a hint.

Audacious doctrines were disguised as allegories, or even witty maxims, and a seeming commonplace often contained a sublime thought. Holy men seemed to be discussing the building of a roof; they spoke of bricks and shingles, while they were actually debating the mysteries of the Torah. Whole theories of life were implied in simple stories told at tea after the *havdalah* ceremony that marked the end of the Sabbath. The power of such *pilpul* penetrated even into the Kabbalah. The later Ashkenazic Kabbalists constructed symbolic labyrinths out of mystic signs; so involved were these labyrinths that only Kabbalists endowed with both mystic passion and intellectual keenness could safely venture into them.

The author of the Revealer of the Deeply Hidden, written in the seventeenth century, interprets in two hundred and fifty-two different ways the portion of the Pentateuch in which Moses pleads with God for permission to enter the Promised Land. The manifest became occult. Everywhere they found cryptic meaning. Even in the part of the Code dealing with civil and criminal law they discovered profound mysteries. Allusions were found in names of towns and countries, as in the name of Poland, which was said to derive from the two Hebrew words, *Po-lin,* "here abide," and to have been inscribed on a note fallen from heaven and found by the refugees from Germany on their eastward journey at the time of the Black Death. On the leaves of the trees, the story goes, are inscribed sacred names, and in the branches are hidden errant souls seeking deliverance through the intermediation of a pious Jew, who in passing would stop to say his twilight prayer under the tree.

In the eyes of these Jews, the world was not a derelict the Creator had abandoned to chance. Life to them was not merely an opportunity for indulgence, but a mission that God entrusted to every individual. Life is at least as responsible an enterprise as the management of a factory. Every man constantly produces thoughts, words, deeds. He supplies these products to the Powers of holiness or the Powers of impurity; he is constantly engaged either in building or in destroying.

Man's task is to restore what has been impaired in the cosmos. Therefore, the Jew is engaged in the service of God. He is rarely dominated by a desire for austere rigorism or a liking for irrational discipline for its own sake. In the main, he is borne up by a sense of the importance of his mission, by the certainty that the world could not exist without the Torah. This sense lends his life the quality of an art whose medium is neither stone nor bronze, but the mystic substance of the universe.

Scientists dedicate their lives to the study of the habits of beetles or the properties of shrubs. Every trifle is significant because it indicates the most intricate qualities of things. The pious Ashkenazic scholars investigated just as passionately the laws that should govern human conduct. They wished to banish chaos from human existence and to civilize the life of man according to the Torah. They trembled over every move, every breath; no detail was treated lightly—everything was serious. Just as the self-sacrificing devotion of the scientist seems torture to the libertine, so the poetry of rigorism jars on the cynic. He does not realize that the question of what benediction to pronounce upon a certain type of food becomes so important because it solves the problem of matching the material with the spiritual. To the uninspired, the Shulhan Arukh is a volume of symphonies whose musical notation they cannot read; to the pious Jew, its signs are full of rhythms and melodies.

In the eighteenth century, the hasidic movement arose and brought heaven down to earth. The Hasidim banished melancholy from the soul and uncovered the ineffable delight of being a Jew. God is not only the creator of earth and heaven. He is also the one "who created delight and joy." He who does not taste paradise in the performance of a precept in this world will not feel the taste of paradise in the other world. "A Jew who does not rejoice in the fact of his being a Jew," said one of the great hasidic teachers, "is ungrateful to heaven. It is a sign that he has failed to grasp the meaning of the daily blessing over his not having been born a heathen." Judaism was as though reborn. The Baal Shem rejuvenated us by a thousand years. A new prohibition was added: "Thou shalt not be old!" and the Jews began to feel life-everlasting in a sacred melody, the Sabbath became the vivid anticipation of the life to come.

Jews ceased to fear the flesh. Do not inflict pain upon it, do not torment it—one should pity the flesh. "Hide not thyself from thine own flesh." One can serve God even with the body, even with the evil inclination; one must only be able to distinguish between the dross and the gold. When a little of the other world is mingled with it, this world acquires flavor. Only without nobility is the flesh full of darkness. The Hasidim have always maintained that the joys of this world are not the highest to which one can achieve, and they found in themselves the passion for spirituality, the yearning for the joys of the world to come.

The perception of the spiritual, the experience of the wonder, become common. Plain men begin to feel what scholars have often failed to sense. The sigh of the contrite heart, a little inwardness, or a bit of self-sacrifice outweighed the merits of him who is stuffed with both erudition and pride. When learning is practiced for its own sake, it may become a kind of idolatry. Excessive *pilpul* may dry up the well of the soul. For that reason renowned scholars sometimes close their Talmud volumes and set out to wander in a self-imposed "exile," far from home, among strangers, to bear humiliation and taste the cup of privation and misery.

There is the story of a scholar who came to visit a rebbe. The scholar was no longer a young man—he was close to thirty—but he had never before visited a rebbe.

"What have you done all your life?" the rebbe asked him.

"I have gone through the whole of the Talmud three times," answered the scholar.

"Yes, but what of the Talmud has gone through you?" the rebbe replied.

Man is no mere reflection of the above; he is a source of light. If he divests himself of the husks, he can illuminate the world. God has instilled in man something of Himself. Israel, in particular, because it lives for the "fulfillment of the Torah," is of unique importance. Hence it is that the fate of His beloved people of Israel is of such concern to God. God is the infinite, "the Hidden of all Hidden," whom no thought can conceive; but when a Jew has almost exhausted his strength in yearning after Him, he would exclaim: "Sweet Father!" It is incumbent upon us to obey our Father in heaven, but God in turn is bound to take pity on His children. And His compassion is abundant indeed. "I wish I could love the saintliest man in Israel as the Lord loves the most wicked in Israel," prayed Rabbi Aaron, the Great.

Jews had always known piety and Sabbath holiness. The new thing in Eastern Europe was that something of the Sabbath was infused into the everyday, into weekdays. One could relish the taste of eternal life in the fleeting moment. In such an environment it was not difficult to believe in the *Neshamah yeterah,* the Additional Soul that every Jew is given for the day of the Sabbath. Jews did not build magnificent synagogues; they built bridges leading from the heart to God.

The present moment overflowed its bounds. People lived not chronologically, but in a fusion of the dimensions of time: they lived with the great men of the past, not only in narrating tales about them, but also in their emotions and dreams. Jews studying the Talmud felt a kinship with its sages. Elijah the Prophet, it was believed, attended circumcision ceremonies, and the spirit of the Holy Guests visited their huts on the days of the Sukkot. The past never died in their lives. Among such Jews there lived the Thirty-six Saints who remain unknown to the people and whose holiness sustains the universe. In their souls simple Jews were always prepared to welcome the Messiah. If Isaiah the Prophet were to rise from his grave and were to enter the home of a Jew even on a plain Wednesday, the two would have understood each other.

Korets, Karlin, Bratzlav, Lubavich, Ger, Lublin—hundreds of little towns were like holy books. Each place was a pattern, an aspect, a way in Jewishness. When a Jew mentioned the name of a town like Medzhibozh or Berdytshev, it was as though he mentioned a divine mystery. Holiness had become so real and so concrete that it was perceptible like beauty.

"Why do you go to see the rebbe?" someone asked an eminent scholar who, although his time was precious, would trudge for days to visit his rebbe on the Sabbath.

"To stand near him and watch him lace his shoes," he answered.

When Hasidim were gathered together, they told each other how the rebbe opened the door, how he tasted his food at the table.

What need was there to discuss faith? How was it possible not to feel the presence of God in the world? How could one fail to see that the whole earth is full of His glory? To preach to these Jews the necessity of observing the six hundred and thirteen commandments would have been superfluous. To live in accordance with the Shulhan Arukh had become second nature. To the Jews this was not enough. A leader of the Musar movement once remarked: "If I thought that I should always remain what I am, I would lay hands on myself. But if I did not hope to be like the Gaon of Vilna, I should not be even what I am."

Outwardly they may have looked plagued by the misery and humiliation in which they lived, but inwardly they bore the rich sorrow of the world and the noble vision of redemption for all men and all beings. For man is not alone in the world. "Despair does not exist at all," said Rabbi Nahman of Bratzlav, a hasidic leader. "Do not fear, dear child, God is with you, in you, around you. Even in the Nethermost Pit one can try to come closer to God." The word "bad" never came to the lips. Disasters did not frighten them. "You can take everything from me—the pillow from under my head, my house—but you cannot take God from my heart."

Miracles no longer startled anyone, and it was no surprise to discover among one's contemporaries a man who attained contact with the Holy Spirit. People ceased to think that their generation was inferior to the earlier; they no longer considered themselves epigones. On the contrary, there were Hasidim who believed that it was easier to receive inspiration from the Holy Spirit in their own day than it had been in the early days of the Talmud. For holiness flows from two sources—from the Temple in Jerusalem and from the Complete Redemption in the time of the Messiah. And we are closer to the time of Redemption than the talmudic sages were to the era of the Temple. The light of the Messiah can already be seen before us, illumining contemporary holy men. "One has to be blind not to see the light of the Messiah," were the words of Rabbi Pinhas of Korets.

The feeling prevailed that man was superior to the angels. The angel knows no self-sacrifice, does not have to overcome obstacles, has no free choice in his actions. Moreover, the nature of the angel is stationary, keeping forever the rank in which he was created. Man, however, is a wayfarer; he always moves either upward or downward; he cannot remain in one place. Man is not only the crown of creation, he can become a participant in the act of creation. The Hasidim realize the wide range of their responsibility, they know that entire worlds wait to be redeemed from imperfection. Not only are we in need of heaven, but heaven needs us as well.

In the days of Moses the Jews had a revelation of God; in the days of the Baal Shem, God had a revelation of Israel. Suddenly there was revealed a holiness in Jewish life that had accumulated in the course of many generations. Ultimately, the "We will do and we will listen," is as important as the "I am the Lord thy God"; and "Who is like unto Thy people, like Israel, a nation one in the earth" is as meaningful to Him as "The Lord is One" is to Israel.

The little Jewish communities in Eastern Europe were like sacred texts opened before the eyes of God. So close were our houses of worship to Mount Sinai. In the humble wooden synagogues, looking as if they were deliberately closing themselves off from the world, the Jews purified the souls that God had given them and perfected their likeness to God. There arose in them an infinite world of inwardness, a

"Torah within the Heart," beside the written and oral Torah. Even plain men were like artists who knew how to fill weekday hours with mystic beauty.

It was no accident that the Jews of Eastern Europe did away with worldly education. They resisted the stream that threatened to engulf the small province of Jewishness. They did not despise science; they believed, however, that a bit of nobility is a thousand times more valuable than all the secular sciences, that praying every day, "My God, guard my tongue from evil," is more important than the study of physics, that meditating upon the Psalms fills man with more compassion than the study of Roman history. They put no trust in the secular world. They believed that the existence of the world was not conditioned on museums and libraries, but on houses of worship and study. To them, the house of study was not important because the world needed it; on the contrary, the world was important because houses of study existed in it. To them, life without the Torah and without piety was chaos, and a man who lived without these was looked upon with a sense of fear. They realized quite well that the world was full of ordeals and dangers, that it contained Cain's jealousy of Abel, and the evil cruelty of Sodom, but they also knew that there was in it the charity of Abraham and the tenderness of Rachel. Harassed and oppressed, they carried, deep within their hearts, a contempt for the "world," with its power and glory, with its bustling and boasting. Jews who at midnight lamented the glory of God that is in exile and spent their days peddling were not insulted by the scorn of their enemies or impressed by their praises. They knew the world and did not turn it into an idol. The so-called progress did not deceive them, and the magic of the twentieth century did not blind them. They knew that the Jews were in exile, that the world was unredeemed. Their life was oriented to the spiritual, and they could therefore ignore its external aspects. Outwardly a Jew might have been a pauper, but inwardly he felt like a prince, a kin to the King of Kings. Unconquerable freedom was in the Jew, who, when wrapped in tallit and tefillin, consecrated his soul to the sanctification of the Holy Name.

Has there ever been more light in the souls of the Jews in the last thousand years? Could it have been more beautiful in Safed or in Worms, in Cordoba or Pumbeditha?

The present generation still holds the keys to the treasure. If we do not uncover the wealth, the keys will go down to the grave with us, and the storehouse of the generations will remain locked forever.

When Nebuchadnezzar destroyed Jerusalem and set fire to the Temple, our forefathers did not forget the Revelation on Mount Sinai and the words of the prophets. Today the world knows that what transpired on the soil of Palestine was sacred history, from which mankind draws inspiration. A day will come when the hidden light of the East-European period will be revealed.

Brooklyn's Hasidim

Jerome R. Mintz

"The difference between Satmar hasidim and other Jews is this: Once when the time came to put the Torah (the Old Testament) back in the covering, it was too difficult to fit it in, and the man who was putting it in suggested that they cut the Torah to make it fit. Ridiculous? Of course. You have to cut the covering to shape. We will adjust our environment to fit the Torah and not the reverse."

This parable, told by the Satmarer Rebbe (leader) at a Friday night meal, epitomizes the attitudes of the most pietistic hasidic Jews living in the Williamsburg section of Brooklyn. The hasidim are ultra-Orthodox Jews who until World War II were the uneasy residents of the villages and ghettos of central and eastern Europe. Joel Leib (a pseudonym), a Satmar hasid who quoted his Rebbe's parable to me, is a Hungarian Jew who survived the final year of the war in a concentration camp. Today he is one of some 75,000 hasidic Jews who live in Brooklyn, New York.

Lieb's religion dominates his life, as it did in prewar Hungary, and his full beard and black caftan are outward signs of a complete allegiance to his faith. Early each morning and again just before nightfall he prays in the *besmedresh* (house of study), usually with the same quorum of at least ten men; during evenings after prayer, he studies the commentaries on the Torah with another small group.

His wife shares the daily rhythm of religious life, although women's activities are sharply separated from those of the men. Like most hasidic women, she rarely attends public services in the *besmedresh,* where she must sit in a screened balcony with the other women. The most evident signs of her religiosity are her efforts to maintain the ritual purity of her home, her attendance at the ritual bath after her menstrual cycle, her modestly cut, long-sleeved dresses, and the wig she wears to cover her closely shorn hair. Only the housing project where they live, the brownstone houses on the neighboring streets, and the elevated subway connecting Williamsburg to Manhattan testify that the hasidim have been transported to the New World and that their life has changed.

Most hasidim who immigrated here in earlier decades melted rapidly into the larger American Jewish community. Those who arrived in the postwar years, however, refuse to slip quietly into the surrounding society: they almost never intermarry, attend the theater, watch a movie or television, or seek advanced secular education. A large percentage work in the diamond and knit goods industries, while others work at jobs related to the community's religious needs, such as teaching at *yeshivas* (schools) or handling kosher food products.

The Brooklyn hasidic community's social and economic organization closely replicates that of the prewar eastern European villages where hasidic Rebbes and their courts were established. The Rebbes were the descendants of the disciples of the Baal-Shem-Tov and Rabbi Dov Baer, the two figures who initiated the hasidic movement in the mid-eighteenth century. The early hasidim separated themselves from established congregations and initiated a range of religious and social changes: the scholarly rabbi, who decided on questions of law, became subordinate to the inspired Rebbe; a more esoteric liturgy was substituted; prayer and devotion were intensified, and some rituals, such as visiting the ritual bath (a small pool, deep enough for one to completely immerse oneself while standing) were emphasized. As the disciples of the first hasidic leaders gathered their own followings, hasidic dynasties developed, with the Rebbes and their hasidim maintaining mutual loyalty in succeeding generations. The physical center of each group was the *hoyf,* or "court," a term that carried both the physical sense of the courtyard containing the Rebbe's residence, the house of study, the bathhouse, and the shops and storehouses, and the intrinsic dynastic qualities of inherited statuses and loyalties. Each court took its name from the town in which it was settled, for example, Satmar in Hungary, Lubavitch in Russia, Ger in Poland, Bobov in Galicia. Each was largely self-contained, with its own artisans, ritual slaughterers, shopkeepers, and an endless stream of visitors who sought the Rebbe's blessing, contributed financial support, and carried back to their villages tales of the miracles wrought by the Rebbe.

The various hasidic courts, which were once scattered throughout eastern Europe, are now located in this country and in Israel. Here, they are concentrated in three Brooklyn neighborhoods—Williamsburg, Crown Heights, and Borough Park. Most hasidim in Williamsburg are of Hungarian origin and have allegiance to Satmar. The Russian hasidim of Lubavitch are settled in Crown Heights; while the growing community in Borough Park, comprising a range of courts of diverse geographic origins, is strongly influenced by its many American-born hasidim. Each court's size, which varies from fifty to several thousand families (for the Satmar community), is related to the number that survived the war, the percentage that preferred to settle in Israel, and the reputation of its Rebbe.

The strength of the present hasidic community derives in great measure from the intimacy and shared responsibilities within the courts. Each court is attached to a particular Rebbe and bound by special customs and traditions and a common language. Its followers have a shared point of view regarding religious and political matters and an oral literature concerning its Rebbes from the past to the present. Each court maintains its own *yeshiva* and *besmedresh* which are supported by tuition and voluntary contributions, generally 10 to 20 percent of every household's income. The duties and shared obligations develop strong, self-perpetuating bonds, with the sons assuming the loyalities and responsibilities of their fathers.

Like all Orthodox Jews, the hasidim are regulated by the 613 commandments *(mitsves)* of the Old Testament and by the elaborations of rabbinical interpretation. The *mitsves* embrace every area of human activity and are the moral and legal guides for daily life. Each Jew's personal fate, as well as the destiny of the community, is believed to hinge cn the fulfillment of the laws. The hasidim, more fervent and punctilious than other Orthodox Jews, are considered to be zealots of the law.

In accordance with the most pervasive commandment, the hasidim honor the Sabbath *(Shabbes)* and the holy days, pray three times each day, bind phylacteries *(tefillin)* to the forehead and arm each morning, eat only kosher food, and use separate kitchenware for milk products and for meat.

The Sabbath is divinely mandated and its observance is public and communal. From Friday sundown until Saturday night all work comes to a halt and a sense of solemnity and celebration descends over the neighborhoods. On Friday afternoon Joel and his fellow hasidim return home early from work. The shops close on the avenue and cars and trucks are parked, except for those of outsiders who pass through the quiet streets. The men come to the basement of the *besmedresh* where they step into the ritual bath to purify themselves in honor of the holy *Shabbes.* They wear silk caftans, and those who are married wear round fur hats with twelve spokes of fur. It is an emulation of the dress of the nobility of two centuries ago, now worn in celebration of the holy day and as a symbol of the hasidim's exalted state. That night and the following day are times for intense prayer, for periods of study, for visiting, strolling, and for meeting with the Rebbe and the court.

During the *Shabbes* the men congregate three times for

communal meals. The hasidim are famous for the third meal, which takes place late Saturday afternoon. The Rebbe, dressed in a resplendent robe and fur hat, is seated at a long table. At the table are learned rabbis and illustrious members of the court. A newly married hasid has the seat of honor next to the Rebbe. The rest of the followers crowd before the table, those in the rear standing on benches, to observe the smallest motion of their Rebbe, be it lifting his spoon or stroking his beard. Individual hasidim catch the Rebbe's eye and toast him with a glass of brandy or beer and, in return, receive his blessing. The Rebbe is customarily served large platters of food—fish, chicken, bread, and soup—but he eats sparingly from the portions. The remains of each dish are then divided into small pieces and passed out to the hasidim, with the Rebbe or his assistant designating the recipient. The tidbits that the hasidim receive are not meant to satisfy their appetite; rather, the morsels enable them to share in the Rebbe's holiness and power. Most of the food is divided in an orderly way, but there are moments when the desire to partake results in chaotic scrambling. The food is passed among the followers until everyone has tasted it or until the supply is exhausted.

After the meal, in the growing darkness, the Rebbe says *toyreh,* his teachings. His talk is often set in mystical terms intertwined with biblical and talmudic allusions. At times, the Rebbe presents his thoughts as if in a semitrance, interweaving examples from the past with problems of the present. He may urge his followers to worship with fervor or insist that they preserve every vestige of the past as a shield —or he may warn his followers against riding the subway during rush hour when contact with women is unavoidable. Often the Rebbe's *toyreh* concludes with the prayer for the coming of the Messiah.

The laws are the primary factor in the development of the hasidic ethos. Fear of contamination through purposeful or accidental failure to carry out the *mitsves* helps create a pervasive anxiety that begins early in life. At the age of two, children are taught to make a blessing when they awaken and before each meal. When young men reach sufficient maturity to be present at the Rebbe's table to listen to his teachings, each is certain that he is being directly addressed.

The tensions in fulfilling the laws would be insupportable if they were not introduced gently and balanced by the acceptance of human frailty and by the warmth and affection that are characteristic of hasidic life. Hasidic children play in the heart of the *besmedresh,* sometimes disturbing prayers and spilling over into the corridors and offices. For children, the house of study is their playground; for adults, it is the center of their lives. Among many of the most dedicated hasidim the religious law is compensated by sympathy and understanding for the problems of young people.

Although every hasid is observant of the laws, the Rebbe's zeal and insight are considered to be on a different scale from that of other hasidim. As a Lubavitcher hasid described it, the Rebbe "worships God every second of the day with all his heart and soul." Because of his prayer, his piety, and his family lineage, the Rebbe is thought to be in contact with enormous spiritual power.

Despite his importance in the community, the Rebbe is not lost to the individual hasid. Several times each week the Lubavitcher Rebbe remains in his office throughout the night to receive individual hasidim who come for his blessing or for his counsel. Although the Satmar Rebbe is 89 years old, he still receives his followers individually at his retreat in Belle Harbor, New York. The Lubavitcher Rebbe is celebrated for stimulating Orthodoxy among less religious Jews, and the Satmar Rebbe is known for his fierce determination to maintain every vestige of law and custom and for his opposition to the government of Israel. Notwithstanding their general fame and public responsibilities, the Rebbes' personal relationships with their hasidim are crucial for the maintenance of their courts.

Hasidim approach their Rebbe with a wide range of motives and needs. Some come for compassion, other require advice or a blessing, and some seek a miracle. They petition their Rebbe to help them overcome an illness in the family, the conflicts in a bad marriage, the curse of poverty and ill-fortune. To fend off potential danger, the Rebbes are also asked to decide on and to bless any family affair or business venture. A hasid will rarely make an important decision or pass through a crisis without visiting the Rebbe to ask for his blessing.

While its Rebbe provides a spiritual center of gravity, a court also requires legal, administrative, and practical organization. These are tasks not usually expected of the Rebbe, whose otherworldliness and spiritual stature generally remove him from the administration of mundane affairs. Orthodox Jewry has always maintained its own legal system to resolve such matters as divorce, contracts, and torts, and it is customary for the Rebbe to designate rabbis who decide such issues. The Rebbe also customarily names a committee of rabbis and learned laymen to administer the *besmedresh,* the *yeshiva,* and the ritual bath.

Despite the intense faith and strong traditions of the hasidim, the community would not flourish without new forms of organization. Survival for each court depends upon responses to problems involving neighborhood relations, jobs, housing, and government agencies. Today the Rebbe must name men with wide practical experience as court managers to match the needs of the community with the ways of the modern world. With the help of "culture brokers" within the community, the hasidim have used the techniques of contemporary society to perpetuate and strengthen their community.

The Satmar court, for example, now has community services that include a private school system for more than 5,000 children, a weekly newspaper, an interest-free loan service, summer camps, an employment agency, a bus service linking Borough Park and Williamsburg, and community butcher shops whose profits support the *yeshivas.* The court also operates a medical and dental clinic, a pharmacy, and an emergency first aid and ambulance service. There is a new *besmedresh,* which holds more than 7,000 people, as well as a new ritual bathhouse for the women. To meet the housing needs of its growing population, the court purchased several hundred acres in Monroe Township, New York, where it will build a satellite community and develop local industry and job opportunities. One such community is already flourishing in nearby Monsey. To meet the loss of jobs in New York City due to the recession in the knitting and diamond industries, the Satmar hasidim have obtained federal aid to initiate programs to retrain unemployed hasidim as mechanics, machine repairmen, computer programmers, bookkeepers, and secretaries—after first assuring the Rebbe that these types of employment would not conflict with Orthodox responsibilities.

Because of the size and unity of their court, the Satmar hasidim have become an important voting bloc in their neighborhood and district. In 1972 they voted to defeat Allard Lowenstein's bid for John Rooney's congressional seat because of their interest in government support for parochial schools. Their voting power, however, was dealt a sharp blow in 1974 when the New York State reapportionment plan redrew state senate and assembly districts, thereby dividing the 35,000 hasidim in Williamsburg into two districts.

The hasidim do not object to their community being the minority in a nonwhite voting district, but they oppose having their community divided. They have brought suit in federal court, contending that the redistricting minimizes their voting strength and denies them their constitutional rights to equal protection and due process as hasidim and as white voters. The Supreme Court has agreed to hear what promises to be a landmark case in the determination of racial and ethnic prerogatives.

The hasidim are threatened by internal as well as external change. The growing hasidic population has resulted in greater geographic spread; as a consequence, social controls within the courts have been weakened. Some hasidim have expressed distress over the contrast between the appearance of religiosity and true piety. They distinguish between the *frum* (observant) who obey the basic tenets of Orthodox Judaism, and the *ehrlicher* (honest) hasid whose piety requires him to do more than the law requires.

With their continued zeal, the hasidim are not likely to discard their Orthodox traditions as did earlier immigrants. Rather, there is the likelihood of dramatic counterreactions. These might take forms already seen in hasidim—revitalized leadership and more intense perception of Orthodoxy. The most immediate threat to the hasidim, however, is the advanced age of their most distinguished leaders. When a Rebbe dies, his place is usually taken by his son, although leadership can fall to a son-in-law, a grandson, or a devoted disciple.

The process of determining succession often intensifies conflicts between factions and can result in a court's division or dissolution. In the stress of selecting a Rebbe, differences resulting from geographic distance, size, or ideology may become exacerbated. The fracturing of an overextended court can mean survival for the faction that chooses wisely and dispersion for the one that does not. For this reason, the maintenance of the court is uppermost in the minds of the hasidim when a new Rebbe must be named. They must choose as heir someone who will enable the court to continue. With the death of the Stoliner Rebbe in 1955, his followers in Israel chose to follow an established Rebbe there, while those in this country decided to wait for the Rebbe's infant grandson to grow up. Since that time, the faction in Israel has dwindled. In Brooklyn, however, the court has grown. The grandson, now the Rebbe, is twenty-two years old and has been married to his first cousin for one year. He keeps an office in his parents' home in Borough Park. Young and untested, the Rebbe must still prove himself as a leader and teacher, but his presence has enabled the Brooklyn court to remain intact.

The problem of leadership may not be so easy to solve for the Lubavitch and Satmar courts, whose Rebbes are old and without direct heirs. For the hasidim, however, tragedy has supernatural ramifications portending messianic redemption. It signals the culmination of a great design. Expressing his faith, Joel Lieb says: "In the darkest hour the Messiah will come." It is this devotion to their mystical and social heritage, together with their loyalty to the law and to their leaders, that enable the hasidim to flourish in twentieth-century New York.

Jewish Identity in the Works of Elie Wiesel*

Maurice Friedman

To speak of Elie Wiesel within the context of the theme "Jewish Identity in Contemporary French Literature" is to confront a double paradox.

The first paradox is that Elie Wiesel is properly counted among the distinguished contemporary French writers of our time. Born in Rumania, or more exactly the city of Sighet in Transylvania, raised as a Hasidic Jew with no real contact with Christian culture, deported at the age of fifteen to Auschwitz and liberated by the American army at Buchenwald, sent after liberation to a camp for Jewish refugee children in France, it was only at the age of sixteen or seventeen that Wiesel came to live in Paris and taught himself to speak and write in French. To say of a man who speaks flawless Hungarian, Yiddish, Hebrew, English, and other languages that French is not his native language is a considerable understatement. Even his published writing has not been exclusively French. The first long version of *Night* was written in Yiddish. His newspaper reports during the time when he served as a journalist at the United Nations and elsewhere were written in Yiddish, Hebrew, and English, as well as French. The lectures which formed the basis for his two books *Célébrations Hassidique (Souls on Fire: Portraits and*

* This essay is largely based on the chapter "Elie Wiesel: The Job of Auschwitz" in Maurice Friedman, *The Hidden Human Image* (New York: Delta Books, 1974). It was given as a paper for a section on "Jewish Identity in Contemporary French Literature" for the annual meeting of the Modern Language Association, New York City, December, 1976.

Legends of the Hasidic Masters) and *Célébrations Biblique (Messengers of God: Biblical Portraits and Legends)* were both originally given in English at the 92nd Street YMHA-YWHA in New York City.

For all that, Elie Wiesel is above all a contemporary *French* writer. Even when he has helped translate his own works into English, he has first of all written them in French. The only partial exception is the difference between the French book about the Soviet Jews, *Les Juifs du Silence,* which is more novelistic, and his English book *The Jews of Silence,* which is more documentary.

Even Wiesel's residence in America for the last fifteen years has not changed his primary identity as a French writer* —an identity which has been recognized by the French literary world through the Prix Medici and many other specifically French honors and distinctions. In the light of this fact, I asked Elie, long before he got married, why he lived in New York City rather than in Paris. "Because one can be more alone in New York than any city in the world," he replied. The fact that he lived at that time in the Master's Hotel directly below the office of the famous American psychologist Rollo May and that neither he nor my other friend Rollo had ever heard of each other, bore witness to Elie's self-chosen isolation.

---

* Wiesel himself says of his choice to be a French writer: "Had I wanted to write in Hungarian, I would have had an easier task but I didn't want to; I even tried to forget Hungarian. The Hungarian language reminded me too much of the Hungarian gendarmes and they were brutal. . . .

It's easier to learn a language than to forget one. I could have written in Hebrew or in Yiddish. Why I chose French, I don't know; maybe because it was harder. I'm sure that symbolically it meant something to me; it meant a new home. The language became a haven, a new beginning, a new possibility, a new world. To start expressing myself in a new language was a defiance. The defiance became even stronger because the French language is Cartesian. Reason is more important than anything else. Clarity. French is such a non-mystical language. What I try to transmit with or in and through that language is mystical experiences. So the challenge is greater." *Harry James Cargas in conversation with Elie Wiesel* (New York: Paulist Press, 1976), p. 65 f.

More than any other fiction writer of universal stature of our time, with the possible exception of Isaac Bathshevi Singer, Wiesel writes in the fullest sense of the term as a Jew. Yet his work is permeated by the spirit of Albert Camus. Although he first attained fame through his discovery by the French Catholic novelist André Mauriac, it is the spirit of Camus that Wiesel carries forward, as no other writer that I know. Elie likes to tell a story that Camus told him about an event that Camus himself witnessed. During the Nazi occupation of France, a Nazi officer chanced to overhear the conversation of two young Parisians caught up in the current vogue of French existentialist literature. The one said to the other that life is not worth living. The Nazi came up to the youth and asked him if he meant what he said. Swallowing hard, the young man stuck by his nihilism. The officer forced the young man to go into the back of a restaurant where, followed by the crowd of people in the restaurant, he made the youth stand against a wall, pulled out his pistol, cocked it, and prepared to shoot him. The last moment the officer lowered his pistol and said to the frightened boy, "It is worth living, isn't it?"

The second paradox is that of Jewish identity itself. Since the Jew in the diaspora always lives in a majority culture that is non-Jewish and, with the exception of those who live in exclusively Jewish communities, speaks, reads, and writes in the language of the country where he or she lives, he cannot have the sense of Jewish identity that comes naturally to the Frenchman as a Frenchman. This is one of the reasons that Sartre in his masterful essay, "Portrait of an Anti-Semite," sees the Frenchman who feels himself rooted in the land as bearing an impenetrable hostility to the relatively rootless and therefore "evil" Jew who may outdo him in academic competition but has no similar claim to an identity with French soil.

The problem of Jewish identity is complicated and permeated in our day by three factors—the more or less complete cultural, though not religious, assimilation of the diaspora Jew into the dominant milieu, the Nazi extermination of six million Jews, and the identification of many diaspora Jews with the state of Israel. For these reasons. we must discuss the problem of Jewish identity for the contemporary Jew in order to understand it in the works of Elie Wiesel—the paradigmatic diaspora Jewish writer of our time.

The problem of Jewish identity cannot be understood by recourse to a definition, such as the fruitless debates of earlier times as to whether being Jewish is a religious, racial, cultural, or national phenomenon. Rather we must ask what, along with the simple fact of being identified as a Jew, the contemporary Jew responds to. For one modern Jew, Jewishness is a culinary matter. For another, it is a type of music and dance. For a third, it is a form of nationalism, very much "like all the other nations." For a fourth, it is the Hebrew language. For a fifth, it is the eleven-hundred-year-old heritage of Yiddish language and culture. For a sixth, it is "ethical monotheism," a religious creed without any necessary cultural or national implications. For a seventh, it is a "civilization." The fragmented character of Jewish identity is not mere difference of opinion but so many illustrations of assimilation. Even the post-World War II recrudescence of "Jewish" novels in America is, like Philip Roth's *Portnoy's Complaint* and Saul Bellow's *Herzog,* a new stage of assimilation in which fragments of Jewish culture—the Jewish mother, Jewish food, and Jewish humor—are themselves taken over by the general culture. It is significant that Saul Bellow and not Elie Wiesel was awarded the Nobel Prize in Literature; for the former's appeal is indeed more "universal."

The rise of officially sanctioned anti-semitism in Nazi Germany, the Holocaust, and more recently the anti-Semitism, disguised as anti-Zionism, of the Soviet Union and the "Third World" have radically changed this situation for many Jews, as has the voluntary complicity of innumerable American businesses with the Arab boycott not only of companies that do business with Israel but also of companies with American

Jews in key positions. Above all it is the Nazi extermination of six million Jews that has demanded a new response of the contemporary Jew and with it a new understanding of Jewish identity. Even those who fear no repetition of what happened in Germany are appalled by the fact that it was Jewish identity, and nothing else, that brought so many millions to a grotesque and inhuman death. Some rationalize what happened by the fact that without it there might have been no state of Israel. But most are forced to question what positive meaning can exist in being Jewish that might alleviate the terrible absurdity of men being put to death merely because others define them as Jewish. These questions have had a strong influence on the resurgence of temple and synagogue membership in America, on the re-adoption of many formerly cast-off religious forms, and on the tendency of intellectuals to identify themselves as Jewish even when they have little positive content to give this term.

Another decisive change that confronts the twentieth century Jew is the existence of the State of Israel. Israel lives the "cultural pluralism" that American Jews talk of as the ideal. While Jewish culture in America is becoming an increasingly homogenized blend of East European food, synagogue membership, and suburban American values, Israel has become the melting pot that America once was. Israel shatters the illusions of those who wish to identify Jewishness with some particular cultural heritage in which they feel at home.

The contemporary Jew must also respond to the weakening of the old liberal certainties. Darwin, Marx, Einstein and Freud have made it increasingly difficult for us to cling to our eighteenth- and nineteenth-century assumptions of enlightened values, universal order, benign and rational human nature, and inevitable progress. It is not just "universal values" that have been shattered but the human image itself—the image which gave former ages and cultures some direction for meaningful personal and social existence. This loss is particularly devastating for the modern Jew. A great many twentieth-century Jews have inherited moral values from their parents without having inherited that Jewish way of life in which such values were originally grounded. Their children, as a result, do not even inherit the moral values, and it becomes increasingly clear that what we took to be the sure ground of liberal, rational, common-sense morality is really an abyss.

In the face of Auschwitz, Hiroshima, Biafra, Vietnam, Arab-Israeli hostility, Third World terrorism, and the continued threat of nuclear war, the young Jew knows that much of what has been handed down to him is inadequate for confronting the concrete situations in which he finds himself. He may, as a result, join the ranks of those who rebel against the "death of God," the alienation of modern man, and the life of the "Modern Exile," as I have described these in my book *Problematic Rebel: Melville, Dostoievsky, Kafka, Camus**. If he does, he is likely to fall into one of the two types of "Modern Rebel" that I describe in *Problematic Rebel* or a mixture of the two. He may become a "Modern Promethean," rejecting all meaning with Nietzsche and Sartre and proclaiming the free invention of values to replace those that no longer exist. Or he may become a "Modern Job," one who rebels against meaninglessness for the sake of meaning, one whose contending takes place within the "Dialogue with the Absurd," one who trusts even while he opposes and, in the words of Martin Buber, "withstands this meaninglessness to the end until through suffering and contradiction meaning shines forth anew."

The most impassioned complaint, the most moving embodiment of "the Job of the gas chambers" is found in the work of Elie Wiesel, as in the man himself for those of us who know him. His slim volumes form one unified outcry, one sustained protest, one sobbing and singing prayer. In the first, *Night,* Wiesel tells the story of how he was deported with his family from his Hungarian-Jewish village when he was a child of fifteen, how his mother and sister were meta-

---

* 2nd revised, enlarged, and radically reorganized edition (The University of Chicago Press and Phoenix Books (paperback), 1970).

morphosed into the smoke above the crematories, how he and his father suffered through Auschwitz, Buchenwald, and forced winter marches until finally, just before liberation, his father died. For Wiesel the "death of God" came all at once, without preparation—not as a stage in the history of culture but as a terrifying event that turned the pious Hasidic Jew into a Modern Job whose complaint against "the great injustice in the world" can never be silenced.

> Never shall I forget those flames which consumed my Faith forever. Never shall I forget that nocturnal silence which deprived me, for all eternity, of the desire to live. Never shall I forget those moments which murdered my God and my soul and turned my dreams to dust. Never shall I forget these things, even if I am condemned to live as long as God Himself. Never.

On a later day when he watched the hanging of a child with the sad face of an angel, he heard someone behind him groan, "Where is God? Where is He? Where can He be now?" and a voice within him answered: "Where? Here He is—He has been hanged here, on these gallows." When after the liberation of Buchenwald he looked at himself in a mirror, a corpse gazed back at him. "The look in his eyes, as they stared into mine, has never left me."

Wiesel's novels are continuous with the autobiography. In *Dawn* he places this same boy, now called Elisha, in the position of a Jewish terrorist, killing English soldiers in an effort to secure the independence of the Jewish state in Palestine. Elisha had wanted to study philosophy at the Sorbonne in order to rediscover the human image that had been destroyed for him by the extermination camps: "Where is God to be found? In suffering or in rebellion? When is a man most truly a man? When he submits or when he refuses? Where does suffering lead him? To purification or to bestiality?" Instead Elisha gives his future to the "Movement," the first group in his knowledge which changes the destiny of the Jew from that of victim to executioner. It is he himself who must execute the English hostage, Captain John Dawson, whom the Movement has sentenced to die as a reprisal for the hanging by the British of one of their number. He comes to realize, in taking upon himself an act so absolute as killing, that he is making his father, his mother, his teacher, his friends into murderers. He cannot rid himself of the impression that he has donned the field-gray uniform of the Nazi S. S. officer. His victim-to-be is sorry for Elisha and troubled by him—an eighteen-year-old turned terrorist—while Elisha tries in vain to hate him as if the coming of the Messiah were dependent upon the Jews finally learning "to hate those who have humiliated and from time to time exterminated them." But when he kills John Dawson, he feels that he has killed himself, that he himself has become the night.

Next to Camus' *The Plague,* the clearest presentation in literature of the progression through the Modern Promethean to the Modern Job is Wiesel's novel *The Town Beyond the Wall.* After the war and the extermination camps, Michael went to Paris and lived in utter solitude in order to seek his God, to track him down. Even in his determination not to give in so easily as Job, even in his insistence that he will be a match for God and will defy his inhuman Justice, he still remains within his dialogue with his God. "He took my childhood; I have a right to ask Him what He did with it." Michael combines the Modern Promethean and the Modern Job, and he shows the link between them: In our time man *has* to go through the first to reach the second, but he may not remain in the first. At the death of the "little prince"—a Jewish boy pampered by the Nazis in the concentration camps only to die under a truck in Paris—Michael's suffering leads him to the verge of madness.

An immense wrath, savage and destructive, welled up suddenly in Michael. His eyes flashed. The little prince's death—this death—was too unjust, too absurd. He wanted to pit himself against the angel as Jacob had: fell him with a blow, trample him. One gesture, just one, but a gesture in proportion to his misery.

Through the aid of his friend Pedro, who works the Black Market, Michael returns after the war to his native Hungarian city. Arrested by the police, Michael is forced to say "prayers," i.e., to stand eight hours at a stretch before a wall without moving, eating, or drinking. In person and later, when Michael is in prison, through his internalized voice, Pedro warns Michael against the mad revolt which tempts him.

"You frighten me, Pedro said. "You want to eliminate suffering by pushing it to the extreme: to madness. To say 'I suffer, therefore I am' is to become the enemy of man. What you must say is 'I suffer, therefore you are.' Camus wrote somewhere that to protest against a universe of unhappiness you had to create happiness. That's an arrow pointing the way: it leads to another human being. And not via absurdity."

These, of all Pedro's words, are the ones that later come to Michael's aid.

Michael finds the alternative to going mad in making himself responsible for his prison cellmate, a young boy who is completely silent and, until he responds to Michael's heartbreaking efforts, completely out of touch. In bringing Eliezer back into dialogue Michael brings himself back to humanity. Pedro has taught Michael and Michael teaches Eliezer the necessity of clinging to humanity. "It's in humanity itself that we find both our question and the strength to keep it within limits." To flee to a nirvana through a considered indifference or a sick apathy "is to oppose humanity in the most absurd, useless, and comfortable manner possible." Like Doctor Rieux in *The Plague,* Michael recognizes that "It's harder to remain human than to try to leap beyond humanity."

Malach, the Hebrew word that is usually translated "angel," actually means "messenger." *The Gates of the Forest* is the story of the lasting effect of two "messengers" on the life of Gregor, a young Jewish refugee. Gavriel, the nameless messenger to whom he gives his own Hebrew name, and the much more tangible Leib the Lion, accompany him—in person or in memory—through the spring when he hides from the Nazis in a cave in the forest, through summer when he plays the role of a feebleminded mute in the village where Maria, the former family servant, passes him off as her nephew, through autumn when he joins the partisans fighting under the leadership of his childhood friend, Leib the Lion, and through winter when he seeks a way forward in postwar New York where he has gone with his wife Clara, once the girl friend of Leib.

Gavriel tells Gregor that the Messiah has already come, that he is among men, that nonetheless the horror has taken place, and that all that is left is to learn to laugh in the face of the horror—a terrible, mad laugh that defies the absurd. It is the laugh of a man poised midway between the Modern Promethean and the Modern Job and holding the tension of both. The message which this messenger brings Gregor is that of the "final solution," the unsuspected extermination of the Jews. His father will not come back. No one will come back. His family has left without hope of return.

When the Hungarian soldiers come with dogs, Gavriel gives himself up to prevent their discovering Gregor. Before going, he tells Gregor of how he discovered the Messiah in a simple beadle who at night wept for the destruction of the Temple, for the exile of Israel and that of the Shekinah. When the Nazis came, Gavriel went to Moshe the Silent and demanded that he do his duty and disobey God for the sake of saving from annihilation the people of the witness, the martyr people, the people of the covenant. But the "Messiah" laid down his arms without resisting and let himself be taken prisoner and executed. "I tell you, Gregor," says Gavriel, "that hope is no longer possible nor permitted: . . . the Messiah has come and the world has remained what it was: an immense butchery." When Gregor goes to live with Maria in her village and impersonates a deaf-mute, he is forced to play Judas at the school play and is almost killed in the frenzy of the crowd. "Miraculously" casting off his dumbness and speaking with the voice of a prophet, he forces the people, including the priest, to beg Judas' pardon—for it is *he,* not Jesus, who is the crucified one. Yet Gregor resists his desire for vengeance. When he announces that he is not the son of Maria's sister Illeana but a Jew, a smile not of victory but of pity illuminates his face.

Escaping to the forest, he makes contact with a band of Jewish partisans and rediscovers his childhood friend Leib the Lion. When they were boys, Leib had taught him to fight the gang of children that descended on them on their way to school with cries of "dirty Jews!" and "Christ-killers!" on their lips. The mythic proportions that Leib took on then in Gregor's eyes are now realized in fact in his role as leader of the Jewish partisans, a latter-day Bar Kochba. Gregor informs Leib of what has been known for a long time already in Washington, London, and Stockholm but which no one had taken the trouble to radio to the Jews of Transylvania—that the deported Jews were not being taken to factories or labor camps but to extermination centers. The shocked and almost unbelieving Leib orders an attempt to liberate Gavriel from prison to ascertain the truth of Gregor's report and is captured himself in the process.

Gregor makes the Promethean laughter of Gavriel and the Jobian courage of Leib his own, and they sustain him and give him strength until that distant day in postwar New York when he is confronted by a Hasidic rabbi who recognizes both his suffering and his pride. When Gregor admits that what he wants is that the rebbe cease to pray and that he howl instead, the rebbe, with a movement of revolt, says to him, slowly, accentuating every word and stopping after every phrase: "Who has told you that force comes from a cry and not from prayer, from anger and not from compassion? . . . The man who sings is the brother of him who goes to his death fighting." The dancing, the singing, the joy of the

Hasid is *in spite of* the fact that all reason for dancing, singing, and joy has been taken from him.

> "He's guilty; do you think I don't know it? That I have no eyes to see, no ears to hear? That my heart doesn't revolt? That I have no desire to beat my head against the wall and shout like a madman, to give rein to my sorrow and disappointment? Yes, he is guilty. He has become an ally of evil, of death, of murder, but the problem is still not solved."

The revolt of the Modern Promethean is unmasked by the rebbe as only a romantic gesture. It still leaves the question of what to do, of how to live, of the direction, if any, from which salvation and hope must come.

Unable to bear any longer the way his wife Clara betrays him by remaining faithful to her first lover, the dead Leib, Gregor has resolved to leave her. Now, after joining a *minyan* in reciting the *kaddish*—the prayer for the dead—he knows that he will return to Clara to take up again the battle of winning her back to the present, to life. It does not matter whether or not the Messiah comes, Gregor realizes, or the fact that he is too late. If we will be sincere, humble, and strong, the Messiah will come—every day, a thousand times a day—for he is not a single man but all men. When Clara learns to sing again and Gregor to weep, it will be he that sings and weeps in them.

The original title of Wiesel's book *Chants des Morts* ("Songs of the Dead") might well be the title of all his books. But so also might be the English title, *Legends of Our Time*. Elie Wiesel, as anyone knows who has ever heard him speak, belongs to the oldest profession in the world, that of the storyteller—the person who preserves the awesome life of the tribe in the form of myths and legends—dramatic events —rather than of connected historical accounts. In a series of poignant and powerful writings, he has woven together words and silence into tales of unexampled beauty and terror. In each successive work he has wrested an image of humanity from his Dialogue with the Absurd—his contending with the Nazi holocaust and the monstrous shadow which it cast on his life. The Job of Auschwitz "will always take the side of man confronted with the Absolute." God's presence, or his absence, at Treblinka or Maidanek "poses a problem which will forever remain insoluble." Nor does it matter that "loss of faith for some equaled discovery of God for others." Both stood within the Modern Job's Dialogue with the Absurd: "Both answered the same need to take a stand, the same impulse to rebel. In both cases it was an accusation."

"My generation has been robbed of everything, even of our cemeteries," says Wiesel in *Legends of Our Time.* Where there are no cemeteries, the dead refuse to stay dead, and the living must give them proper burial through creating a structure within which mourning can take place. The whole of Wiesel's writing is just such a work of mourning, of witnessing to the living dead: "The act of writing is for me often nothing more than the secret or conscious desire to carve words on a tombstone: to the memory of a town forever vanished, to the memory of a childhood in exile, to the memory of all those I loved and who, before I could tell them I loved them, went away." These include his playmates, his teachers, Moshe the Madman, the beadle, and his family—all from the town of Sighet. But they also include men whom he knew in the extermination camps, such as the man who went to his death laughing after he had fasted on Yom Kippur as a Job of Auschwitz must fast: "Not out of obedience, but out of defiance."

"Man defines himself by what disturbs him and not by what reassures him." Elie Wiesel lets himself be disturbed, and he disturbs us by insisting, in the face of *all* who turn away from it, on "the guilt we share." Witnessing the trial of Eichmann, Wiesel conducts a worldwide trial: of the indigenous populations of Hungary and Poland whose eagerness to become *Judenrein* alone made it possible for "the cattle trains with their suffocating human cargo" to "roll swiftly into the night"; of "the whole outside world, which looked on in a kind of paralysis and passively allowed" the murder of six million Jews, a number that could never have been reached had Roosevelt, Churchill, and the pope let loose an avalanche of angry protestations; of the American Jewish community which did not use its political and financial powers to move heaven and earth to save five to ten thousand Jews from murder each day; of Chaim Weizmann who put off for two weeks the messenger of the Holocaust who had told him that "every passing day meant the lives of at least ten thousand Jews" ("How did Brand not go stark raving mad?" Wiesel asks.); of Gideon Hausner, Ben-Gurion, and the Israelis who tried Eichmann without crying out "in a voice loud enough to be heard by three generations: We never attempted the impossible—we never even exhausted the possible." From this trial, Wiesel concludes that "with the advent of the Nazi regime in Germany, humanity became witness to what Martin Buber would call an eclipse of God." It was above all, in fact, in the name of the "Job of Auschwitz," that Buber called this an age of the "eclipse of God."

It is Auschwitz that will engender Hiroshima and perhaps that extinction of the human race by nuclear warfare that "will be the punishment for Auschwitz, where, in the ashes, the hope of man was extinguished." At the time of the Holocaust, those outside did not speak out. "One need only glimpse through the newspapers of the period to become disgusted with the human adventure on this earth." Nor were the inmates of the camps ignorant of this. Their seemingly weak "acceptance" of their death became, in consequence, "an act of lucidity, a protest" not only against their torturers, but also against the rest of humanity that had abandoned, excluded, and rejected them. "It is as though every country—and not only Germany—had decided to see the Jew as a kind of subhuman species" whose disappearance did not weigh on the conscience since the concept of brotherhood did not apply to him.

In Wiesel's haunting and compelling novel of the Six Day War, *A Beggar in Jerusalem,* the Holocaust and the threat of extermination that seemed to hover over the people of the state of Israel on the eve of the Six Day War fuse into one reality. "They were alone," writes Wiesel, "as earlier in Europe in the time of *Night.*" Perhaps it was the overwhelming feeling that Wiesel himself was the first to articulate— that we could not allow this extermination to happen twice in one lifetime—that gives this book a different time sense from all his other novels. In all of them there are flashbacks and the easy—and enormously painful—intermingling of what has been and what is. But only in *A Beggar* are all the ages present simultaneously. One of the circle of "beggars" who sit before the Wall during the long and story-laden nights after the Six Day War tells of when he came up to the man Jesus as he hung on the cross and said to him, "They will kill millions of your people in your name," at which Jesus wept so bitterly that the man who stood beneath him wept too. In *A Beggar,* as in *One Generation After,* there appears the bitter irony that alive, Jesus, the Jew, is the enemy of mankind; whereas once he is safely dead he becomes their God. "We have been crucified six million times," Wiesel seems to say, "and no amount of worship of the crucified ones will stay the hand of the next slayer who comes looking for a victim."

In 1967 when Elie came as a favor to me to lecture at Manhattanville College of the Sacred Heart, where I was the first non-Catholic Professor of Philosophy and Religion in the one hundred forty years of the College's history, he prefaced his talk by the statement that this was only the second time in his life that he had spoken before a Catholic audience. "When I was a child in Sighet, I used to turn my face away from the Catholic church—not out of hatred but out of fear." Later Manhattanville invited Elie to give its commencement address and gave him an honorary doctorate. In 1973 I took my course in "Judaism and Literature" at Temple University to hear Elie lecture at a Reform temple in Philadelphia. Among the students was a mature Catholic woman in the forefront of those who are shaping a new Catholicism in our day. This woman reacted so strongly to a comment of Elie about Jesus that henceforth she could not read his works or write about him without extreme, belligerent antipathy. What Elie said was that Jesus must bear some responsibility for what has been done in his name in the two millenia since he lived. My own first thought was that Elie spoke out of discomfort with the liberal and in many ways assimilated temple in which he spoke. My wife said that it clearly arose out of his identification with the European Jews and his consequent antagonism to that traditional Christian anti-semitism that had supplied the structures (the yellow badge and the ghetto) to the Nazis and that had expressed itself in the willing cooperation of the non-Jewish populations of Eastern Europe in the Nazi extermination of the Jews. When I asked Elie about it, he explained it as a reaction against the growing Christian campaign to convert young Jews to Christianity. It was not an antipathy to Christianity as such but to its presumption in trying to capture the Jewish youth that angered Elie, even as his gratitude for André Mauriac's preface to *Night* was tempered by the latter's statement, "Did I speak of . . . the Crucified, whose Cross has conquered the world? Did I affirm that the stumbling block to his faith was the cornerstone of mine, and that the conformity between the Cross and the suffering of men was in my eyes the key to that impenetrable mystery whereon the faith of his childhood had perished?" In the light of Wiesel's recently published conversations with Kargas, it is clear that both my wife's explanation and Elie's are necessary to understand the statement which he also repeats there: "Whether he was the Christ is for Christians to decide. As far as the Jews are concerned, he may be retroactively guilty for all the murders and massacres that were done in his name. I believe that the Christians betrayed the Christ more than the Jews did." "The Christ" is not the historical man Jesus first of all but the symbol, and it is this which may make sense of Wiesel's retroactive attribution of guilt. His real accusation, in any case, is neither against Jesus nor against Christ but against Christianity and Christians.

His first accusation concerns the Christian responsibility for the Holocaust:

Auschwitz would not have been possible without Christianity. John XXIII understood this. The fact that Hitler was never excommunicated; the fact that, I think, over twenty percent of the S. S. killers were practicing Christians; the fact that Pius XII never spoke up means that Christianity's role, or the Christian Church's role—both Protestant and Catholic—was so dominant in the fact that so many Jews could have been killed.

His second accusation concerns the Christian desire to convert the Jew.

If the Christians give up their dream to convert Israel (Israel never tried to convert the Church) then I'm sure we can find some common ground. . . . For many centuries the Christian defined himself by the suffering he imposed on the Jew. The more the Jew suffered, the better a Christian was. Theologically, the Christian saw that he was *the* Jew, the true Jew; the true Israel was the Church. The others had to suffer for not becoming part of the new concept of Judaism.*

The plot of *A Beggar of Jerusalem,* insofar as there is one, is the story of two men, David and Katriel, the one present throughout, the other both present and absent. We come to feel that David and Katriel are one person even before David is recognized by Katriel's wife Malka, whom he has never met before yet who is his wife. Nor is it clear to David which one of them, himself or Katriel, is "the beggar of Jerusalem" —the man who will come and tell you your own story in such a way that you will recognize in it your life and death.

Commenting on those Jews who wished, before the Six Day War, to define themselves simply as men and only accidentally as Jews, Wiesel neatly reverses the formula and sug-

---

* *Harry Kargas in conversation with Elie Wiesel,* p. 34 f.

gests that in our day "one cannot be a man without assuming the condition of the Jew." The old dream of universalism, by doing away with Jewishness, was a lost, a false dream. "As a Jew I believe that to be a Jew is to be an opening. But when the Jew is Jewish he speaks on behalf of everybody," says Wiesel to Kargas and adds, "At one point or another, every person becomes Jewish—the moment he becomes authentic he genuinely—though metaphorically—becomes Jewish. And every Jew is universal the moment he is genuine." In accepting his own condition, his own identity, the Jew gives himself to his people and through it to the entire world, to mankind. Any attempt to oppose Jewishness to universalism would be impossible and unfeasible, says Wiesel, and "not in line with our concept of history." "The Jew is the most exposed person in the world today," wrote Martin Buber in 1933. The inhumanity which has been unleashed upon the Jew since then so threatens the humanity of all persons that only in sharing that exposure can any person today become human. Today we must all suffer with the "Modern Exile" or lose our birthright as human beings.

This state of exile is also the state of God today, *A Beggar in Jerusalem* suggests. The Messiah does not dwell above in glory, but below in the suffering and exposure of men. God too has need of a witness: "In the beginning was the Word; the Word is the history of man; and man is the history of God." The Shekinah, the indwelling Glory of God, remains in Jerusalem yet follows all Jews everywhere into exile. The Shekinah dwells in the contradiction, and the greatest and most tormenting contradiction of all is to kill for the sake of God men who are created in the image of God: "He who kills kills God. Each murder is a suicide of which the Eternal is eternally the victim." This contradiction is similar to the question that haunts Elie Wiesel throughout each of his novels: How is it possible to live for the living without betraying the dead?

The answer to this question lies in bringing forth from its concealment the hidden human image. If man is created in the image of God, then the only way that that image can be transmitted is through transmitting the image of the human. It is for this that a whole people set out to march for a third time, and with the living marched the dead: "Israel conquered because its army, its people included six million additional names." Only Elie Wiesel in our generation has been capable of uniting the Holocaust and the emergence and survival of the state of Israel without denying the mystery or reality of either or turning one into historical cause and the other into historical effect. In this sense, all of Elie's other books were preparations for *A Beggar in Jerusalem;* for only here do the living fight *with* the dead and not against them, only here is it possible for David to stay with Malka despite their loyalty to Katriel.

In what he himself says will be his final book on the Holocaust, *One Generation After,* Wiesel repeatedly asserts that in the Holocaust man betrayed his image and that whether or not the murder of a million children makes historical sense, it denies and condemns man. The Job of Auschwitz hears above all the command to witness to what has happened, recalling and telling every detail, writing down his testimony moments before dying in agony, surviving in order to be able to tell—to howl against the wall of death that crushed a whole people. It is only this—and the hope that someone might listen to this recounting—that enables the Job of Auschwitz to continue at all. Nothing so concisely sums up Elie Wiesel's mission as a person and as a writer as his own sentence, "I do not demand of the raconteur that he play the role of master but that he fulfill his duty as messenger and as witness." What it means to "hold fast to one's integrity" in this calling of messenger and witness Wiesel has shown us in every one of his novels and stories and in *Night* and *The Jews of Silence.*

Wiesel's identification with the state of Israel does not entail a hatred for Israel's enemies. The victorious Jew "is no longer a victim, but he will never become a torturer" or seek to break the will of the vanquished. That he *does* identify himself with the state of Israel Wiesel leaves in no doubt. Although he says that only those whom Eichmann killed could decide what to do with him, he tells Kargas, "What Israel does—maybe I'm too weak and too inhibited and also too Jewish to criticize or to say one way or another—what Israel does, Israel does. And does it for me." At the same time he makes clear that Israel is not for him a matter of nationalism in the modern sense: "I think that the secularists were wrong when they wanted to have a nation like all the others. They were wrong because Israel *cannot* be a nation like all others. It is impossible. It's a counter-sense, it's a nonsense, really, a contradiction in terms." The state of Israel in no way cancels out the extermination of six million Jews. It may nonetheless be permitted to the Job of Auschwitz—the survivor who trusts *and* contends and holds fast to the integrity of the human in so doing—to see in Israel "a victory over the absurd and the inhuman." "I belong to a generation," writes Wiesel, "that has not known many such victories." This victory is not incompatible with the continued exile of the Shekinah, the mark of an unredeemed world, as the last chapter of *A Beggar in Jerusalem* makes clear.

> A victor, he? Victory does not prevent suffering from having existed, nor death from having taken its toll. How can one work for the living without by that very act betraying those who are absent?

When the General Assembly of the United Nations voted to label Zionism "racist," Elie, who was in Paris at the time, wrote an article entitled, "The Honor of Being a Zionist," which was published on the front page of *Paris Soir*. "I had not strongly identified myself as a Zionist before," Elie said to me, "but in the face of this I had to." This stand is fully consistent with Wiesel's self-definition in his conversations with Kargas: "Mainly, my position in the Jewish community is really the position of a witness from within and defender from without," a position which he links with the duties and privileges of a storyteller, a writer. This same position is expressed in Wiesel's concern with "the Jews of silence"—the

Jews of the Soviet Union the discrimination against whom Wiesel has done more than any other person in the world to make known. *Simhat-Torah,* the day of rejoicing in the giving of the Torah, "will henceforth be associated with the Jews of silence," Wiesel testifies after going to Moscow for a second time to see the thousands of young Jews, deprived of their heritage, publicly affirming and celebrating their existence as Jews. "For those who participate in their dancing, each moment becomes privileged: a victory over silence." From these Soviet Jews Wiesel learned that those who make of their Judaism a song are of equal value with those who make of it a prayer. "The staunchest Hasid could learn from the most assimilated Jewish student in Moscow how to rejoice and how to transform his song into an act of belief and defiance." Out of a situation of constraint these young Jews made an act of choice, out of what should break and humiliate them they drew their force of resistance. This witness to the Jews of silence is also a reproach on Wiesel's part to the silence of the Jews in other parts of the world in the face of Soviet discrimination against two million of their brethren.

In *One Generation After,* Wiesel tells a young German of the New Left that if he does not despise his guilty fathers, he will become inhuman himself and unworthy of redemption. Wiesel demands that he face up to the reality of the past or become guilty of the Holocaust himself. "I shall not hate you," Wiesel declares in an echo of Camus' "Letter to a Nazi Friend" that he quotes from at the head of this essay, but "I shall denounce, unmask and fight you with all my power." In "To a Young Jew of Today" God himself is brought to trial as he was by Job and two and a half millennia later by the Hasidic rebbe Levi Yitzhak of Berditshev. "If God is an answer, it must be the wrong answer." There is no answer: "the agony of the believer equals the bewilderment of the non-believer." All there is, is a question which man must live and formulate and in so doing challenge God. This challenge is permissible, indeed required. "He who says no to God is not necessarily a renegade. . . . One can say anything as long as it is for man, not against him, as long as one remains inside the covenant." Here contending means faithfulness; to betray the present means to destroy the past, whereas to fulfill oneself means choosing to be a link "between the primary silence of creation and the silence that weighed on Treblinka."

The task of the Job of Auschwitz is contending for meaning within the Dialogue with the Absurd. If he rakes over the ashes of the Holocaust, it is because "to be a Jew today . . . means to testify," to bear witness with fervent, if saddened, joy to the Israel that is and to bear witness with "restrained, harnessed anger, free of sterile bitterness" to the world of the six million Jews that is no longer. "For the contemporary Jewish writer, there can be no theme more human, no project more universal."

"Was it not a mistake to testify, and by that very act, affirm their faith in man and word?" asks Wiesel, and replies for himself, "I know of at least one who often feels like answering yes." This note of doubt and bitterness also belongs to the Job of Auschwitz as it did to the original Job. He would be a dishonest rebel if he did not sometimes say with Wiesel: "Nothing has been learned; Auschwitz has not even served as a warning. For more detailed information, consult your daily newspaper." The storyteller is left with a sense of guilt and impotence. Writing itself is called in question; for by its uniqueness the Holocaust defies literature. The storyteller who sees himself essentially as a witness realizes in anguish that he cannot "approach this universe of darkness without turning into a pedlar of night and agony." The messenger unable to deliver his message knows that "no image is sufficiently demented, no cry sufficiently blasphemous to illustrate the plight of a single victim, resigned or rebellious." And yet the story had to be told for the sake of our children. "We needed to face the dead again and again, in order. . . . to seek among them, beyond all contradiction and absurdity, a symbol, a beginning of promise." Finding promise in the Dialogue with the Absurd is intimately linked for Wiesel with his identity as a Jew:

I'm convinced that if I had not been Jewish I would not have accepted the awesome responsibilities of bringing life into this world. It is really the Jew in me that says that we must go on, we must build endurance, no matter what. We must show that although there is no hope, we must invent hope. Although the world is not worthy to have its own children, we must bring these children, hoping that we should change the world.*

It is precisely this tension between the powerful urge to keep silent and the equally powerful call to witness that forms the heart of Wiesel's novel *The Oath.* Set in two time periods before and after the Holocaust, *The Oath* only gradually reveals itself as the most terrifying of Wiesel's works in its suggestion of the possibility of the permanent eclipse of the hidden human image. It is, by the same token, a powerful comment on the Holocaust itself—not just as a sickness of the Nazis or of modern man but of humanity. In the first instance, this is European, Christian humanity, but in the end it is the human as such that is tainted by senseless hatred and ultimate stupidity

The Oath is structured around a dialogue between an old man with a terrible secret protected by a solemn communal vow and a young man contemplating suicide who just thereby tempts him to break his vow. On a deeper level still, it is the hidden image of Moshe the Madman, a recurrent figure through each of Wiesel's works, and the story of Kolvillàg, a small town somewhere between the Dnieper and the Carpathians which represents all the towns and cities in the world. The name of the old man is Azriel, but he is also called by some Katriel. Like Wiesel's own teacher, whom he portrays in "The Wandering Jew" in *Legends of Our Time,* Azriel is a mysterious figure, someone equally at ease quoting from the Talmud or Mao Tse-tung, master of seven ancient tongues and a dozen living ones, "haughty with the powerful, humble with the deprived," and above all a *Na-venadnik,*

Harry James Kargas in conversation with Elie Wiesel, p. 111.

one whose destiny is never to put down roots in any one place. Azriel's chronicler father and his mad teacher Moshe, by making him the repository of their tragic truths, doomed him to be survivor, a messenger, and a perpetual exile—revealing and attaching himself to no one, watching over the inhabitants of the secret world inside him. In his daydreams it is not he but his village that is roaming the roads in search of help and redemption: He is but a link, the hyphen between countless communities.

There is nothing paradoxical in this; for Azriel's message is the message of silence—of events too monstrous to be told, too bewildering to be imagined. It is the silence of the Holocaust, the burden of which the youth of today have inherited without its mystery. The Exterminating Angel has turned all men into victims, not least those who attempt to use its services. The culmination of fanaticism and stupidity affects equally victims and executioners. "Whoever kills, kills himself; whoever preaches murder will be murdered. One may not accept any meaning imposed on death by the living. Just as every murder is a suicide, every suicide is a murder." To kill the other, like the sin of Cain, is to murder the brother in oneself. To kill oneself is to murder oneself in one's brother.

A central motif in *The Oath,* as in *The Gates of the Forest,* is messianism—the inverted messianism of a cursed century. Man clamors for the Messiah, but he is fascinated by death. The Christian Messiah expires on the cross, leaving others to bear his shame. But the Jewish Messiah survives all generations, perhaps ashamed to reveal himself or ashamed for a world in which men claim to be brothers and are nothing but wild, solitary beasts. "In these days exile is becoming ever harsher. To have hope in God is to have hope against God." "What is the Messiah," said Moshe to Azriel, "if not man transcending his solitude in order to make his fellow-man less solitary?" "Every truth that shuts you in, that does not lead to others, is inhuman." In defying Moshe's vow of silence, Azriel is allowing Moshe, the hidden image of the human, to speak through him to the young man. Conversely, in forcing Azriel to reinvent a meaning to his quest, the young man is unwittingly helping Azriel even as Azriel is helping him. "May God save you not from suffering but from indifference to suffering," Moshe had said to Azriel, and it is out of gratitude to the young man for saving him from this indifference that Azriel breaks his oath.

Moshe is a great Kabbalist with miraculous powers who channels his fervor into prayer, study—and madness. Moshe takes as his only disciple Azriel, the son of Shmuel—the chronicler responsible in his generation for the Book of Kolvillàg. Both—Shmuel and Moshe—are trying to attain the same messianic goal, the one through memory of the past, the other through imagination of the future. When the Jews of Kolvillàg are threatened with a pogrom triggered by the disappearance of a Christian hoodlum who torments birds and children alike, Moshe takes it upon himself to save the community by meeting the prefect's demand for a Jewish name on which to pin the supposed murder. Beaten into unconsciousness by the sadistic sergeant to whom he "confesses," Moshes takes on the role of a Modern Job. "Nothing justifies suffering," he thinks, but "nobody is required to explain it, only to fight it." One cannot confer a meaning on death.

"To turn death into a philosophy is not Jewish. To turn it into a theology is anti-Jewish. Whoever praises death ends up either serving or totally ignoring it. . . . We . . . consider death the primary defect and injustice inherent in creation. To die for God is to die against God. For us, man's ultimate confrontation is only with God."

"What is essential," Moshe tells the boy Azriel, "is to live to the limit. Let your words be shouts or silence but . . . nothing in between. Let your desire be absolute and your wait as well. . . . Whoever walks in the night, moves against night."

Moshe's desire to be a martyr for the sake of Israel is not

granted, for once stirred up, the senseless hatred will not stop until everything is destroyed. Through the intervention of the friendly prefect, Moshe is allowed to summon the whole of the Jewish community to an extraordinary session where he sweeps everyone up into his own rebellion against the traditional Jewish task of pleasing God by becoming the illustrations of their own tales of martyrdom. Jewish memory, it was held, robbed the executioner of his final victory by preventing his attempts to erase the evidence of his cruelty, haunting his conscience, and warning humanity present and future of his crimes. Murdered, plundered, humiliated, oppressed, expelled from society and history, forbidden the right to laugh or sing or even cry, the surviving Jews turned their ordeal into a legend destined for men of good will. "The more they hate us, the more we shout our love of man." But now, says Moshe the Madman, the time has come to put an end to this Jewish role of being mankind's memory and heart. "Now we shall adopt a new way: silence." By refusing to testify anymore, we can break the link between suffering and the history of suffering, thereby forestalling future abominations. With all the mystic power till now held in check, Moshe leads the whole community to take an oath that whoever may survive the massacre and humiliation which await the Jews of Kolvillàg will go to their graves without speaking of it, and he seals this oath by placing the entire people of Israel under the sign of the *Herem*—the dread word of excommunication and damnation!

What rules in Kolvillàg just before the attack is fear, fear "ready to rob you of vision and life and of your very desire to go on living." "Heralding disaster, fear becomes disaster." Fear operates in the besieged community of Kolvillàg exactly as the plague in Camus' Oran:

Fear is absorbed and communicated like poison or leprosy. Once contaminated by fear, you too become a carrier. And you transmit it the way primary experience is transmitted: involuntarily, unwittingly, almost clandestinely; from eye to eye, from mouth to mouth.

A father describes a pogrom to his daughter as worse than hell; for in hell there is no blind cruelty, no gratuitous savagery, no desecration, no trampled innocence. A pogrom is "insanity unleashed, demons at liberty, the basest instincts, the most vile laughter." Even the Hasidic rebbe says, "We were wrong . . . to try, wrong to hope. . . . A Jew must not expect anything from Christians, man must not expect anything from man."

When the attack comes it is "primitive and absolute hate," an apocalyptic vision of "horsemen and beasts" which announces "the explosion and end of the world." This terrifying inhuman night does not stop at destroying the Jews but spreads to all, the killers and the killed. "It is a night of punishment, of supreme ultimately stupidity," Moshe says to the prefect who tries in vain to save him. "They kill themselves by killing, they dig their own graves by murdering us, they annihilate the world by destroying our homes." What follows is a babel of mutual murder that spares no one. "The killers were killing each other, senselessly, with swords, hatchets and clubs. Brothers and sisters striking one another, friends and accomplices strangling one another." Here the two voices of Elie Wiesel—the memory of Shmuel and the silence of Moshe—are united in an unbearable vision of a "Second Coming"; "Suddenly I understood with every fiber of my being why I was shuddering at this vision of horror: I had just glimpsed the future." The narrative, which dooms the youth to survive while allowing Azriel to return to Kolvillag to die in his stead, Azriel concludes in the name of his mad friend Moshe, the "last prophet and first messiah of a mankind that is no more."

The most sublime and impassioned protest of this Job of Auschwitz is neither novel, play, nor essay but the cantata *Ani Maamin,* which in November 1973 was performed at Carnegie Hall to music composed for it by the great French composer Darius Milhaud. It is the haunting and powerful plaint of Abraham, Isaac, and Jacob, the traditional intercessors for Israel, who, in the face of the Holocaust, turn to God and then away from God to Israel to share the fate of the exterminated millions and the tormented survivors. Maimonides' statement of perfect faith that, though the Messiah tarry, he will come, is not here the affirmation of those pious Jews who went to their deaths in the gas chambers singing these words as a hymn. It is Wiesel's and our affirmation *despite* God and *despite* man, an affirmation that is as much contending as trust. It is the Dialogue with the Absurd embodied and voiced by the man who, more than any other living human being, has become in his own person the "Job of Auschwitz." This Job of Auschwitz is not the person who was exterminated, but, as Buber stated when he coined the phrase, that *survivor* of the Holocaust who does not put up with faceless fate but struggles for redemption *with* and *against* our "cruel and kind Lord" whose revelation in our times is only deepening of his hiddenness.

> Who is the Jew? How is he to be identified, to identify himself? The answer is found in authenticity. " 'We are Jews only by accident; we are men and that is all.' Yet, here they are: Jews again. And men. Because there comes a time when one cannot be a man without assuming the Jewish condition." . . . "The Jews are God's memory and the heart of mankind. We do not always know this, but the others do, and that is why they treat us with suspicion and cruelty."*

This is not a definition of Jewish identity that all or even most Jews would agree with. Yet it is Elie Wiesel's own vision of Jewish identity—the one that he witnesses for and lives by.

---

* *Harry Kargas in conversation with Elie Wiesel*, p. 123.

A New Age Judaism

Philip Mandelkorn

What is a Jew? Many of us asked ourselves this question. We were raised by Jewish parents in not-such-Jewish homes. Yet, we celebrated Passover and the High Holidays. Some of our families were more observant. But it's only in the last several years that most of us have been waking to a personal Jewish identity.

Rabbi Arthur Green calls us *neo-Hasidim.* That perceptive theologian has been aware of this metamorphosis since we started "coming home" in the late 1960's.

But we are not returning to traditional Hasidism of this day. We choose what we like from all Jewish ways—including the Hasidim of the last centuries—and we borrow just as freely from Zen, Sufi, and Yoga practices. No apologies. We mean to worship God with all devotion and joy. In order to do that, we'll use any method or technique we can lay our hands on.

Right from the start it wasn't easy being Jewish in America. We knew we weren't Christians, but most of us were pretty secular kids. In some cases our families were *shul-* or temple-goers. In some of our homes Yiddish was spoken and with it came lots of ethnic trimmings.

But that's just part of the Judaism we're talking about now. As children in pluralistic America, we weren't part of our Old World heritage. Then we wanted to be just plain Americans —not different.

Don't forget, back in those days when we began, some Jews were getting their noses shortened and changing their names. Those were different times. Today we grow full beards and the nose looks fine. The women aren't straightening their hair to look like somebody else, and as a people, we're beginning to accept who we are—wherever we are. We have discovered our roots go back further than the ghettos and the pogroms—all the way back to the Middle East in the time of David and his mighty men. We are the children of Israel.

After all, it was our father Jacob who showed us the way when he wrestled with God. Now we're wrestling within ourselves to be whole again and totally dedicated.

This all began unexpectedly for most of us. God "zapped" us with His light, and we became personally aware of His presence. Somewhere along the way we glimpsed how it all is. Something happened, and suddenly there we were in a special sort of place. During those moments it was crystal clear that God is not just a concept. He really does exist and is in our midst right now.

As children we might have imagined God as some lofty Father figure—awesome and distant. But the God we have begun to know in this generation isn't like that. Whatever He is (or She is—such Holiness is beyond gender, beyond forms) our human minds stretch to their limits to understand. Still His presence is beyond description. But He graciously does let us experience Him a little now and then. During those moments our hearts and consciousness expand enough to realize something marvelous is happening everywhere, and somehow we are each part of this exquisite and timeless reality.

At the time we didn't realize it, but we had already begun to live a new age Judaism based almost totally on a direct spiritual relationship with God. We are not another sect within 20th century Jewish worship styles. In fact, we come from diverse backgrounds, from totally assimilated Jews to the very Orthodox. However, we share a common focus in our spiritual life. A persistent, almost irrational devotion compels us today more than any laws, rituals or traditions which we do not purposely avoid but which no longer define the patterns or the practice of our faith.

There's no other way to say it: the new age is another level of consciousness, a spiritual awakening that is spreading across the continent and probably around the globe. When it first blossoms inside someone a period of exhilaration follows: "Oh, it's really wonderful to be alive. No matter all the troubles on earth, everything after all is okay, and it's going on forever."

Just about everyone who wakes to this awareness becomes interested in one religion or another. For Jews, usually this means more thoroughly investigating ethnic and religious Jewish life. Until we fully accept our Jewish identities we cannot uncover who we are and why we're here.

Yiddishkeit was for many a fresh spring on the long journey home. Fortunately in America these days, being ethnic is admired. We can thank American blacks for that. More than a decade ago as a people in America they had begun searching for their origins—before slavery. That's when they stopped trying to look white.

We've stopped trying to look white too. This melting-pot nation already has melted down too many of us. After three and four generations in America we had lost our footing. Isolated and insulated in big companies and in big cities, there wasn't any satisfaction. It was all so dry. Besides, we'd seen an earlier generation exerting themselves to earn a good living—to what end? Country clubs, scotch and water? No satisfaction there either.

Who am I? What is this Jewish thing? Who is chosen? We knew the gruesome history of Jews in Europe. Are we chosen for heartaches and oppression? And in our country we'd seen plenty of Jewish bums and Jewish thieves. So we wondered: is this all an ego trip? These questions made us restless. Maybe if we found a teacher, or moved to another place, a different community for a while, we might find that peace again.

Israel. Probably no other single experience had such positive effect on our Jewish identity. One way or another, many among us decided to visit Israel. Whether this pilgrimage was a short trip, a college tour or a hippie trek, we got there, wandered through Tel Aviv and bathed in the Mediterranean. The first time we went it was amazing. All the people around were speaking Hebrew, like Italians speak Italian. The whole country—almost everyone—they're all Jews.

Out on the *kibbutzim* we picked carrots and hauled garbage, fed the cows and played chess with the elders. We learned a little modern Hebrew and played with the kids. At the end of the day we watched the sunset over the desert that earlier in the afternoon we had helped irrigate. We ate fresh melons, thick sour cream, and we began to know a little more about our heritage.

Before bondage. Before the ghettoes. Before the dispersals into other lands. This patch of ground where Jacob buried Rachel our Mother. Something in the air around these pastel hills.

Jerusalem. Holy city for Muslims, Christians and Jews. What happened to our minds here is not clear. It wasn't exactly that we fell in love with all Israelis. They're like other people, a mixed bag with a hearty pioneer style. We couldn't say this nation is the most picturesque. Probably we could take lusher photographs in the Caribbean. Jerusalem is not so breath-taking as San Francisco. But still, there's something so familiar about this place, the winding streets of the Old City, the Wall where people just naturally pray.

Israel planted a seed inside. By the time we returned to the United States, almost all self-consciousness about being Jewish in Protestant America had disappeared. In its place a tender plant was growing. We were in the process of accepting our Jewish identities—not reluctantly—but with new and even reckless pride.

Slowly we changed over our homes. Some put up posters or paintings of Jerusalem on the walls. On our doorways we affixed *mezzuzahs*. We began frequenting Jewish book stores and searching in earnest for a worship community with others who felt this way too. We tried to persuade our families and other Jews we knew to see the treasures in *Yiddishkeit* that we were discovering. That was frustrating for everyone, and it was our mistake—zeal of youth and lack of insight. Only later we realized that in most cases each of us was "the Jew" in the family. Our relatives still loved us, but they frankly thought we had gone overboard with all this "religious stuff."

Maybe they were right, but there was no turning back. Seeds inside were sprouting. We were caught up in the spirit. Somehow we had to express the devotion bubbling up inside. We went in and out of dozens of synagogues and temples joining in the services, desperately hoping to find a conducive environment. Usually it was disappointing. We traveled to Brooklyn and tried to join Hasidic services there. But the traditional Hasidim stared at us.

In time, it became obvious we would have to find others who had gone through similar experiences and design with them our own forms of worship. Some dropped out of seminaries because the professors and administrators there simply wouldn't—or couldn't—respond to a spiritual quest. Some tried mixing with other religious traditions, but that didn't work well because we already had begun to wrap ourselves in Torah. The voices inside spoke to us with peculiarly Jewish inflections. Like it or not, we were Jews and that was the way we worshipped best.

So we struck out on our own. Scattered across the North American continent, isolated at first from most others who were going through similar spiritual experiences, we began to develop a new age Judaism. We discovered a devotional spontaneity which could sometimes be communicated. We had already found that devotional singing and dancing help the worshipper rise up. It wasn't long before we were drawn to study past Hasidic teachers. Among the Jews of their day we found a sub-culture of pious people who were serious in their spiritual commitments, yet, it seemed, still light-hearted.

We romanticized these people. Of course they weren't all spiritual giants. Some among them were probably narrow-minded. They had suffered in a time of persecution. Some Hasidic dynasties in fact became nepotistic and corrupt. But those were later generations.

In its purest form, the movement burgeoned in the early 18th Century under the inspirational example of Israel ben Eliezer, who became known as the *Ba'al Shem Tov,* Master of the Good Name. Whether or not Hasidic story-tellers, such as Martin Buber, Meyer Levin and Elie Wiesel, laundered that history for contemporary readers was of more interest to scholars than to us.

For in those tales and teachings we found our soul brothers, people who danced and sang on the Sabbath. They too were rebels in their day, carrying the message that each of us can be a torch in the hands of God. No intermediaries needed. Hardly a book necessary. You don't even have to know rabbinic Hebrew to be a pious Jew, they encouraged one another. You can study and pray in your mother tongue. Sing to God from the heart. Be virtuous and loving. Rise up in your devotion.

Those Hasidim were singing our song. At night under the stars we danced on the beach. Alone in the forest or on a farm road in the moonlight we called to Him. Three A.M. on quiet city streets we looked up at the constellations, and He answered us.

We began studying the Torah. At first it wasn't easy getting into that thick history book with its genealogy, war stories and repetitive language. It seemed dry. But in time we each found our own gate in. Some came to Torah through the book of Proverbs. Others discovered a living scripture through the Song of Songs.

I used the psalms of David as a ladder to scale the walls. Step at a time, those songs lift the singer to expanded consciousness. While doing so, the psalmist refers frequently to significant experiences of the children of Israel as they crossed the wilderness with Moses and Aaron. Without realizing it, we became familiar with our ancestors again.

We began to read more carefully the first five books in the Bible, not as we knew them as children, but with newly-opened eyes, aware that all this before us is in God's name. Such study showed us that the incidents in Torah are much more than they appear at first. We would focus on one story or section, breaking down a specific passage to discover therein yet another story, and still another one inside that. All these years the Bible tales from our childhood were lodged in our psyches. With a little effort we were rediscovering them again—but this time on a deeper level.

Meanwhile we had begun to meditate on Hebrew letters as centering devices, not exactly the way Rabbi Abraham Abulaffia did it in the 13th Century, but more as Zen and Yoga students today might use these holy letter-symbols as *yantras* to focus the mind and go within. Each letter, we found, is a sort of key that opens the gate of intuition. If we dared, we might come to discover our real selves on this soulful pathway home. I used to draw the letters in different colors and put them around my home, on the desk, on the mirror or beside my bed.

Slowly these keys reached in, and the door opened.

Our knowledge of Hebrew was improving slowly. After hurried study for *bar mitzvah* or confirmation, we only knew prayers from childhood and at services could follow along without knowing the actual meanings of many Hebrew words. So we simply prayed in English. Wrapped in a big *tallis* we felt safe and unselfconscious. There we would sing the psalms or make up our own prayers. We came to like the big prayer *tallesim* of traditional Jews. At the same time it was both a meditation robe and a tent of meeting. We bought them or made them ourselves with many colors, like Joseph's coat. And in these we wrapped ourselves to thank and praise God and to wrestle with Him. For from our Torah study we had seen that Abraham, Jacob and Moses wrestled with God in their day. And afterall, these are our teachers.

Sometimes we'd visit a local congregation for a regular evening or Sabbath service, sitting unobtrusively in the back, hoping not to draw attention to our own style of worship. Besides, we wanted to be free to leave if lip service prayers made us too restless. Often these excursions were disappointing. Either a choir-on-high utterly sapped our enthusiasm or the cantor sang opera style arias from the prayer book. It was entertaining, but was this the place to pray? We shifted in the seats, staring at the words before us.

"Doesn't anyone feel this stuff?" To escape the emotionless room we would close our eyes and dive deep inside searching for our *kavannah,* some real devotion. "There must be something I feel thankful for today. Surely there's a recent experience or emotion that makes me want to praise God. Yes, here it is . . . " When we found it, we offered it up, and then something started to happen.

At least we were beginning to get in touch. Whatever other people's states of mind, no one had to see or hear us. But there a few feet away an older woman is into something genuine. And now a man in front has caught on. Before long it seemed the whole congregation was moved by a genuine emotion. Even the cantor had changed from performing to praying. We rose, as one group, almost as one voice. Our prayers moved off the walls and ceilings, where they had stopped before, and sailed up where they were intended to go.

Some of us began to fast—not just on Yom Kippur—but this time to clean our bodies, purify our minds, and find deeper insights in Torah. Sometimes we tried to do *t'shuvah,* to return to God each week before the Sabbath. Maybe we could clear away the guilt which had slipped in like soot in the air from the inconsiderate actions and thoughts we had allowed during the past week.

As our studies continued, we began investing the Sabbath with special care. We tried to make of it a holy day, a weekly retreat from worldly problems; and we discovered all the Jewish holidays. There are dozens of them, each with its own spiritual significance. By studying the appropriate readings in Torah a few days before each holy period, we primed our psyches to re-experience these cosmic rhythms.

Thus, the years became enriched. More than just the passing seasons, we began to feel new cycles and patterns in our lives, and without realizing it at first, we had begun to align ourselves with these special breath patterns of God. Jewish holy festivals became spiritual punctuations in our lives, a time of insight, a means of coming to know God better, and allowing our inner natures to flower.

We were moving the *mezzuzahs* off our door posts and into our hearts. Each time we saw the little container that held the *sh'ma* affirmation, we were reminded again that there is only one God who is the life in all of us. Sometimes in moments of devotion, we might whisper God's name aloud. No lightning consumed us then. For in those moments we felt ourselves offering self-sacrifice and atonement not only for ourselves and our families, but for all humanity.

Naturally the crest of a new wave does not go on forever. Those early gusts that lifted us so high, slowly turned back to the shore again. And we too came down to earth.

After the early 1970's, the spiritual movement began to change. At this point we had become friends with one another here and there. We had started worshipping and studying together. More often than not, we gathered in small informal fellowships—*havorot*—which evolved by participatory worship. We took turns leading services. Instead of big buildings with congregational rabbis, we met in living rooms or in small classrooms of temples and synagogues. In these informal settings we prayed as we liked—with a new group of friends who had come to their own Jewish identity by a different route.

The ethnic Jewish renaissance had spread across America, through the large East and West Coast cities at first and then into the Midwest and South. Jewish identity was more popular everywhere. Hundreds of thousands of U.S. and Canadian Jews, most of them with better Jewish education than ours, were enthusiastically turning to a richer practice of their faith.

These were not neo-Hasidim by Art Green's definition. Their Jewish identity was based more on ethnic heritage and a desire to mix with their own kind, and let their Jewishness come out. We soon learned these people would be close friends, and with them we would make *minyonim* or congregational quorems. Obviously it was God's plan for us to grow side-by-side, at least for some years. Our own spiritual enthusiasm needed grounding in the tradition. Their ethnic underpinnings and Jewish schooling needed a shot of joyous worship and a little mysticism. Besides, in any one city, so far there just weren't enough of us to make a *minyon*. The timing was right. Both groups needed to meet other Jews who preferred informal worship styles and participatory services.

By sheer numbers they took over. The small Jewish communities in which we found ourselves became less spontaneous in style, more traditional in practice and liturgy.

It was time to do our homework, to learn about our tradition, to study not only the mystics and kabbalists, but to include as well the sages of Talmud from the time of the Bible to the present. It was time to learn Hebrew better too, so we could open the still-hidden doorways in Torah.

Our meditations and studies had begun to merge. By now we were focusing on different attributes of God hoping to emulate Him. As we contemplated abstract divine qualities; such as compassion, peace, equanimity and love; we aimed to take on these characteristics personally.

We continued to study Hasidic teachings of the *Ba'al Shem Tov* and his followers. Our new friends in the *havorot* shared our enthusiasm for the wisdom and piety of that time. Among several interpreters of Hasidism, the writings of the late Martin Buber were particularly helpful during the first years of Jewish studies. His theology was tough to plow through, perhaps because the German translation came out sluggish and complicated. Perhaps it was Buber's own style. But his Hasidic stories were lyric gems that surprised our souls and made us cry—all the time giving us the cream of Hasidic spirituality. From the jewels he passed along we began building our small altars.

We began studying the teachings of the late Abraham Heschel whose soul reached in with love and warmed us through. Heschel was a well of compassion, a mystic practically from our own time. He was an *halakhic* Jew, observant according to traditional tenets. His outlook was so enlightened and universal that we could no longer postpone seriously considering taking on a traditional Jewish lifestyle.

That in fact is what this later period was all about—each of us finding his or her own way of practicing Judaism. Most of us—both the men and the women—had already found the large *tallesim* useful in worship. But few really could work up any honest enthusiasm about regularly *leying t'fillin,* the black leather straps of the prayer phylacteries with boxes of scriptural quotations which traditional Jews regularly put on their arms and foreheads six mornings each week. Still we inched closer to traditional practices. No doubt, that way of Jewish worship was a gold mine.

At first it was particularly hard for the women among us. They could get only so close, but no further without feeling rebuffed. Because they were not counted in the *minyonim,* nor called to the Torah like the men, much less being honored actually to *layn* or chant the Hebrew in the Torah scrolls themselves, they felt cool toward this form of Jewish observance, and their feelings were hurt. It was harder for them at first to separate the bitter from the sweet.

But Orthodoxy still had a lot to teach us all. They knew how to "give with a *shukle,*" to move in rhythm during worship that somehow raised up the energy of devotion. Like Hasidim, some of them would punctuate prayer with their whole bodies. This we learned and took for our worship. They knew about the meeting times—dawn and dusk—when the world is neither day nor night, when God's presence is reached between the halves.

Orthodox youngsters, moreover, had a lot of *ruach,* a high-spirited, almost football cheering soul-flavor, and a fierce pride in their heritage. These too we gratefully took and used to good effect.

As much as we enjoyed these forays into traditional Judaism, most did not stay and adopt this as their way of life. After all we have been and we continue to be eclectic seekers. When our traditional hosts insisted that their way was the only legitimate Jewish worship, then we began to ease away. We'd already seen too much to accept that proposition. We knew too many children of God both inside and out of our own tradition. And we knew from our own experiences that all sincerely loving offerings to God are accepted.

It took us a few years not to want some sort of approval or credentials from traditional Jews or contemporary Hasidim. This they would grant only if we lived and worshipped as they did. However, as we became more grounded through discipline and study, our self-confidence grew. We began to accept ourselves and look only to God Himself to recognize the authenticity of our lives. By this point we had stopped proselytizing our relatives, and they—almost—had stopped wringing their hands over our way of life.

Our Judaism cannot be assigned to narrow categories. It's neither Orthodox nor Reform; it's not Hasidic as practiced today nor is it Reconstructionist nor Conservative. It's an on-going, open-ended *kavannah* relationship which even now continues to design its own forms of worship and practice.

The Sabbath, for example, had become very important to us. We learned to prepare for it ahead of time. By getting things done earlier in the week so we wouldn't have to do them on Friday nights and Saturdays, we paved the way for a day of peace. A no-hassles day. A day without guilt about not doing something that otherwise should be done. Every weekday there are plenty of things we "ought" to do in our worldly coming and going. But on the Sabbath, God has quite clearly advised us *not* to do any of that busy buzzing. No regrets for taking a day off and catering to our spiritual growth.

Toward that end we cleaned our homes before Friday afternoon, and in advance bought groceries for the weekend. We cooked everything we needed for Friday and Saturday so we wouldn't have kitchenwork during the Sabbath. A day completely free, a day to worship—with others if we wanted to. Usually that helped.

But sometimes we simply stayed home, or went for quiet walks and reflected, or read a section from the Bible, or just took it easy with each other. Imagine, a day without guilt or worries. For bakers, a day without baking. For drivers, a day without driving. For painters, a day without painting.

But for non-painters, well, it might be a day for painting. We chose from the traditional practices those that spoke relevantly to us. We found it useful not to drive around in city traffic on the Sabbath, and to avoid housework or daily labor. But some found it more restful to ride to services than to walk. Some who never had time to write during the week-days chose to write on the Sabbath. Everyone observed this holy day as he chose, and none among us would judge.

Some of us became traditionally observant, trying out the lifestyle of an *halakhic* Jew. Usually they lived this way for a year or so and then eased off a little. Some went back to Israel or moved into Hasidic communities in New York. But those were mostly our new friends, Americans who had come to define themselves through what began as an ethnic Jewish identity, and in turn led to more traditional observance.

They believed the more "Jewish" they became, the more fulfilling their lives would be. Many simply equated being more *halakhic* with being more Jewish. Like new converts, they immersed themselves in traditional lifestyle which they believed would make them more authentically Jewish.

Sometimes they revisited the *havorot*, their early community friendships, and tried subtly or openly to convince us of their way. We deserved it. In a sense, we had done something similar to our own families. An eye for an eye. Those were awkward moments for everyone. It ended with a good hug, but we had to let each other go.

Another week passes, churning all the swirls of our day-to-day melodramas. Why are we living in this world in this day? Friday afternoon. We slip away from work a little early and into the nearby woods to walk alone and prepare ourselves for the coming Sabbath. Maybe He will take us up again, back to our real home, out of the hurries and worries, beyond the demanding egos of passing ambitions. Dusk settles slowly in the branches. Sabbath comes on gently. We stand looking through pine needles, waiting for the first stars to appear, like heralds.

Seasons pass. Worship becomes integral to the fabric of our lives. The insights He allows into our expanding consciousness enrich the mosiac we glimpsed at during those first exhilarating flights of the soul.

We've found small groups with whom we study a bit of *Talmud, hasidus, midrash* and even the *Zohar* or the *Book of Splendor.* We study mostly in English, but we're making "connections." Something we thought about or read about years back suddenly falls into place with something happening today.

When it comes to the whole Bible, we're still selective students. But we have already read the Five Books of Moses several times. We have our favorite psalms and passages from the prophets. This type of study will last a lifetime. Torah, in its broadest sense, is all the wisdom in our tradition, both written and oral. The books are endless; the teachings are infinite; insights flow from an eternal fountain.

The books are simply an excuse to get together and study the teachings. Even in our countless disagreements over interpretations of a specific teaching or line from scripture, still the sparks of truth are flying and everyone is uplifted. Who designed such marvelous inquiry? Our feet are in dust of the earth; our heads are in heaven.

Despite traditional warnings, we've dipped into kabbalis-

tic texts for years, ever since we began to "see" a little better
how everything is laced together. There are plenty of English primers. The scholarly writing of Gershom Scholem are
useful. We also enjoy the late Louis Ginsberg's *Legends of
the Jews,* a compilation of Talmudic and midrashic tales
chock full of more "connections."

We read different translations of the psalms and other
biblical books, attempting sometimes to write our own. We
study more Hebrew hoping one day to read both Hebrew
and Aramaic without vowels.

Wasn't it delightful to discover that since every Hebrew
word in the Torah scrolls has no vowels each can therefore
be read with literally half a dozen different meanings from
the same root letters. The sages have suggested that the way
humanity understands Torah varies from age to age. In future times, the same letters will tell an even richer tale than
we perceive today.

Why not look to that time now? We must first digest thousands of years of Jewish scholarship, insights already realized
and passed along. Can anyone do such a thing in one lifetime? It doesn't matter. After all, one need not eat the entire
blintz to fully taste its delicious filling.

Among our favorite hasidic teachers of the 1800's was
Rebbe Nachman of Bratslav who would tell his disciples it's
not necessary to read the *Zohar,* for example, so carefully—at
least not the first time through. Instead, just skim along, he
said, not bothering at first to stop and study the sections you
don't understand. Get the feel of the whole work, the flavor
of the teachings. He was telling his students even then, let
the media be the message. Later on, he recommended, if you
desire to study one portion or another in detail, you may do
so.

That's exactly how we study the teachings of Rebbe Nachman himself, or the *Tanya* of Rebbe Shneur Zalman. First

time through, the get-acquainted method. There's also the dip-in-for-a-cup-of-soup method. In this way, we study small sections of Maimonides, Rashi, Rav Kook and Rebbe Eliemelekh. We dip into *gemara, mishnah* or *midrash* for small tastes of wisdom from different times in the evolution of our tradition.

Of course, we enjoy the insights of those sages, but even more important we are sampling the whole menu of that time and mind. There's a vast storehouse of illumination available to us from the rabbinic sages. It goes back to our earliest dispersals from Israel and even before.

Being carried away from our own land wasn't all bad for us. Dispersed through the nations of the world, we learned how to be ingenious and adjust. We suffered and found humility again. As a people we grew in wisdom from our experiences and from rubbing elbows with the learned of other cultures. Constantly we enriched former understandings with new insights, until we had again built a holy temple. This time it was outside time and space and indestructible in the hearts of students of truth.

By definition wisdom is open-ended. In our history there is not one way. There is not only one interpretation. As Rabbi Isaac Luria of Safed taught, every soul will naturally have its own personal perception of God's truth. None is higher or lower ultimately. Each generation then is called on to reinterpret scripture to find therein fuller concepts and instructions in the tradition which has been passed to this point.

One such modern innovation that many observe these days might be called a new *kashrut*. We choose to eat no flesh at all. We try not to participate in the killing of any animals which God created. Perhaps if we lived in the arctic and had to eat meat to survive, we would do so without guilt. But in these more temperate climes, we are expanding our understanding of God's compassion to see His love for all sentient life.

Even with plant life, we try to be more sensitive. If possible, we choose the fruits that come most easily from the trees in order to leave something alive and still maturing on the vine.

It's clear now that God is guiding us on earth. It's obvious too that we still have a lot of work to do on ourselves, remaking our characters almost from scratch. We must in time eliminate every vestige of selfish egoism in order to become pure channels of God's light and in this way experience full happiness.

As we stumble forward, God stands nearby like a father with His arms outstretched. When we fall He lifts us up again. He teaches us patience and persistence. We say He is omnipotent. He must have made us this way, capable of error and remorse. He has given us enough free will to wish to live right. Certainly, He could have created us perfect from the start—like angels. So it must be a high game of His design. We err and ask His pardon. It's our nature to err—we're human. It's God's nature to forgive. When we perform our small penitences and return to Him again, then He pours His love down into the world through our open hearts. In this way we are God's partners in bringing compassion to the world.

Part of our penitence is taking on daily discipline which includes study, prayer and meditation. We try to eat healthier food because the meals we take in, it's now evident, are offerings in His temple—these our bodies. And step by step we begin to control our actions and speech, and with time, our thoughts. In a way, we are neo-Hasidim after all. Our disciplines are not exactly the same. Our practice of Judaism is different too. But we seek what they sought and we are remaking our lives to reach it.

It's another age here in America. We are ecumenical Jews. Our vision is universal. We are Jewish in our worship, in our lifestyle. But we have kin in every great religious tradition.

What is happening to our consciousness is obviously also happening among Christians, Muslims, Hindus and Buddhists. It's happening to the educated and the illiterate, to blacks and to whites, to all races and all peoples. A new age of spiritual illumination has begun. In time every soul will awaken to more refined perceptions of reality.

We are children of one Father. We are cells in one great organism which includes all life. And as we wake to this expanding understanding, we see one another as unique manifestations of the Holy One who made us breathe and live and help each other.

God's presence is in our midst. He has provided a vast network of various pathways by which humans can come to know Him according to their varying tastes and temperaments. As we grow, He encourages us. For every step we move towards God, he takes ten steps to meet us.

Sometimes He graces us with insights too sublime to say in words. Whether qualified or not, maybe we've become kabbalists after all. Kabbalah literally means "to receive." We are surely receiving something wonderful and holy. If we sometimes receive intuitive perceptions too subtle to describe, perhaps these are the so-called "secrets" or esoteric wisdom people have referred to over the ages. If that's the case, anyone can know such secrets.

When we took on our Jewish identities we became more comfortable with ourselves. That helped us relate more familiarly with the One we worship. This led to deeper Torah study which in turn changed the way we understood ourselves. Our Jewish identity has begun to move inward. The outward manifestations are not as important as when we began. Nowadays we try to go a little earlier to services, or to a retreat with our congregations, in order to help set up for the others. Later we stay for the clean-up. Being Jewish is getting simpler.

Keeping the Sabbath special and peaceful has now become a habit in our lives. If by chance we get involved doing other things on Saturdays, we really miss that peaceful day. Being Jewish is not so much *mezzuzahs* and colorful *tallesim* as it is helping the widow next door get her groceries when there's ice on the sidewalk. It's feeding poor people and listening to troubled people. Being Jewish is never appearing empty-handed to someone in need and it's helping pay for repair of the Torah scrolls.

Jewish identity has come to mean helping all people everywhere whenever it's possible to do that. It's mixing into enterprises that bring more justice in the world. It's recognizing Moslems, Christians, Buddhists and Hindus as our brothers and sisters too; it's perfecting little things in life, and loving parents even if they didn't raise us exactly right.

Being Jewish is serving God by serving His creation as anonymously as we can. And it's studying Torah until that is integral in our lives, until we become steady in wisdom and compassion ourselves. Without retaliating, it's forgiving the people who have persecuted us. At the same time, if ever we or our families are attacked, it's vigorously and successfully defending ourselves. Being Jewish is letting someone else at the intersection go first.

Finally, we begin to understand: whoever chooses God is *chosen* by Him. These are the chosen people. We should be so chosen!

We have nearly reached the point where we don't *need* our Jewish identities any longer. We don't intend to turn away from all that we have been discovering, but we are coming to understand Judaism as a great and holy *path*—not the goal. Surely all the ethnic and religious treasures are useful along the way. But there comes a time when we transcend even our most precious self-images to discover that essentially all are one in God. From that vantage there is no Jewish or non-Jewish identity. In this fullness there are no categories, definitions or limitations.

Does that mean we'll never *daven* again or sing a blessing in Hebrew? From now on are all traditions dispensed with?

We're each a unique flower on God's tree of life. We come from the same source, but each has his or her particular fruitfulness. When the mind returns from transcendent awareness, life goes on more richly and devotion deepens. Now that we have begun to understand, probably we'll be better Jews than ever.

Moses asks: "Who is sending me to free the people?" "I am that I am," says the Lord. There's no measuring God, and we His children have no measure either.

We've begun to shed our pride and neuroses. Maybe something from Him is starting to rub off. After all, we've been wrestling with Him through the ages, like Jacob wrestled with the angel until God blessed him and called him Israel.

Intellectual Roots

PART II

Intellectual Roots

Introduction

Judaism has profoundly touched and shaped Western thought and philosophy. Beyond its most obvious contribution, monotheism, it has offered the world some of its greatest minds, ideas and insights. Because of the dominant emphasis on scholarship and learning in Jewish culture, Jewish thought has come to represent the epitome of reason and intellect, even during times when these qualities were temporarily extinguished in all other quarters. The strength of the Jewish intellectual tradition resides in its breadth, the quality of its participants, the disciplines it has fostered and its ability to tolerate and generate change within itself.

Two elements run through Jewish thought, the rabbinic and the mystical. Representing two sides of human nature, they complement and enhance each other. Unfortunately, for many years the mystical aspects of Judaism were suppressed and unavailable to the learner, lost in an age of reason which placed little value on the intuitive or the spiritual. Only with the work of Gershom Scholem and Martin Buber was it re-introduced into Western thought. Mysticism holds that there is a hidden order to the universe, that there is reason and purpose even in the most illogical and senseless happenings of life. The goal of the mystic is to directly discover (experience) this order and, as a consequence, God's Presence in the world. Together, this belief and the task of searching for evidence of God's emanations on earth have occupied and given comfort and solace to the Jew throughout the demeaning and often senseless ordeal of diaspora. Perhaps, a similar chaos in contemporary life is responsible for the unprecedented interest in mysticism today. In "The Mystical Elements of Judaism," this section's first offering, Abraham Heschel explores Jewish mysticism at length: its motivation, doctrines and practice. In so doing, he lays bare

the wisdom and lessons available in this little known or appreciated tradition for the scrutiny of the modern Jew.

Two Jewish theologians have particularly distinguished
themselves in the world of contemporary thought: Abraham
Heschel, the author of two articles in the present volume,
and Martin Buber. In the works of these two men one finds
an understanding and interpretation of Judaism which is un-
canny in its relevance to modern living. One also discovers,
in the life of each, a sincere dedication to principled action
and a willingness to speak out against immorality, cruelty and
injustice, irrespective of their source. While Heschel's influence has remained primarily in the Jewish community, the
works of Buber are read and appreciated by Christian and
Jewish theologians alike. Buber's decision to repeatedly criticize the Israeli government for policy and activities contrary
to his own principles of true encounter and dialogue and the
alienation it caused him, has led some analysts to estimate
that his ideas have had greater influence in Christian than in
Jewish circles. Whether true or not, Buber's greatest facility
was his ability to anticipate decades ahead of time the critical
social and intellectual trends of today. In his concept of "I
and Thou" he foreshadowed both the growing contemporary
concern for humanism and the idea of multidimensional experiencing in the person. In his focus on the need for community he anticipated the counterculture of the late 1960's
and its experimentation with the intentional community.
And in his fascination with the Hasidim he previewed the
present day interest in mystical experience, psycho-religious
cults and non-Western modes of thought. His insightfulness
is nowhere more evident than in his writings on the meaning
of Jewish identity. In "Martin Buber's 'Speeches on Judaism':
A Classic of Jewish Identity," Maurice Friedman presents
Buber's existential thoughts on the topic and, in addition,
shows the modern Jew how his Jewishness may be viewed as
both a challenge to self-actualized and intentional living and
a symbol of the universal need for greater morality in contemporary life.

No academic discipline has been more influenced by Jewish thought than has the field of psychology. In its first seventy years of existence its Jewish practitioners have played a disproportionately important role in its shaping and development. The names of Sigmund Freud, Alfred Adler, Otto Rank, Wilhelm Reich, Erich Fromm, Max Wertheimer, Kurt Koffka, Kurt Lewin and Abraham Maslow stand shoulders above the rest in significance. Psychologist David Baken has gone a step further in suggesting that psychoanalysis, the single most influential theory in psychology's history, was derived indirectly from Jewish mysticism. In his controversial book, *Sigmund Freud and the Jewish Mystical Traditional,* Bakan shows how the basic assumptions and patterns of psychoanalytic thought had their origins in traditional Jewish beliefs and themes. In a similar manner Dov Peretz Elkins, in the third article of Part II, explores the relationship between Judaism and humanistic psychology, a particularly popular orientation in current psychological thought. In "Judaism and Personal Growth" he stresses the importance of mutual influence between these two intellectual sources, showing not only how Judaism has effected humanistic psychology, but also how the Human Potential Movement can help to revitalize the contemporary practice of Judaism.

Perhaps, above all else, Jewish thought's greatest asset is its flexibility and tolerance for change. This is the subject of Irving Greenberg's provocative essay, "Judaism and History: Historical Events and Religious Change." In it he makes the very important point that the Jewish religion has changed radically over its long history. Beginning with the Exodus model of redemption, he shows how historical crises have altered the Jewish conception of God and, as a consequence, the practice of its ritual and observance. He ends his article with speculation as to the yet unfelt consequences of the Holocaust on religious Judaism. Although change is essential for the survival of all traditions, it is not always positively received at the time of its inception. There has always been some resistance to innovation from segments of the Jewish community, and the same is true today. But resistance does not eliminate the possibility of change; it only slows the process somewhat by increasing the amount of effort and time required for actualization. In Professor Greenberg's article the Jew of today can find a precedent and justification for contemplating religious innovation aimed at better meeting contemporary needs and demands. Those already deeply enmeshed in the task of changing the Jewish lifestyle and religion—the Women's Movement, political activists, the neo-Hasidim, members of Havurot and other alternative communal forms, advocates of liturgical renewal—can take heart in the contention that such activity is not only tolerated but, in fact, expected and demanded by the Jewish tradition.

The Mystical Element in Judaism

Abraham J. Heschel

1. *The Meaning of Jewish Mysticism*

There are people who take great care to keep away from the mists produced by fads and phrases. They refuse to convert realities into opinions, mysteries into dogmas, and ideas into a multitude of words, for they realize that all concepts are but glittering motes in a sunbeam. They want to see the sun itself. Confined to our study rooms, our knowledge seems to us a pillar of light; but when we stand at the door that opens out to the Infinite, we see how insubstantial is our knowledge. Even when we shut the door to the Infinite and retire to the narrow limits of notions our minds cannot remain confined. Again, to some people explanations and opinions are a token of wonder's departure, like a curfew after which they may not come abroad. In the cabbalists, the drive and the fire and the light are never put out.

Like the vital power in ourselves that gives us the ability to fight and to endure, to dare and to conquer, which drives us to experience the bitter and the perilous, there is an urge in wistful souls to starve rather than be fed on sham and distortion. To the cabbalists God is as real as life, and as nobody would be satisfied with mere knowing or reading about life, so they are not content to suppose or to prove logically that there is a God; they want to feel and to enjoy Him; not only to obey, but to approach Him. They want to taste the whole wheat of spirit before it is ground by the millstones of reason. They would rather be overwhelmed by the symbols of the inconceivable than wield the definitions of the superficial.

Stirred by a yearning after the unattainable, they want to make the distant near, the abstract concrete, to transform the soul into a vessel for the transcendent, to grasp with the senses what is hidden from the mind, to express in symbols what the tongue cannot speak, what the reason cannot conceive, to experience as a reality what vaguely dawns in intuitions. "Wise is he who by the power of his own contemplation attains to the perception of the profound mysteries which cannot be expressed in words."

The cabbalist is not content with being confined to what he is. His desire is not only to *know* more than what ordinary reason has to offer, but to *be* more than what he is; not only to comprehend the Beyond but to concur with it. He aims at the elevation and expansion of existence. Such expansion goes hand in hand with the exaltation of all being.

The universe, exposed to the violence of our analytical mind, is being broken apart. It is split into the known and unknown, into the seen and unseen. In mystic contemplation all things are seen as one. The mystic mind tends to hold the world together: to behold the seen in conjunction with the unseen, to keep the fellowship with the unknown through the revolving door of the known, "to learn the higher supernal wisdom from all" that the Lord has created and to regain the knowledge that once was in the possession of men and "that has perished from them." What our senses perceive is but the jutting edge of what is deeply hidden. Extending over into the invisible, the things of this world stand in a secret contact with that which no eye has ever perceived. Everything certifies to the sublime, the unapparent working jointly with the apparent. There is always a reverberation in the Beyond to every action here: "The Lord made this world corresponding to the world above, and everything which is above has its counterpart below . . . and yet they all constitute a unity"; "there being no object, however small, in this world, but what is subordinate to its counterpart above which has charge over it; and so whenever the thing below bestirs itself, there is a simultaneous stimulation of its counterpart above, as the two realms form one interconnected whole."

Opposed to the idea that the world of perception is the bottom of reality, the mystics plunge into what is beneath the perceptible. What they attain in their quest is more than a vague impression or a spotty knowledge of the imperceptible. "Penetrating to the real essence of wisdom . . . they are resplendent with the radiance of supernal wisdom." Their eyes perceive things of this world, while their hearts reverberate to the throbbing of the hidden. To them the secret is the core of the apparent; the known is but an aspect of the unknown. "All things below are symbols of that which is above." They are sustained by the forces that flow from hidden worlds. There is no particular that is detached from universal meaning. What appears to be a center to the eye is but a point on the periphery around another center. Nothing here is final. The worldly is subservient to the otherworldly. You grasp the essence of the here by conceiving its beyond. For this world is the reality of the spirit in a state of trance. The manifestation of the mystery is partly suspended, with ourselves living in lethargy. Our normal consciousness is a state of stupor, in which our sensibility to the wholly real and our responsiveness to the stimuli of the spirit are reduced. The mystics, knowing that we are involved in a hidden history of the cosmos, endeavor to awake from the drowsiness and apathy and to regain the state of wakefulness for our enchanted souls.

It is a bold attitude of the soul, a steadfast quality of consciousness, that lends mystic character to a human being. A man who feels that he is closely enfolded by a power that is both lasting and holy will come to know that the spiritual is not an idea to which one can relate his will, but a realm which can even be affected by our deeds. What distinguishes the cabbalist is the attachment of his entire personality to a hid-

den spiritual realm. Intensifying this attachment by means of
active devotion to it, by meditation upon its secrets, or even
by perception of its reality, he becomes allied with the dynamics of hidden worlds. Sensitive to the imperceptible, he
is stirred by its secret happenings.

Attachment to hidden worlds holds the cabbalist in the
spell of things more basic than the things that dominate the
interest of the common mind. The mystery is not beyond and
away from us. It is our destiny. "The fate of the world depends upon the mystery." Our task is to adjust the details to
the whole, the apparent to the hidden, the near to the distant. The passionate concern of the cabbalist for final goals
endows him with the experience of surpassing all human
limitations and powers. With all he is doing he is crossing the
borders, breaking the surfaces, approaching the lasting
sources of all things. Yet his living with the infinite does not
make him alien to the finite.

2. *The Exaltation of Man*

In this exalted world man's position is unique. God has
instilled in him something of Himself. Likeness to God is the
essence of man. The Hebrew word for man, *adam,* usually
associated with the word for earth, *adamah,* was homiletical-
ly related by some cabbalists to the expression, "I will ascend
above the heights of the clouds; I will be like *(eddamme)* the
Most High" (Is. 14:14). Man's privilege is, as it were, to aug-
ment the Divine in the world, as it is said, "ascribe ye
strength unto God" (Ps. 68:35).

Jewish mystics are inspired by a bold and dangerously
paradoxical idea that not only is God necessary to man but
that man is also necessary to God, to the unfolding of His
plans in this world. Thoughts of this kind are indicated and
even expressed in various Rabbinic sources. "When Israel
performs the will of the Omnipresent, they add strength to
the heavenly power; as it is said, 'To God we render
strength!'" When, however, Israel does not perform the will

of the Omnipresent, they weaken—if it is possible to say so—the great power of Him Who is above; as it is written "Thou didst weaken the Rock that begot thee" (Deut. 32:18). In the *Zohar* this idea is formulated in a more specific way. Commenting on the passage in Ex. 17:8, "Then came Amalek and fought with Israel in Rephidim," R. Simeon said: "There is a deep allusion in the name 'Rephidim.' This war emanated from the attribute of Severe Judgment and it was a war above and a war below . . . The Holy One, as it were, said: 'When Israel is worthy below, My power prevails in the universe; but when Israel is found to be unworthy, she weakens My power above, and the power of severe judgment predominates in the world.' So here, 'Amalek came and fought with Israel in Rephidim,' because the Israelites were 'weak' (in Hebrew: *raphe,* which the *Zohar* finds in the name 'Rephidim') in the study of the Torah, as we have explained on another occasion." Thus man's relationship to God should not be that of passive reliance upon His Omnipotence but that of active assistance. "The impious rely on their gods . . . the righteous are the support of God." The Patriarchs are therefore called "the chariot of the Lord." The belief in the greatness of man, in the metaphysical effectiveness of his physical acts, is an ancient motif of Jewish thinking.

Man himself is a mystery. He is the symbol of all that exists. His life is the image of universal life. Everything was created in the spiritual image of the mystical man. "When the Holy One created man, He set in him all the images of the supernal mysteries of the world above, and all the images of the lower mysteries of the world below, and all are designed in man, who stands in the image of God." Even the human body is full of symbolic significance. The skin, flesh, bones and sinews are but an outward covering, mere garments, even though "the substances composing man's body belong to two worlds, namely, the world below and the world above." The 248 limbs and 365 sinews are symbols of the 613 parts of the universe as well as of the 248 positive and 365 negative precepts of the Torah. Man's soul emanates from an upper region where it has a spiritual father and a spiritual mother, just as the body has a father and mother in this world. The souls that abide in our bodies are a weak reflection of our upper souls, the seat of which is in heaven. Yet, though detached from that soul, we are capable of being in contact with it. When we pray we turn toward the upper soul as though we were to abandon the body and join our source.

Man is not detached from the realm of the unseen. He is wholly involved in it. Whether he is conscious of it or not, his actions are vital to all worlds, and affect the course of transcendent events. In a sense, by means of the Torah, man is the constant architect of the hidden universe. "This world was formed in the pattern of the world above, and whatever takes place in this earthly realm occurs also in the realm above." One of the principles of the *Zohar* is that every move below calls forth a corresponding movement above. Not only things, even periods of time are conceived as concrete entities. "Thus over every day below is appointed a day above, and a man should take heed not to impair that day. Now the act below stimulates a corresponding activity above. Thus if a man does kindness on earth, he awakens loving-kindness above, and it rests upon that day which is crowned therewith through him. Similarly, if he performs a deed of mercy, he crowns that day with mercy and it becomes his protector in the hour of need. So, too, if he performs a cruel action, he has a corresponding effect on that day and impairs it, so that subsequently it becomes cruel to him and tries to destroy him, giving him measure for measure." Even what we consider potential is regarded as real and we may be held accountable for it: " . . . just as a man is punished for uttering an evil word, so is he punished for not uttering a good word when he had the opportunity, because he harms that speaking spirit which was prepared to speak above and below in holiness."

The significance of great works done on earth is valued by their cosmic effects. Thus, *e.g.,* "When the first Temple was completed another Temple was erected at the same time, which was a center for all the worlds, shedding radiance upon all things and giving light to all the spheres. Then the worlds were firmly established, and all the supernal casements were opened to pour forth light, and all the worlds experienced such joys as had never been known to them before, and celestial and terrestrial beings alike broke forth in song. And the song which they sang is the Song of Songs."

Endowed with metaphysical powers man's life is a most serious affair; "if a man's lips and tongue speak evil words, those words mount aloft and all proclaim 'keep away from the evil word of so-and-so, leave the path clear for the mighty serpent.' Then the holy soul leaves him and is not able to speak: it is in shame and distress, and is not given a place as before . . . Then many spirits bestir themselves, and one spirit comes down from that side and finds the man who uttered the evil word, and lights upon him and defiles him, and he becomes leprous."

Man's life is full of peril. It can easily upset the balance and order of the universe. "A voice goes forth and proclaims: 'O ye people of the world, take heed unto yourselves, close the gates of sin, keep away from the perilous net before your feet are caught in it!' A certain wheel is ever whirling continuously round and round. Woe to those whose feet lose their hold on the wheel, for then they fall into the Deep which is predestined for the evildoers of the world! Woe to those who fall, never to rise and enjoy the light that is stored up for the righteous in the world to come!"

3. *The En Sof and His Manifestations*

Mystic intuition occurs at an outpost of the mind, dangerously detached from the main substance of the intellect. Operating as it were in no-mind's land, its place is hard to name, its communications with critical thinking often difficult and uncertain and the accounts of its discoveries not easy to decode. In its main representatives, the cabbala teaches that man's life can be a rallying point of the forces that tend toward God, that this world is charged with His presence and every object is a cue to His qualities. To the cabbalist, God is not a concept, a generalization, but a most specific reality; his thinking about Him full of forceful directness. But He who is "the Soul of all souls" is "the mystery of all mysteries." While the cabbalists speak of God as if they commanded a view of the Beyond, and were in possession of knowledge about the inner life of God, they also assure us that all notions fail when applied to Him, that He is beyond the grasp of the human mind and inaccessible to meditation. He is the *En Sof,* the Infinite, "the most Hidden of all Hidden." While there is an abysmal distance between Him and the world, He is also called All. "For all things are in Him and He is in all things . . . He is both manifest and concealed. Manifest in order to uphold the all and concealed, for He is found nowhere. When He becomes manifest He projects nine brilliant lights that throw light in all directions. So, too, does a lamp throw brilliance in all directions, but when we approach the brilliance we find there is nothing outside the lamp. So is the Holy ancient One, the Light of all Lights, the most Hidden of all Hidden. We can only find the light which He spreads and which appears and disappears. This light is called the Holy Name, and therefore All is One."

Thus, the "Most Recondite One Who is beyond cognition does reveal of Himself a tenuous and veiled brightness shining only along a narrow path which extends from Him. This is the brightness that irradiates all." The *En Sof* has granted us manifestations of His hidden life: He had descended to become the universe; He has revealed Himself to become the Lord of Israel. The ways in which the Infinite assumes the form of finite existence are called *Sefirot.* These are various aspects or forms of Divine action, spheres of Divine emanation. They are, as it were, the garments in which the Hidden God reveals Himself and acts in the universe, the channels through which His light is issued forth.

The names of the ten *Sefirot* are *Keter, Hokhmah, Binah, Hesed, Geburah, Tiferet, Netsah, Hod, Yesod, Malkut.* The transition from Divine latency to activity takes place in *Ket-*

er, the "supreme crown" of God. This stage is inconceivable, absolute unity and beyond description. In the following *Sefirot, Hokhmah* and *Binah,* the building and creation of the cosmos as well as that which divides things begins. They are parallel emanations from *Keter,* representing the active and the receptive principle.

While the first triad represents the transition from the Divine to the spiritual reality, the second triad is the source of the moral order. *Hesed* stands for the love of God; *Geburah* for the power of justice manifested as severity or punishment. From the union of these emanates *Tiferet,* compassion or beauty of God, mediating between *Hesed* and *Geburah,* between the life-giving power and the contrary power, holding in check what would otherwise prove to be the excesses of love.

The next triad is the source of the psychic and physical existences—*Netsah* is the lasting endurance of God, *Hod* His majesty, and *Yesod* the stability of the universe, the seat of life and vitality. *Malkut* is the kingdom, the presence of the Divine in the world. It is not a source of its own but the outflow of the other *Sefirot;* "of itself lightless, it looks up to the others and reflects them as a lamp reflects the sun." It is the point at which the external world comes in contact with the upper spheres, the final manifestations of the Divine, the *Shekinah,* "the Mother of all Living."

The recondite and unapproachable Self of God is usually thought of as transcendent to the *Sefirot.* There is only a diffusion of His light into the *Sefirot.* The *En Sof* and the realm of His manifestations are "linked together like the flame and the coal," the flame being a manifestation of what is latent in the coal. In the process of the emanation, the transition from the Divine to the spiritual, from the spiritual to the moral, from the moral to the physical, reality takes place. The product of this manifestation is not only the visible universe but an endless number of spiritual worlds which exist beyond the physical universe in which we live. These

worlds, the hidden cosmos, constitute a most complex structure, divided into various grades and forms which can only
be described in symbols. These symbols are found in the
Torah, which is the constitution of the cosmos. Every letter,
word or phrase in the Bible not only describes an event in the
history of our world but also represents a symbol of some
stage in the hidden cosmos. These are the so-called *Raze
Torah,* the mysteries, that can be discovered by the mystical
method of interpretation.

The system of *Sefirot* can be visualized as a tree or a man
or a circle, in three triads or in three columns. According to
the last image the *Sefirot* are divided into a *right* column,
signifying Mercy, or light, a *left* column, signifying Severity,
the absence of light, and a *central* column, signifying the
synthesis of the right and left. Each *Sefirah* is a world in itself,
dynamic and full of complicated mutual relations with other
Sefirot. There are many symbols by which each *Sefirah* can
be expressed, *e.g.,* the second triad is symbolized in the lives
of each of the three Patriarchs. The doctrine of *Sefirot* enables the cabbalists to perceive the bearings of God upon this
world, to identify the Divine substance of all objects and
events. It offers the principles by means of which all things
and events can be interpreted as Divine manifestations.

The various parts of the day represent various aspects of
Divine manifestation. "From sunrise until the sun declines
westward it is called 'day,' and the attribute of Mercy is in the
ascendant; after that it is called 'evening,' which is the time
for the attribute of Severity . . . It is for this reason that Isaac
instituted the afternoon prayer *(Minhah),* namely, to miti-
gate the severity of the approaching evening; whereas Abraham instituted morning prayer, corresponding to the
attribute of mercy."

The plurality into which the one Divine manifestation is
split symbolizes the state of imperfection into which God's
relation to the world was thrown. Every good deed serves to
restore the original unity of the *Sefirot,* while on the other

hand, "Sinners impair the supernal world by causing a separation between the 'Right' and the 'Left.' They really cause harm only to themselves, . . . as they prevent the descent of blessings from above . . . and the heaven keeps the blessings to itself." Thus the sinner's separation of the good inclination from the evil one by consciously cleaving to evil separates, as it were, the Divine attribute of Grace from that of Judgment, the Right from the Left.

4. *The Doctrine of the Shekinah*

Originally there was harmony between God and His final manifestations, between the upper *Sefirot* and the tenth *Sefirah*. All things were attached to God and His power surged unhampered throughout all stages of being. Following the trespass of Adam, however, barriers evolved thwarting the emanation of His power. The creature became detached from the Creator, the fruit from the tree, the tree of knowledge from the tree of life, the male from the female, our universe from the world of unity, even the *Shekinah* or the tenth *Sefirah* from the upper *Sefirot.* Owing to that separation the world was thrown into disorder, the power of strict judgment increased, the power of love diminished and the forces of evil released. Man who was to exist in pure spiritual form as light in constant communication with the Divine was sunk into his present inferior state.

In spite of this separation, however, God has not withdrawn entirely from this world. Metaphorically, when Adam was driven out of Eden, an aspect of the Divine, the *Shekinah,* followed him into captivity. Thus there is a Divine power that dwells in this world. It is the Divine Presence that went before Israel while they were going through the wilderness, that protects the virtuous man, that abides in his house and goes forth with him on his journeys, that dwells between a man and his wife. The *Shekinah* "continually accompanies a man and leaves him not so long as he keeps the precepts of the Torah. Hence a man should be careful not to go on the road alone, that is to say, he should diligently keep the pre-

cepts of the Torah in order that he may not be deserted by
the *Shekinah,* and so be forced to go alone without the ac-
companiment of the *Shekinah.* "The *Shekinah* follows Israel
into exile and "always hovers over Israel like a mother over
her children." Moreover, it is because of Israel and its observance of the Torah that the *Shekinah* dwells on earth. Were
they to corrupt their way, they would thrust the *Shekinah*
out of this world and the earth would be left in a degenerate
state.

The doctrine of the *Shekinah* occupies a central place in
the cabbala. While emphasizing that in His essence "the Holy
One and the *Shekinah* are One," it speaks of a cleavage, as
it were, in the reality of the Divine. The *Shekinah* is called
figuratively the *Matrona* (symbolized by the Divine Name
Elohim) that is separated from the King (symbolized by the
ineffable Name *Hashem*) and it signifies that God is, so to
speak, involved in the tragic state of this world. In the light
of this doctrine the suffering of Israel assumed new meaning.
Not only Israel but the whole universe, even the *Shekinah,*
"lies in dust" and is in exile. Man's task is to bring about the
restitution of the original state of the universe and the reun-
ion of the *Shekinah* and the *En Sof.* This is the meaning of
Messianic salvation, the goal of all efforts.

"In time to come God will restore the Shekinah to its place
and there will be a complete union. 'In that day shall the
Lord be One and His Name One' (Zech. 14:9). It may be said:
Is He not now One? no; for now through sinners He is not
really One. For the Matrona is removed from the King
. . . and the King without the Matrona is not invested with
His crown as before. But when He joins the Matrona, who
crowns Him with many resplendent crowns, then the supernal Mother will also crown Him in a fitting manner. But now
that the King is not with the Matrona, the supernal Mother
keeps her crowns and withholds from Him the waters of the
stream and He is not joined with her. Therefore, as it were,
He is not one. But when the Matrona shall return to the place
of the Temple and the King shall be wedded with her, then

all will be joined together, without separation and regarding this it is written, 'In that day shall the Lord be One and His Name One.' Then there shall be such perfection in the world as had not been for all generations before, for then shall be completeness above and below, and all worlds shall be united in one bond."

The restoration of unity is a constant process. It takes place through the study of the Torah, through prayer and through the fulfillment of the commandments. "The only aim and object of the Holy One in sending man into this world is that he may know and understand that *Hashem* (God), signifying the *En Sof*, is *Elohim (Shekinah)*.This is the sum of the whole mystery of the faith, of the whole Torah, of all that is above and below, of the written and the oral Torah, all together forming one unity." "When a man sins it is as though he strips the *Shekinah* of her vestments, and that is why he is punished; and when he carries out the precepts of the law, it is as though he clothes the *Shekinah* in her vestments. Hence we say that the fringes worn by the Israelites are, to the *Shekinah* in captivity, like the poor man's garments of which it is said, 'For that is his only covering, it is his garment for his skin, wherein he shall sleep.'"

5. *Mystic Experience*

The ultimate goal of the cabbalist is not his own union with the Absolute but the union of all reality with God; one's own bliss is subordinated to the redemption of all: "we have to put all our being, all the members of our body, our complete devotion, into that thought so as to rise and attach ourselves to the *En Sof*, and thus achieve the oneness of the upper and lower worlds."

What this service means in terms of personal living is described in the following way:

Happy is the portion of whoever can penetrate into the mysteries of his Master and become absorbed into Him, as it were. Especially does a man achieve this when he offers up his prayer to his Master in intense devotion, his will then becoming as the flame inseparable from the coal, and his mind concentrated on the unity of the lower firmaments, to unify them by means of a lower name, then on the unity of the higher firmaments, and finally on the adsorption of them all into that most high firmament. Whilst a man's mouth and lips are moving, his heart and will must soar to the height of heights, so as to acknowledge the unity of the whole in virtue of the mystery of mysteries in which all ideas, all wills and all thoughts find their goal, to wit, the mystery of *En Sof*.

The thirst for God is colored by the awareness of His holiness, of the endless distance that separates man from the Eternal One. Yet, he who craves for God is not only a mortal being, but also a part of the Community of Israel, that is, the bride of God, endowed with a soul that is "a part of God." Shy in using endearing terms in his own name, the Jewish mystic feels and speaks in the plural. The allegory of the Song of Songs would be impertinent as an individual utterance, but as an expression of Israel's love for God it is among the finest of all expressions. "God is the soul and spirit of all, and Israel calls Him so and says: (My soul), I desire Thee in order to cleave to Thee and I seek Thee early to find Thy favor."

Israel lives in mystic union with God and the purpose of all its service is to strengthen this union: "O my dove that art in the clefts of the rock, in the covert of the cliff" (Song of Sol. 2:14). The "dove" here is the Community of Israel, which like a dove never forsakes her mate, the Holy One, blessed be He. "In the clefts of the rock": these are the students of the Torah, who have no ease in this world. "In the covert of the steep place": these are the specially pious among them, the saintly and God-fearing, from whom the Divine Presence never departs. The Holy One, blessed be He, inquires concerning them of the Community of Israel, saying, "Let me see thy countenance, let me hear thy voice, for sweet is thy voice"; "for above only the voice of those who study the

Torah is heard. We have learned that the likeness of all such is graven above before the Holy One, blessed be He, Who delights Himself with them every day and watches them and that voice rises and pierces its way through all firmaments until it stands before the Holy One, blessed be He."

The concepts of the cabbala cannot always be clearly defined and consistently interrelated. As the name of Jewish mysticism, "cabbala" (lit.: "received lore"), indicates, it is a tradition of wisdom, supposed to have been revealed to elect Sages in ancient times and preserved throughout the generations by an initiated few. The cabbalists accept at the outset the ideas on authority, not on the basis of analytical understanding.

Yet the lips of the teachers and the pages of the books are not the only sources of knowledge. The great cabbalists claimed to have received wisdom directly from the Beyond. Inspiration and Vision were as much a part of their life as contemplation and study. The prayer of Moses: "Show me, I pray Thee, Thy glory" (Ex. 33:18) has never died in the hearts of the cabbalists. The conception of the goal has changed but the quest for immediate cognition remained. The Merkaba-mystics, following perhaps late prophetic traditions about the mysteries of the Divine Throne, were striving to behold the celestial sphere in which the secrets of creation and man's destiny are contained. In the course of the centuries the scope of such esoteric experiences embraced a variety of objectives. The awareness of the cabbalists that the place whereon they stood was holy ground kept them mostly silent about the wonder that was granted to them. Yet we possess sufficient evidence to justify the assumption that mystic events, particularly in the form of inner experiences, of spiritual communications rather than that of sense perceptions, were elements of their living. According to old Rabbinic teachings, there have always been Sages and saints upon whom the Holy Spirit rested, to whom wisdom was communicated from heaven by a Voice, through the appearance of the spirit of Elijah or in dreams. According to the *Zohar,*

God reveals to the saints "profound secrets of the Holy Name which He does not reveal to the angels." The disciples of Rabbi Simeon ben Yohai are called prophets, "before whom both supernal and terrestrial beings tremble in awe." Others pray that the inspiration of the Holy Spirit should come upon them. The perception of the unearthly is recorded as an ordinary feature in the life of certain Rabbis. "When R. Hamnuna the Ancient used to come out from the river on a Friday afternoon, he was wont to rest a little on the bank, and raising his eyes in gladness, he would say that he sat there in order to behold the joyous sight of the heavenly angels ascending and descending. At each arrival of the Sabbath, he said, man is caught up into the world of souls." Not only may the human mind receive spiritual illuminations; the soul also may be bestowed upon higher powers. "Corresponding to the impulses of a man here are the influences which he attracts to himself from above. Should his impulse be toward holiness, he attracts to himself holiness from on high and so he becomes holy; but if this tendency is toward the side of impurity, he draws down toward himself the unclean spirit and so becomes polluted."

Since the time of the prophet Joel the Jews have expected that at the end of days the Lord would "pour out His spirit upon all flesh" and all men would prophesy. In later times, it is believed, the light of that revelation of mysteries could already be perceived.

The mystics absorb even in this world "something of the odor of these secrets and mysteries." Significantly, the Torah itself is conceived as a living source of inspiration, not as a fixed book. The Torah is a voice that "calls aloud" to men; she calls them day by day to herself in love . . . "The Torah lets out a word and emerges for a little from her sheath, and then hides herself again. But she does this only for those who understand and obey her. She is like unto a beautiful and stately damsel, who is hidden in a secluded chamber of a palace and who has a lover of whom no one knows but she. Out of his love for her he constantly passes by her gate, turning his eyes toward all sides to find her. Knowing that he is always haunting the palace, what does she do? She opens a little door in her hidden palace, discloses for a moment her face to her lover, then swiftly hides it again. None but he notices it; but his heart and soul, and all that is in him are drawn to her, knowing as he does that she has revealed herself to him for a moment because she loves him. It is the same with the Torah, which reveals her hidden secrets only to those who love her. She knows that he who is wise of heart daily haunts the gates of her house. What does she do? She shows her face to him from her palace, making a sign of love to him, and straightaway returns to her hiding place again. No one understands her message save he alone, and he is drawn to her with heart and soul and all his being. Thus the Torah reveals herself momentarily in love to her lovers in order to awaken fresh love in them."

6. *The Torah—A Mystic Reality*

The Torah is an inexhaustible esoteric reality. To enter into its deep, hidden strata is in itself a mystic goal. The Universe is an image of the Torah and the Torah is an image of God. For the Torah is "the Holy of Holies"; "it consists entirely of the name of the Holy One, blessed be He. Every letter in it is bound up with that Name."

The Torah is the main source from which man can draw the secret wisdom and power of insight into the essence of things. "It is called Torah (lit.: showing) because it shows and reveals that which is hidden and unknown; and all life from above is comprised in it and issues from it." "The Torah contains all the deepest and most recondite mysteries; all sublime doctrines both disclosed and undisclosed; all essences both of the higher and the lower grades, of this world and of the world to come are to be found there." The source of wisdom is accessible to all, yet only few resort to it. "How stupid are men that they take no pains to know the ways of the Almighty by which the world is maintained. What prevents them? Their stupidity, because they do not study the

Torah; for if they were to study the Torah they would know
the ways of the Holy One, blessed be He."

The Torah has a double significance: literal and symbolic.
Besides their plain, literal meaning, which is important, valid
and never to be overlooked, the verses of the Torah possess
an esoteric significance, "comprehensible only to the wise
who are familiar with the ways of the Torah." "Happy is
Israel to whom was given the sublime Torah, the Torah of
truth. Perdition take anyone who maintains that any narrative in the Torah comes merely to tell us a piece of history
and nothing more! If that were so, the Torah would not be
what it assuredly is, to wit, the supernal Law, the Law of
truth. Now if it is not dignified for a king of flesh and blood
to engage in common talk, much less to write it down, is it
conceivable that the most high King, the Holy One, blessed
be He, was short of sacred subjects with which to fill the
Torah, so that He had to collect such commonplace topics as
the anecdotes of Esau, and Hagar, Laban's talks to Jacob, the
words of Balaam and his ass, those of Balak, and of Zimri, and
such-like, and make of them a Torah? If so, why is it called
the 'Law of Truth?' Why do we read 'The Law of the Lord
is perfect . . . The testimony of the Lord is sure . . . The
Ordinances of the Lord are true . . . More to be desired are
they than gold, yea, than much fine gold' (Ps. 19:8–11). But
assuredly each word of the Torah signifies sublime things, so
that this or that narrative, besides its meaning in and for
itself, throws light on the all-comprehensive Rule of the
Torah."

"Said R. Simeon: 'Alas for the man who regards the Torah
as a mere book of tales and everyday matters! If that were so,
we, even we, could compose a torah dealing with everyday
affairs, and of even greater excellence. Nay, even the princes
of the world possess books of greater worth which we could
use as a model for composing some such torah. The Torah,
however, contains in all its words supernal truths and sublime mysteries. Observe the perfect balancing of the upper
and lower worlds. Israel here below is balanced by the angels

on high, of whom it says: 'who makest thine angels into winds' (Ps. 104:4). For the angels in descending on earth put on themselves earthly garments, as otherwise they could not stay in this world, nor could the world endure them.

"Now, if thus it is with the angels, how much more so must it be with the Torah—the Torah that created them, that created all the worlds and is the means by which these are sustained. Thus had the Torah not clothed herself in garments of this world the world could not endure it. The stories of the Torah are thus only her outer garments, and whoever looks upon that garment as being Torah itself, woe to that man—such a one will have no portion in the next world. David thus said: 'Open thou mine eyes, that I may behold wondrous things out of Thy law' (Ps. 119:18), to wit, the things that are beneath the garment. Observe this. The garments worn by a man are the most visible part of him, and senseless people looking at the man do not seem to see more in him than the garments. But in truth the pride of the garments is the body of the man, and the pride of the body is the soul. Similarly the Torah has a body made up of the precepts of the Torah, called *gufe torah* (bodies, main principles of the Torah), and that body is enveloped in garments made up of worldly narratives. The senseless people only see the garment, the mere narrations; those who are somewhat wise penetrate as far as the body. But the really wise, the servants of the most high King, those who stood on Mt. Sinai, penetrate right through to the soul, the root principle of all, namely to the real Torah. In the future the same are destined to penetrate even to the super-soul (soul of the soul) of the Torah . . . "

How assiduously should one ponder over each word of the Torah, for there is not a single word in it which does not contain allusions to the Supernal Holy Name, not a word which does not contain many mysteries, many aspects, many roots, many branches! Where now is this "book of the wars of the Lord"? What is meant, of course, is the Torah, for as the members of the Fellowship have pointed out, he who is engaged in the battle of the Torah, struggling to penetrate into her mysteries, will wrest from his struggles an abundance of peace.

7. *The Mystic Way of Life*

A longing for the unearthly, a yearning for purity, the will to holiness, connected the conscience of the cabbalists with the strange current of mystic living. Being puzzled or inquisitive will not make a person mystery stricken. The cabbalists were not set upon exploring, or upon compelling the unseen to become visible. Their intention was to integrate their thoughts and deeds into the secret order, to assist God in undoing the evil, in redeeming the light that was concealed. Though working with fragile tools for a mighty end, they were sure of bringing about at the end the salvation of the universe and of this tormented world.

A new form of living was the consequence of the cabbala. Everything was so replete with symbolic significance as to make it the potential heart of the spiritual universe. How carefully must all be approached. A moral rigorism that hardly leaves any room for waste or respite resulted in making the cabbalist more meticulous in studying and fulfilling the precepts of the Torah, in refining his moral conduct, in endowing every-day actions with solemn significance. For man represents God in this world. Even the parts of his body signify Divine mysteries.

Everything a man does leaves its imprint on the world. "The Supernal Holy King does not permit anything to perish, not even the breath of the mouth. He has a place for everything, and makes it what He wills. Even a human word, yes, even the voice, is not void, but has its place and destination in the universe." Every action here below, if it is done with the intention of serving the Holy King, produces a "breath" in the world above, and there is no breath which has no voice; and this voice ascends and crowns itself in the supernal world and becomes an intercessor before the Holy One, blessed be He. Contrariwise, every action which is not done with this purpose becomes a "breath" which floats about the world, and when the soul of the doer leaves his body, this "breath" rolls about like a stone in a sling, and it "breaks the spirit." The act done and the word spoken in the service of the Holy One, however, ascend high above the sun and become a holy breath, which is the seed sown by man in that world and is called *Zedakah* (righteousness or loving-kindness), as it is written: "Sow to yourselves according to righteousness" (Hos. 10:12). This "breath" guides the departed soul and brings it into the region of the supernal glory, so that it is "bound in the bundle of life with the Lord thy God" (I Sam. 25:29). It is concerning this that it is written: "Thy righteousness shall go before thee; the glory of the Lord shall be thy reward" (Is. 58:8). That which is called "the glory of the Lord" gathers up the souls of that holy breath, and this is indeed ease and comfort for them; but the other is called "breaking of spirit." Blessed are the righteous whose works are "above the sun" and who sow a seed of righteousness which makes them worthy to enter the world to come.

Everything a man does leaves its imprint upon the world: his breath, thought, speech. If it is evil, the air is defiled and he who comes close to that trace may be affected by it and led to do evil. By fulfilling the Divine precepts man purifies the air and turns the "evil spirits" into "holy spirits." He should strive to spiritualize the body and to make it identical with the soul by fulfilling the 248 positive and 365 negative precepts which correspond to the 248 limbs and the 365 sinews of the human body. The precepts of the Torah contain "manifold sublime recondite teachings and radiances and resplendences," and can lift man to the supreme level of existence.

The purpose of man's service is to "give strength to God," not to attain one's own individual perfection. Man is able to stir the supernal spheres. "The terrestrial world is connected with the heavenly world, as the heavenly world is connected with the terrestrial one." In fulfilling the good the corresponding sphere on high is strengthened; in balking it, the sphere is weakened. This connection or correspondence can be made to operate in a creative manner by means of *kaw-wanah* or contemplation of the mysteries of which the words and precepts of the Torah are the symbols. In order to grasp the meaning of those words or to fulfill the purpose of those precepts one has to resort to the Divine Names and Qualities which are invested in those words and precepts, the mystic issues to which they refer, or, metaphorically, the gates of the celestial mansion which the spiritual content of their fulfill- ment has to enter. Thus, all deeds—study, prayer and ceremonies—have to be performed not mechanically but while meditating upon their mystic significance.

Prayer is a powerful force in this service and a venture full of peril. He who prays is a priest at the temple that is the cosmos. With good prayer he may " build worlds," with im- proper prayer he may "destroy worlds." "It is a miracle that a man survives the hour of worship," the Baal Shem said. "The significance of all our prayers and praises is that by means of them the upper fountain may be filled; and when it is so filled and attains completeness, then the universe below, and all that appertains thereto, is filled also and re- ceives completeness from the completion which has been consummated in the upper sphere. The world below cannot, indeed, be in a state of harmony unless it receives that peace and perfection from above, even as the moon has no light in herself but shines with the reflected radiance of the sun. All our prayers and intercessions have this purpose, namely, that the region from whence light issues may be invigorated; for then from its reflection all below is supplied." "Every word of prayer that issues from a man's mouth ascends aloft through all firmaments to a place where it is tested. If it is genuine, it is taken up before the Holy King to be fulfilled, but if not it is rejected, and an alien spirit is evoked by it." For example, "it is obligatory for every Israelite to relate the story of the Exodus on the Passover night. He who does so fervently and joyously, telling the tale with a high heart, shall be found worthy to rejoice in the *Shekinah* in the world to come, for rejoicing brings forth rejoicing; and the joy of Israel causes the Holy One Himself to be glad, so that He calls together all the Family above and says unto them: 'Come ye and hearken unto the praises which My children bring unto Me! Behold how they rejoice in My redemption!' Then all the angels and supernal beings gather round and observe Israel, how she sings and rejoices because of her Lord's own Redemption—and seeing the rejoicings below, the supernal beings also break into jubilation for that the Holy One possesses on earth a people so holy, whose joy in the Redemption of their Lord is so great and powerful. For all that terrestrial rejoicing increases the power of the Lord and His hosts in the regions above, just as an earthly king gains strength from the praises of his subjects, the fame of his glory being thus spread throughout the world."

Worship came to be regarded as a pilgrimage into the supernal spheres, with the prayerbook as an itinerary, containing the course of the gradual ascent of the spirit. The essential goal of man's service is to bring about the lost unity of all that exists. To render praise unto Him is not the final purpose. "Does the God of Abraham need an exaltation? Is He not already exalted high above our comprehension? . . . Yet man can and must exalt Him in the sense of uniting in his mind all the attributes in the Holy Name, for this is the supremest form of worship." By meditating upon the mysteries while performing the Divine precepts, we act toward unifying all the supernal potencies in one will and bringing about the union of the Master and the Matrona.

Concerning the verse in Ps. 145:18, "The Lord is nigh to all them that call upon Him, to all that call upon Him in truth," the *Zohar* remarks that the words "in truth" mean in possession of the full knowledge which enables the worshiper perfectly "to unite the letters of the Holy Name in prayer . . . On the achievement of that unity hangs both celestial and terrestrial worship . . . If a man comes to unify the Holy Name, but without proper concentration of mind and devotion of heart, to the end that the supernal and terrestrial hosts should be blessed thereby, then his prayer is rejected and all beings denounce him, and he is numbered with those of whom the Holy One said, 'When ye come to see my countenance, who hath required this from your hand, to tread my courts?' All the 'countenances' of the King are hidden in the depths of darkness, but for those who know how perfectly to unite the Holy Name, all the walls of darkness are burst asunder, and the diverse 'countenances' of the King are made manifest, and shine upon all, bringing blessing to heavenly and earthly beings."

The lower things are apparent, the higher things remain unrevealed. The higher an essence is, the greater is the degree of its concealment. To pray is "to draw blessings from the depth of the 'Cistern,' from the source of all life . . . Prayer is the drawing of this blessing from above to below; for when the Ancient One, the All-hidden, wishes to bless the universe, He lets His gifts of Grace collect in that supernal depth, from whence they are to be drawn, through human prayer, into the 'Cistern,' so that all the streams and brooks may be filled therefrom." The verse in Psalm 130:1, "Out of the depths have I called Thee," is said to mean not only that he who prays should do so from the depths of his soul; he must also invoke the blessing from the source of all sources.

8. *The Concern for God*

The yearning for mystic living, the awareness of the ubiquitous mystery, the noble nostalgia for the nameless nucleus, have rarely subsided in the Jewish soul. This longing for the mystical has found many and varied expressions in ideas and doctrines, in customs and songs, in visions and aspirations. It is a part of the heritage of the psalmists and prophets.

There were Divine commandments to fulfill, rituals to perform, laws to obey—but the psalmist did not feel as if he carried a yoke: "Thy statues have been my songs" (119:54). The fulfillment of the *mitzvot* was felt to be not a mechanical compliance but a personal service in the palace of the King of Kings. Is mysticism alien to the spirit of Judaism? Listen to the psalmist: "As the hart panteth after the water brooks, so panteth my soul after Thee, O Lord. My soul thirsteth for God, for the Living God; when shall I come and appear before God?" (42:2–3). "My soul yearneth, yea even pineth for the courts of the Lord; my heart and my flesh sing for joy unto the Living God" (84:3). "For a day in Thy courts is better than a thousand" (84:11). "In Thy presence is fulness of joy" (16:11).

It has often been said that Judaism is an earthly religion, yet the psalmist states, "I am a sojourner in the earth" (119:-19). "Whom have I in heaven but Thee? And beside thee I desire none upon earth" (73:25). "My flesh and my heart faileth; but God is the rock of my heart and my portion forever" (73:26). "But as for me, the nearness of God is my good" (73:28). "O God, Thou art my God; earnestly will I seek Thee; my soul thirsteth for Thee, my flesh longeth for Thee in a dry and weary land, where no water is . . . for Thy lovingkindness is better than life. My soul is satisfied as with marrow and fatness; . . . I remember Thee upon my couch and meditate on Thee in the nightwatches . . . My soul cleaveth unto Thee, Thy right hand holdeth me fast" (63:2, 4, 6, 7, 9).

In their efforts to say what God is and wills, the prophets sought to imbue Israel with two impulses: to realize that God is holy, different and apart from all that exists, and to bring into man's focus the dynamics that prevail between God and man. The first impulse placed the mind in the restful light of the knowledge of unity, omnipotence, and superiority of God to all other beings, while the second impulse turned the hearts toward the inexhaustible heavens of God's concern for man, at times brightened by His mercy, at times darkened by His anger. He is both transcendent, beyond human understanding, and at the same time full of love, compassion, grief, or anger. The prophets did not intend to afford man a view of heaven, to report about secret things they saw and heard but to disclose what happened in God in reference to Israel. What they preached was more than a concept of Divine might and wisdom. They spoke of an inner life of God, of His love or anger, His mercy or disappointment, His interest or participation in the fate of Israel and other nations. God revealed Himself to the prophets in a specific state, in an emotional or passionate relationship to Israel. He not only demanded obedience but He was personally concerned and even stirred by the conduct of His people. Their actions aroused His joy, grief or disappointment. His attitude was not objective but subjective. He was not only a Judge but also a Father. He is the lover, engaged to His people, who reacts to human life with a specific *pathos,* signified in the language of the prophets, in love, mercy or anger. The Divine pathos which the prophets tried to express in many ways was not a name for His essence but rather for the modes of this reaction to Israel's conduct which could be changed by a change in Israel's conduct. Such a change was often the object of the prophetic ministry.

The prophets discovered the holy dimension of living by which our right to live and to survive is measured. However, the holy dimension was not a mechanical magnitude, measurable by the yardstick of deed and reward, of crime and punishment, by a cold law of justice. They did not proclaim a universal moral mechanism but a spiritual order in which justice was the course but not the source. To them justice was not a static principle but a surge sweeping from the inwardness of God, in which the deeds of man find, as it were, approval or disapproval, joy or sorrow. There was a surge of Divine pathos, which came to the souls of the prophets like a fierce passion, startling, shaking, burning, and led them forth to the perilous defiance of people's self-assurance and contentment. Beneath all songs and sermons they held conference with God's concern for the people, with the well out of which the tides of anger raged.

There is always a correspondence between what man is and what he knows about God. To a man of the *vita activa,* omnipotence is the most striking attribute of God. A man with an inner life, to whom thoughts and intuitions are not less real than things and deeds, will search for a concept of the inner life of God. The concept of inner life in the Divine Being is an idea upon which the mystic doctrines of Judaism hinge. The significance of prophetic revelation lies not in the inner experience of the prophet but in its character as a manifestation of what is in God. Prophetic revelation is primarily an event in the life of God. This is the outstanding difference between prophetic revelation and all other types of inspiration as reported by many mystics and poets. To the prophet it is not a psychic event, but first of all a transcendent act, something that happens to God. The actual reality of revelation takes place outside the consciousness of the prophet. He experiences revelation, so to speak, as an ecstasy of God, who comes out of His imperceivable distance to reveal His will to man. Essentially, the act of revelation takes place in the Beyond; it is merely directed upon the prophet.

The knowledge about the inner state of the Divine in its relationship to Israel determined the inner life of the prophets, engendering a passion for God, a *sympathy* for the Divine pathos in their hearts. They loved Israel because God loved Israel, and they frowned upon Israel when they knew that such was the attitude of God. Thus the marriage of Hosea was an act of sympathy; the prophet had to go through the experience of being betrayed as Israel had betrayed God. He had to experience in his own life what it meant to be betrayed by a person whom he loved in order to gain an understanding of the inner life of God. In a similar way the sympathy for God was in the heart of Jeremiah like a "burning fire, shut up in my bones and I weary myself to hold it in, but cannot" (20:9).

The main doctrine of the prophets can be called *pathetic theology.* Their attitude toward what they knew about God can be described as religion of sympathy. The Divine pathos, or as it was later called, the *Middot,* stood in the center of their consciousness. The life of the prophet revolved around the life of God. The prophets were not indifferent to whether God was in a state of anger or a state of mercy. They were most sensitive to what was going on in God.

This is the pattern of Jewish mysticism: to have an open heart for the inner life of God. It is based on two assumptions: that there is an inner life in God and that the existence of man ought to revolve in a spiritual dynamic course around the life of God.

Martin Buber's "Speeches on Judaism": A Classic of Jewish Identity*

Maurice Friedman

What makes Martin Buber's epoch-making "Speeches On Judaism" not merely an event in the history of Central European Jewry but of relevance today, more than sixty years after they were written, is the revolutionary existentialist element in them which turned the "Jewish Question" from an abstract question about whether Jews are to be considered members of a race, nation, or common creed to that of the deepest personal meaning of Judaism to the Jew himself. Buber had already anticipated this approach in his emphasis upon cultural as opposed to merely political Zionism. But now he went a step further to understand Jewishness as an existential choice that is made to create the future out of the inheritance of the past.

The Western Jew is a divided man because his community of land, speech, and custom is different from his community of blood. Yet the blood is the deepest level of force of the soul, for it has given us something that determines in every hour each tone and color of our lives. The great heritage of the ages that we bring with us into the world is the destiny, action, suffering, pain, misery, and disgrace of the fathers and mothers—from the fight of the prophets to the detached

---

* This essay is based on a chapter from the not yet fully cut version of Maurice Friedman, *Encounter on the Narrow Ridge: Milestones in the Life of Martin Buber* (New York: E.P. Dutton, 1978). A translation of all Buber's early "Speeches on Judaism" is to be found in the first section of Martin Buber, *On Judaism,* ed. by Nahum N. Glatzer (New York: Schocken Books).

intellectuality of the modern Jew. The inner division of the Jew will remain until he recognizes that the blood is the formative element in his life. This recognition does not mean a choice that would free him from the influence of his environment. We are, said Buber, in a more pregnant sense than any other civilized people, a mixture. But we do not want to be the slaves but the masters of this mixture. The choice means a decision about which shall be the ruling element and which the ruled in us. When out of deep self-knowledge we shall have said Yes to our whole Jewish existence, then we shall no longer feel ourselves as individuals but as a people, for each will feel the people in himself. My soul is not with my people, rather my people *is* my soul.

"When I was a child," Buber concluded, "I read an old Jewish saying that I could not understand . . . :'Before the gates of Rome sits a leprous beggar and waits. He is the Messiah.' Then I went to an old man and asked him: 'For what does he wait?' And the old man answered me something that . . . only much later I learned to understand. He said: 'For you.'"

In the second of his "Three Speeches on Judaism"—"Judaism and Mankind"—Buber universalized the inner duality of the Jew to a psychological dualism characteristic of all men, perhaps indeed, the most essential and decisive factor of human life. Whether it is experienced as personal choice, external necessity, or pure chance, man experiences his inner way as a movement from crossroad to crossroad. What has made the Jewish people a phenomenon of mankind is that in it this polarity is more dominant than elsewhere and the striving for unity stronger.

The Indian idea of redemption is clearer and more unconditional than the Jewish, Buber stated. Yet it means becoming free not from the duality of the soul but from the soul's entanglement in the world. The Indian redemption means an awakening, the Jewish a transformation; the Indian a laying aside of illusion, the Jewish a laying hold of the truth; the

Indian a negation, the Jewish an affirmation; the Indian takes place in the timeless, the Jewish means the way of mankind. The Jewish idea is, like all historical views, the less essential but the more moving. It alone can say like Job, "I know that my Redeemer liveth." From it the Messianic idea of Judaism derives its humanity. And when in Jewish mysticism duality was carried even into the conception of God, the Jewish idea of redemption rose to the height of the Indian: it became the idea of the redemption of God—of the reunification of the essence of God, which is removed from things, with the glory of God, which wandering, straying, and scattered lives among the things of the world.

The Jewish mystic carried forward in glowing inwardness the ancient striving for unity. Yet this striving is carried forward today, Buber claimed, by each person who wins unity out of his soul, who decides in himself for the pure, the free, the fruitful, by each who drives the money-changers out of his own temple. The people too must also decide and reject the negative, the play-actors, the covetous, the gamblers, the cowardly slaves of the community. For the expulsion of the negative, in a people as in individuals, is the way to becoming one. The distinction here is between those who choose and those who let happen, between those who have a goal and those who have petty ends, between those who create and those who destroy.

Buber demanded a decisive turning of the whole being, and he called this turning "The Renewal of Judaism." The concept of evolution that dominates the typical man of this time, he said, is the concept of gradual change coming from the working together of many little causes. "When I speak of renewal," Buber said, "I am aware that I am leaving the ground of this age and am entering that of a new, coming one. For I mean by renewal nothing at all gradual . . . but something sudden and enormous, . . . no continuation and betterment, but radical turning and transformation. Indeed, just as I believe that in the life of an individual man there can be a moment of elemental revolution, a crisis and shattering and a new becoming from the roots to all branches of existence, just so I believe in it for the life of Judaism."

Because of his firm belief that the renewal of Judaism must take place as a revolutionary turning of the whole existence, Buber was critical of the claim of liberal and Reform Judaism to be a renewal of Judaism. Rationalization of the faith, simplification of the dogma, relaxing of the rituals—all this is negation, nothing but negation! This is not a renewal of Judaism but its continuation in an easier, more elegant, more European, salon-like form. The prophets certainly spoke of the insignificance of all ceremonies, but not in order to make the religious life easier. They sought rather to make it more difficult, to make it genuine and whole, to proclaim the holiness of the *deed.* Prophetic Judaism demanded that man live unconditionally, that he be whole at every hour and in all things, and that he *realize* his feelings of God at all times. This meant the realization of three interrelated tendencies—the striving for unity, for the deed, and for the future. These tendencies find their strongest expression in Messianism—the deepest original idea of Judaism. In Messianism the relativity of a far time is transformed into the absolute of the fullness of time. Here, for the first time the Absolute was proclaimed as the goal—the goal in mankind and to be realized through it. This unconditional demand Buber tried to renew in his time for every Jew who was willing to listen and respond as a Jew. "We stand," Buber proclaimed, "in a moment of the greatest tension and of ultimate decision, in a moment with a double face—one looking toward death, the other toward life." The renewal of Judaism means to put aside the dualism between our absolute and our relative life in order that the fight for fulfillment may grasp the whole people, that the idea of reality may penetrate the everyday, *that the spirit may enter into life!* Only then when Judaism extends itself like a hand and seizes every Jew by the hair of his head and bears him in the storm between heaven and earth toward Jerusalem will the Jewish people become ripe to build itself a new destiny.

What is at stake here is not the destiny of the Jewish people alone, Buber asserted, but a new world-feeling to be brought to mankind. The formation of this new world-feeling and the renewal of Judaism are two sides of *one* event. The basic tendencies of Judaism—the striving for unity, deed, and future—are the elements out of which a new world will be constructed. "And so our soul's deepest humanity and our soul's deepest Judaism mean and will the same thing."

Inner division can be overcome by decision, Buber stated, and decision brings unity not only to the divided individual but to the divided world. He who stands in decision knows nothing else than that he must choose, and even this he knows not with his thinking but with his being. He who decides with his whole soul, decides himself to God; for all wholeness is God's image and in each whole being God himself shines forth. In each genuine, united decision the primal meaning of the world fulfills itself in eternal originality. In the province entrusted to him, the united man completes the work of creation; for each thing's completion, the greatest and smallest, touches upon the divine. In appearance the deed is inescapably fixed in the structure of causality, but in truth it works deep and secretly on the fate of the world. When it recollects its divine goal of oneness and cuts itself loose from conditionality, it is free and powerful as the deed of God. This recollection is *teshuva,* turning to God with one's whole existence. When God first planned the world, it is told in the Talmud, he saw that it could not persevere because it had no basis; then he created the turning. *Teshuva,* or the turning, is that renewing revolution in the course of existence for which Buber called in "The Renewal of Judaism."

There are three stages of realization which can be distinguished in Jewish religiousness. In the first, the Biblical stage, it was conceived as an *imitatio Dei.* In the second, the Talmudic stage, the realization of God was conceived as an enhancing of his reality. In the third, Kabbalistic stage, realization was raised to the working of man's action on the fate of God. All three stages, asserted Buber, are united in the conception of the absolute value of the human deed. He who does the deed cannot measure its effect; yet he must say, with the Talmud, "For my sake the world was created" and "Upon me rests the world." What is essential to one's deed is not the What but the How. It is not the content of a deed that makes it truth, but whether it takes place in human conditionality or divine unconditionality. Even "profane" actions are holy if they are performed in holiness, in unconditionality. Unconditionality is the specific religious content of Judaism. Where religiousness is effective in building community, founding religion, where from the life of the individual it enters into the life between men, then the basic feeling that one thing is needful becomes a demand. In the common life of men, as nowhere else, a formless mass is given us in which we can imprint the face of God. The community of man is an important work that awaits us; a chaos that we must order, a diaspora that we must gather, a conflict that we must resolve. But we can only do this if each one of us in his place, in the natural realm of his life together with men, does the right, the uniting, the shaping: because God does not want to be believed in, discussed, or defended by man; he wants to be *realized*.

Judaism and Personal Growth

Dov Peretz Elkins

There is an exquisite balance in Jewish tradition between the needs of the individual and the needs of society.

Hillel's wise and insightful apothegm summarizes the synthesis of these two needs with characteristic brilliance and humanness: If I am not for myself, who will be? If I care only for myself, what am I? If not now, when?

There is a frantic search in the world today, especially in North America, for self-realization and self-fulfillment. After the great disillusionments of the 1960's and early 1970's, including Vietnam, Watergate and other government scandals, and following the frustrations and failures of blacks and other oppressed groups to achieve full and immediate social justice, people turned to the improvement of the irreducible component in society: the individual person. If society as a whole cannot be made right now, let us turn to the individual and make him/her whole. Then perhaps, hopefully, a whole society will follow the making of whole persons.

Another major factor in modern life propelling individuals toward the new fields of human growth and development is the freakish gap between scientific and technological progress and human and ethical advances. With supersonic flights we can travel to Europe in a few hours. By satellite we can view live scenes in Peking. Our weaponry is sufficiently powerful to destroy the world one thousand times in a short few minutes (and yet we are still working diligently to perfect even better weapons). The variety and complexity of consumer goods making life easier and more luxurious is astounding. Medical progress has given longer life to heart patients, and miraculous drugs and other cures give great hope that we will soon extend our lives to 80 or 90. Computers have reduced to hours the tasks which would have occupied countless scientists hundreds of years.

With all this dazzling progress in science and technology people are rightly asking a logical and simple question: Why is there not concomitant growth and development on the part of the individual? If we can communicate with Soviet diplomats across the globe in a few seconds, why cannot we communicate better with our spouses, our children, our neighbors, indeed, our selves? If we can destroy the world in minutes, why cannot we heal people and societies in years? If we can implant new organs and new arteries and make weak and sick hearts beat again, why cannot we help people become more sensitive, more compassionate, more vibrant, more excited?

The movement towards self-fulfillment and self-realization in America today is addressing itself to the sobering and somber conclusion that unless we learn more about the inner depths, the inner space, all the discoveries we have made in outer space are useless. Unless we develop the technology to go in, all the technologies we have invented to go up will prove to be our ultimate undoing.

American Judaism and Personal Growth

One of the tragic aspects of American Jewish life is that for the most part Jewish institutions address themselves neither to the needs of the individual for personal development nor to the needs of the Jewish and general society for justice, wholeness and community. Jewish education has been described as a mile wide and an inch deep. That description can easily apply to all of Jewish institutional life today. Children are bored and alienated in religious schools, adults find precious little of interest and value in Jewish public programming. Mostly negative factors, such as anti-Semitism in the

USSR and in Arab countries, and the threat to Israel's survival, bring Jews to meetings and financial commitments. Little or nothing is done in the realm of social justice any more (the faint sparks of the sixties have turned to smoldering embers). And in the realm of personal development, most Jewish professionals and lay leaders are unfamiliar with and/or afraid of the challenges and risks that come with personal growth.

The major focus of synagogues and their various movements is related to ritual and Jewish law. The chief distinguishing characteristic of synagogues today are the presence or absence of the skullcap and the amount of Hebrew or English in the service. Religious worship is dull, empty and uninspiring.

While the world outside is turning to exciting and dynamic, vibrant and challenging new modalities of being human, the religious traditions of America, including Judaism, are withering on the vine. While people are searching for meaning, direction, fulfillment and personal growth in an age of demoralization and alienation and loneliness, Jewish groups are plugging away at the old methods and the old programs, ignoring the deep human yearnings of the citizenry for a richer, fuller human existence.

"Turning People On"

The journey inward has many paths. For some it is T.M. (transcendental meditation); for others, yoga. Thousands have been turned on to life through *est* (Erhard Seminars Training); countless couples have renewed their marriage through Marriage Encounter. Still others find enriched living through Gestalt, psychosynthesis, journal writing, encounter groups, jogging, and many other methods. The list is endless. All of this potpourri goes by the general appellation: the Human Potential Movement.

The Human Potential Movement is based on a new school

of thought in the behavioral sciences called Humanistic Psychology. Founded by the late Abraham H. Maslow and others, this new approach builds on psychoanalysis and behaviorism, but goes beyond them. It stresses personal meaning, values, fulfillment, peak experiences, aliveness, joy, ecstasy, wholism. Above all, it is person-centered. It believes in the infinite possibilities of human persons to expand their boundaries, stretch their imagination, and grow as persons. It stresses the sanctity and precious healing quality of human relationships. "I want to be my best self, and when I am my best self, I can best reach out to you in meaningful dialog; an I to a thou."

The Human Potential Movement is turning people on to the idea that we have a long way to go towards being fully human, but the longest part of that journey is inward. We have just scratched the surface of fulfilling the potential of that creature which we call human being. Margaret Mead and others estimate that we fulfill only 5 or 10 per cent of our full potential. Our life is a palace in which we choose to live in only one room. We were given a hand, and so far have only learned to utilize a finger.

Through human potential courses, workshops and other similar experiences, people are learning to find more ecstasy, more joy, more depth to their lives. To relate more deeply. To open their souls and hearts. To expand the range of their feelings. To accept themselves as God made them. To heighten their awareness, to lengthen their perception, to broaden their perspective. To live more justly, more authentically, more openly. To let themselves risk the kind of relationship that makes one vulnerable, more open to deep hurt and deep love. To experience their pain and to create their destiny.

In short, the Human Potential Movement has found ways to help people become more human, more alive, more fully functioning. It has snatched the pristine role of religion from the grasp of the religionist. Since modern religion has failed to provide meaning and fulfillment, a substitute has arisen to replace it.

But the new Movement need not replace traditional religion. There is too much beauty, poetry, wisdom, insight and experience, embedded within the traditions of the past for them ever to be replaced. Thus, for those, like myself, already committed to a traditional ethno-cultural religious life, the new Movement comes to enhance and enrich what already is. To give it a new focus, a new color, a new song.

A new synthesis is emerging between the Human Potential Movement and traditional religions. Groups of religionists from all camps are organizing to bring to bear the insights of humanistic psychology on their own backgrounds: literary, historical, educational and religious.

Just as Judaism has been enriched by the winds of change in philosophy and culture by the Persians, the Greeks, the Babylonians, the Europeans, the Americans, in the past, so today it can be enriched and enhanced by the amalgamation of two great traditions—an ancient one and a modern one. Human fulfillment, personal growth, interpersonal relationships, small and large group functioning, can all be aided and enlightened through the interface of these two approaches to life.

Human Potential as Hasidism for the World

If the Human Potential Movement sounds and acts like a religion, it is the Jewish religious heritage which most closely approximates many of its beliefs, attitudes and values. The positive view of the basic nature of human persons, the beauty and worthwhileness of the body, the need for and healthfulness of joy, are all viewpoints shared alike by Judaism and humanistic psychology. Other points of contact will be delineated further in this essay. Generally speaking it is possible to say that there is a remarkable confluence in the liberal, humanistic, moral, optimistic belief systems of the two traditions.

If Judaism and the Human Potential Movement share common viewpoints, it is Hasidic Judaism which most prominently highlights the shared philosophies. For it is in Hasidism at its best that one finds most clearly the ideas and ideal of Judaism which parallel the new "religion" of humanistic psychology and education.

Both Hasidism and the Human Potential Movement grew in an age of widespread despair and alienation, fear and frustration. When there was a need to give persons hope about life, the world, and themselves. In eighteenth century Europe, Jews were in deep depression due to widespread persecution, the raising of false hopes through bogus messianic figures, and a reliance on dry intellectualism and rigid, legalistic ritualism. We have already discussed some of the factors in modern America which have led to the birth of the personal growth movement, including futile war, widespread corruption, mushrooming technology, and a general attitude of anonymity, rootlessness, depersonalization and dehumanization.

In short, both Hasidism and the Human Potential Movement were born at times when people despaired of life and became mired in a rut of mechanical, repetitious drudgery. The new movements gave hope, joy, sanctity, vitality, spontaneity, and direction to their despairing adherents.

Elie Wiesel describes with clarity and precision the revolution in Jewish life that was created by the birth of Hasidism:

> At that moment in Jewish history, it was a powerful, irresistible message. By putting the accent on friendship and love, on impulse rather than asceticism, erudition and the observance of the Law, Hasidism brought back to the fold large numbers of Jews who, faltering under the weight of their burden, came close to conceding defeat
> . . .

What was miraculous was that the Jew suddenly discovered within himself the desire and strength to sing and celebrate life at a time when the sky was darkening with crimson clouds and the threat was becoming closer and more defined. Thanks to the Rebbe, the Hasid could persevere and gradually regain self-confidence; he could claim his place in time and hope . . .

(*Souls on Fire,* pp. 208–9)

Hasidic doctrine enabled its followers to rely on their own inner strength of spirit to overcome life's difficulties and vicissitudes. By emphasizing the spiritual life, joy in all things, the sanctity of family, love and friendship, the close relationship with God and all human beings, Hasidim were able to create their own inner world to substitute for the world of hatred, injustice, poverty and misery on the outside. If the Hasid was a slave to the ruling authorities, he was a king in his own palace. Bei dem Riboneh Shel Olom bistu a Kenig (To the Creator of the Universe you are a King) was a widespread philosophy giving renewed hope and excitement about life to the followers of the Baal Shem Tov.

By the same token, the teachers of the newly-burgeoning Human Potential Movement were able to renew the feelings of hope and joy and sanctity of their followers in a world which was despairing of all goodness, humanness, justice and happiness.

Maslow recognized very clearly that the new psychology was fulfilling the same needs as traditional religion did in its time. He stated that the hope for self-actualization (the term for fulfillment, or salvation, coined by Kurt Goldstein and popularized by Maslow in his famous study of fully evolved human beings) was the very same hope aspired to by the ancient prophets and sages.

If the various extant religions may be taken as expressions of human aspiration, i.e., what people would *like* to become if only they could, then we can see here too a validation of the affirmation that all people yearn toward self-actualization or tend toward it. This is so because our description of the actual characteristics of self-actualizing people parallels at many points the ideals urged by the religions, e.g., the transcendence of self, the fusion of the true, the good and the beautiful, contribution to others, wisdom, honesty and naturalness, the transcendence of selfish and personal motivations, the giving up of "lower" desires in favor of "higher" ones, increased friendliness and kindness, the easy differentiation between ends (tranquility, serenity, peace) and means (money, power, status), the decrease of hostility, cruelty, and destructiveness (although decisiveness, justified anger and indignation, self-affirmation, etc., may very well *increase*).

(*Towards a Psychology of Being,* p. 158)

With the coming of humanistic psychology, the lines between religion and psychology, the ineffable and the precisely defined, the humanities and science, become seriously blurred.

If Christianity distilled the essence of Jewish ethical monotheism and spread it to the world, then it seems that in a similar way the Human Potential Movement is re-learning the lessons of Hasidic Judaism and spreading it to the world. The dream of personal fulfillment, of ecstasy and peak experiences, of joy and richness, of higher values and self-transcendence, of wholeness and happiness, of loving and intense relationships, of sacred community, all of which Hasidism advocated and lived by as much as possible, is now becoming a dream for all human beings through the new movement for personal growth and spiritual development.

There is no small irony in the fact that the major forces in the still growing Human Potential Movement were and are Jewish: Maslow, Fromm, Frankl, Erikson, Schutz, Simon, Kirschenbaum, Perls, Berne, Jourard, Ellis and many others.

The new ideas and methods of humanistic psychology and education, then, are deeply roots in the same forces and trends that have moved Judaism in its time of greatest creativity and adaptiveness. The relationship between the two approaches are remarkably similar, and those aspiring to help persons and communities to live fuller, richer lives, can only benefit by drawing upon the overflowing wells of both Judaism and humanistic directions.

Deeper Jewish Roots of Human Potential Ideas

While the philosophy of Hasidic Judaism most closely approximates the ideas now being grappled with among humanistic leaders, Jewish theology and ideology from its earliest days espoused a *Weltanschauung* which helped give birth to the liberalism, openness and optimism now spreading among modern philosophers and psychologists following the school of Maslow.

I see four major ideas, fundamental to Judaism, which also are the ideological pillars of the new humanistic movement.

1) The idea that the potential for growth in human beings is extraordinary.

In Judaism, human beings are created in the image of God. Furthermore, the world is not finished; we are constantly creating and re-creating it. The greatest sin *(chet)* is missing the mark, not fulfilling our best selves. Growth and self-perfection are a lifelong pursuit. Change is possible and necessary. Return, *teshuva,* to our highest self, is the ultimate goal of life. Persons are here on earth to evolve and grow and develop and learn and expand. God gave us the powers to do this and must do it or end our existence. *De-la moseef yasef* —we either grow or we die.

The ancient rabbis, elucidating the liturgical passage declaring that the New Year is the birthday of the world and of humankind, explain: "Said the Holy One to Israel: My children, if you turn this day, changing your bad ways, you will become new creatures, not the same peoples as before. Then will I consider you as if I had created you new." (Lev. R. 29:12)

2) The idea that one's self takes precedence over others, that one has the obligation to care for and protect oneself.

In the scheme of Jewish holy days, the very personal and individually oriented High Holy Days begin the Jewish year, and are followed by the national-historical holidays of the three pilgrimage festivals. Personal fulfillment leads to community fulfillment and must therefore precede it. The story of Akiba and Ben Petura illustrates the same point, ending with the declaration that "your life takes precedence over that of your brother." Hillel's statement, "If I am not for myself, who will be?" is cut from the same cloth. Likewise the Talmudic statement that one must say always, "For my sake was the world created." So, too, the notion that the value of each individual life is precious, holy, and infinite; equal, in fact, to the entire world.

3) The idea that true growth is spiritual growth.

The Hebrew emphasis on the sanctity of time over material things, the centrality of the Shabbat over the days of the week, point in this direction. The emphasis on study as a means of knowledge and righteous living also stresses the spiritual life. The need for prayer and acts of kindness as fundamental to human living is in the same vein. One who studies Torah, Talmud, Codes, liturgies, and other bedrock Jewish literary contributions, will find one theme running through all these books: the striving for the good life through personal spiritual development.

Who is the real hero, the model, the guru? He who harnesses his own spiritual powers. That is the truest strength, and the only strength. (Compare Avot 4:1)

4) The idea that authentic human relationships, love and intimacy, are the touchstone of successful living.

Love your neighbor as yourself. Honor your parents. Acts of kindness to other humans are a pillar of the universe. As God is holy, so you too be holy, in your dealings with others. Marriage, the family, raising children, being part of the community, all stress the sanctity, the indispensability of significant relationships as a therapeutic, confirming, ennobling, aspect of living. The Jew cares for other Jews, is sensitive to the needs of all people.

Oh chevruta oh metoota—Either community or death.

Why Do Jews Need the Human Potential Movement?

If within traditional Judaism already lie the seeds of the new humanistic approaches, why, then, do Jews need to turn to the Human Potential Movement for spiritual satisfaction and personal development and growth? Would not maintaining an active and committed Jewish life accomplish the same goals of personal and social growth through Judaism?

Judaism has never been alien to alternative sources of truth which do not conflict with its own system. To the contrary, strands of thought and perception of other cultures and civilizations have been eagerly assimilated into the Jewish way of life throughout the centuries. These new infusions of fresh blood into the living body of Judaism have given it renewed vigor and greater adaptability to the needs of each generation.

At a time when traditional religion has fallen into desuetude, when the complexity and overlapping of Jewish organizational life has alienated many young, thoughtful and sensitive Jews, a new infusion of thought and practice into Jewish life in North America (and throughout the world) should be a welcome phenomenon.

Most important of all, the insights, beauty, depth and wisdom of leading pioneers in humanistic studies can make an extremely significant addition to the achievement of the ultimate goal of Judaism: the living of a meaningful, fulfilling mode of human existence. It would be folly to ignore a wellspring of new vigor and dynamism which, in my opinion, has become the foremost contribution to our search for a life of values and self-actualization in the twentieth century.

There are two specific areas in which the Human Potential Movement can make highly significant contributions to the search for meaning and truth in the life of Jews and Jewish groups.

First, there is developing a body of *ideas,* of ways of viewing persons and relationships and the world, containing insights that develop, extend, amplify and embellish Judaism's profound contribution to persons' understanding of themselves and their environment. Such ideas are often closely related to fundamental Jewish notions. At times they expand what is only adumbrated in Jewish sources. In other instances the implicit is made explicit; thoughts and ideas are carried to their next logical progression.

Briefly, I would mention three principle concepts in humanistic psychology which carry forward ideas upon which Judaism touches lightly and in outline form.

The concept of *awareness.* Implied in many of the ideas and rituals of Judaism is the need for awareness of self, others and environment. The most prominent example would be the "beracha," the ritual formula recited on hundreds of different occasions, designed to heighten the awareness and sensitivity of the individual in his/her daily comings and goings. Whether it be eating bread, seeing a rainbow, wearing a new garment, or celebrating a holy day with wine, the beracha lifts the event from a mundane act required for daily subsistence to an experience of transcendence and exaltation.

Many approaches within the Human Potential Movement,

but particularly Gestalt Therapy as developed by Fritz Perls and others, stress the importance of *awareness* as a key to mature living (see for example, *Awareness* by John O. Stevens, Real People Press, 1971, or any of the many books of Fritz Perls). The full development of this significant concept, in addition to exploration of new ways to achieve greater awareness, is a major contribution which anyone who takes the enterprise of living seriously must reckon with.

A second major contribution of humanistic psychology which expands and elaborates on a notion only incipiently dealt with in Jewish tradition is the idea of *existential living,* or living in the "here and now." While Judaism has for the most part been very much present-oriented, rather than other-worldly directed, the nuances and full development of this seminal theme, are significantly carried forward in its treatment by humanistic writers and thinkers. (For further elaboration on the comparison of this idea in Judaism and humanistic psychology, see my study, "Kavanah as Existential Living—Judaism and the 'Here and Now' " in *Humanizing Jewish Life: Judaism and the Human Potential Movement,* A.S. Barnes, 1976, pp. 180–191).

A third important area of common ground between the two great traditions is the whole realm of *interpersonal relationships.* Specifically, the notions of authenticity, self-disclosure, and congruence, are ways of looking at human relationships which carry forward significantly Judaism's ancient search for personal fulfillment through human relationship. (On these subjects, see the works of James Bugental, Carl Rogers, Sidney Jourard, Harry Stack Sullivan and Martin Buber, for example).

When we realize that the most important areas of our living, including child-rearing, marriage, family life, formal and informal education, friendship, community and society living, are dependent upon the quality and depth of human relationships, it is easy to understand how a contribution to the understanding and dynamics of interpersonal relationships would be viewed by Judaism with great favor.

A second realm of contributions to Judaism's search for meaningful existence available through the Human Potential lies in the *techniques* and *technologies* of achieving the goals of life such as those mentioned above (awareness, existential living, intimate and effective relationships).

If it is truly the objective of the Torah to help persons grow and fulfill their unique potential, then the whole range of programs and approaches available at Human Potential workshops, seminars, and training courses, should be warmly welcomed as new and effective means to achieve that objective. Such programs include training in listening skills, assertiveness, conflict resolution, sensory awareness, psychodrama, bio-energetics, value clarification, experiential education, sensitivity groups, awareness exercises, meditation, marriage and family enrichment, Gestalt, psychosynthesis, self concept development, journal writing, guided imagery, and a host of others.

To summarize, Judaism can be viewed as the *text* and the Human Potential Movement as *commentary*. Just as new midrashim have throughout the ages elaborated, expanded, and further developed the foundations of Judaism given in the Torah, so today a new midrash is helping us to re-focus our attention on the eternal questions of finding significance in a confused and demanding world.

Why Does Jewish Life Need the Human Potential Movement?

If Jews as individuals can benefit greatly from the new insights, philosophies and techniques of humanistic schools of thought and practice, then Jewish institutional and community life desperately needs the renewal and challenge available today in the Human Potential Movement. I have dealt in greater detail elsewhere with specific programs for humanizing the synagogue, religious education and Jewish community institutions *(Humanizing Jewish Life)*. Here it must suffice to touch briefly on some of the major thrusts of the programmatic interface between Judaism and humanistic psychology.

First, the synagogue can be made into a more caring and searching community. The use of small groups, such as Havurot and Mishpachot (substitute extended families), of Jewish family life education, retreats, and growth groups, can bring new life and vigor and direction to institutions scarcely meeting the human needs of today's constituents. New liturgical and ritual creations, based on interpersonal experiences, guided imagery, personal artistic expression, sensory awareness, and other methods, can make worship a truly alive and exciting experience, instead of the rote, mechanical exercise it has become in most congregations.

Secondly, Jewish education can be revamped and revitalized by using Value Clarification, experiential and affective education, Gestalt awareness techniques, Kohlberg's approach to moral development, journal writing, magic circle (Human Development Program), role playing, self concept enhancement, transpersonal education, centering, meditation, chanting, and countless other methods to make the educational experience person-centered and growth-oriented. (For scores of specific techniques and classroom exercises, see the writer's volumes, *Clarifying Jewish Values: Value Clarification Activities for Jewish Groups,* Growth Associates, 1977; and *Jewish Consciousness Raising: A Handbook of Exercises,* Growth Associates, 1977).

Other Jewish organizations, such as community federations, Jewish community centers, Jewish family services, can take advantage of new avenues to leadership development training, personal growth programs, group and community development and team building technologies, Jewish family life education through experiential learning, sensitivity and awareness activities, paths to heightened spiritual consciousness such as chanting, meditation, creative writing, and other transpersonal methods.

****

Just as Hasidism brought a new perspective, a renewed enthusiasm, and a revitalized commitment to Jewish living in the eighteenth century, the Human Potential Movement has the capacity of reforming, renewing and re-invigorating Jewish personal, educational, spiritual, institutional and community life.

We are on the edge of a growing revolution of new consciousness and awareness in North America, in which the life of the spirit, personal development, creative community and intimate relationships are receiving higher priorities on the agenda of life for creative persons. Judaism has always been on the frontier of the road to the good life, and it dare not relinquish that role today.

For young and old to find Judaism as an ever sustaining source of inspiration, wisdom and direction, it will have to more actively explore the rich resources available in the Human Potential Movement.

Through enhancing the meaning and quality of daily living by utilizing human potential ideas and techniques, twentieth century Jews will find a new and resounding meaning, in a way never before envisioned, in the ancient admonition of the Torah, "Choose life!"

Judaism and History: Historical Events and Religious Change

Irving Greenberg

I *Historical Event As Revelation: The Jewish Model*

The vast majority of human beings who ever lived, have lived in poverty and oppression, their lives punctuated by sickness and suffering. A small minority of human beings who ever lived escaped damaging illness; even fewer have escaped the ravages of old age (except by dying!) and none have avoided death thus far.

Of the nameless and faceless billions we know little and can say even less. Of the wealthy and the powerful and the creative, whose records we *do* have, we can say: inescapable tragedies were built into their existence, including vulnerability and failure, separation from and loss of loved ones, untimely life and untimely death. Thus, most of humankind know the world as indifferent or hostile. Statistically speaking, human history is unredeemed, and human life is of little value.

Judaism, the Jewish faith, and the Jewish people affirm differently: there is a God who cares, human beings have infinite value. Judaism insists that history and the social-economic-political reality which people live in eventually will be perfected, so that they will corroborate this statement of faith. In short, much of what passes for reality and history, the statistical norm of human existence, is really a deviation from the ultimate reality.

How is this known? Here is the paradox of Jewish existence and revelation. It is known from an actual Jewish experience in history—the Exodus. Mark the paradox: the very idea that history itself is a mistake, a deviation; the very notion that redemption will overcome history comes from an historical experience.

The Exodus became the central, normative, orienting experience of the Jewish tradition. It was judged to be not a one-time event but a norm by which all of life and all other experience can be judged and oriented. It became the interpretive key by which all events are understood. Although the event of Exodus is fleeting and rare, it emerged as the ultimate touchstone of all events. An "orienting experience" means that the event itself makes certain claims. There is a God who cares; that human beings are his creatures and are valuable. It implies that no human power is absolute, for this God transcends human power. It follows that human power is conditional and temporary—at least until the time will come when there is a reality which is consonant with this perfection model. Humans are meant to be free also follows from this experience. Exodus morality means treating people on the basis of freedom and value rather than by power and use, which of course is the usual standard of human behavior throughout history.

At the same time the Exodus is a *model* or an orienting event. It is not reality yet; neither for Jews nor for the whole world. Whatever the divine or miraculous components in it, the event is located in actual history. This is also a very important part of the model. If the event is located in actual history and not just in mythical realms, the event itself does not blot out the rest of reality. The Exodus does not destroy the evil or the status quo of the world. What it does is set up an alternate conception of the world. It is in dialectical tension with the real world. Simultaneously it affirms the real world—the locus where the redemption took place; the place where the ultimate redemption will occur again—yet at the same time the Exodus challenges the normative status quo, and denies that it has ultimate religious or moral value. Built into the central model of Jewish revelation is a tension. There is an insistence that history really counts, that the Exodus itself will not be valid until it is finally realized in history. While at the same time history itself should be taken with a grain of salt. It is not really normative; it is something to be challenged and overcome.

The Jewish tradition places the Exodus in the framework of world history. In the Biblical model the world starts with perfection—the Garden of Eden—the way the world is meant to be. In Platonic terms, we can describe it as a taste of value and social-economic perfection given to men so they will never forget and never be gratified with anything less than the final perfection. After the expulsion from the Garden of Eden and after the Flood, we enter into human history and the real world where the tension of the ideal and the real is acted out. Were it not for the Exodus, humans would have reconciled themselves to the evils that exist in the world and accepted a low value for themselves. The Exodus sets up the tension that must exist until reality is redeemed. Even better, Exodus shows the way to final perfection, by living patterns which at once reconcile ideal and reality in an imperfect world while moving and guiding human action closer to the final perfection. The dialectic is the classic Jewish operative model and it undergirds much of the halachic system.

Thus, history is at once the scene of human activity and divine redemption. The ultimate fulfillment will take place in history. The final redemption will confirm what is now a daring assertion but not much more—the claim that humans have ultimate value; that the structure of reality is embedded in meaning; that there is a God who cares. It follows from all this that hope and not despair is the valid response to the world we live in. Judaism, faith, turns out to be by this analysis not certitude, and not knowledge, but *testimony*. It's a statement of what *will* be; based on an experience already had. It is testimony of the Jewish people derived from its own experience, namely, Exodus, telling itself and the world the ultimate truth—even though the present reality does not sustain it.

As testimony, its credibility is subject to fluctuation, and even refutation. Israel's behavior as well as events in history deeply affect the credibility of this testimony. Thus, Israel's faithfulness, in living by the Exodus and the Covenant which comes out of the Exodus, sanctifies God's name, that is to say, makes God credible. Its deviance, its surrender to status quo in religion and morality, defames God's name—that is to say, makes less credible what it *affirms.*

History is the scene where this testimony is given. The whole world is the audience which hears, or disowns, the testimony—depending on what it sees and hears from the people of Israel. Similarly, God's mighty acts in history, his redemption of Israel, make his own name great and make the testimony credible. Defeats of the Jewish people, disasters, inherently weaken the effect of revelations and statements. Thus, the credibility of faith is also dialectical. Faith is not pure abstraction, unaffected or unshaken by contradictory events; it is subject to "refutation." Yet it is not simply an empirical faith either. A purely empirical faith would be subject to immediate refutation, but, in fact, the people of Israel may continue to testify in exile and after defeat. It may see or hope beyond the present moment to the redemption which will inevitably follow. Thereby, it continues to testify despite the contradition in the present moment. In fact, when the redemption comes, it will be even greater proof of the faith assertions and of the reliability of God's promises— all the greater because it will overcome the present hopeless reality. On the other hand if redemption never came or if Israel lost hope while waiting for redemption, then the status quo would win and Jewish testimony would come to an end. Thus, faith is not a simple product of history, nor is it insulated from history. It is testimony anchored in history, in constant tension with it, subject to revision and understanding as well as to fluctuation in credibility due to the unfolding of events.

Where does Israel get the strength to go on testifying despite the contradictions of reality. Out of the memories of the Exodus! That memory includes a covenant—promises made to the Jewish people that it will be eternal—so long as it lives by the Exodus and the God who was revealed to it in that event. Thus, much of Jewish religion consists of reliving the event of the Exodus. Passover *literally* reenacts the event starting with the eating the bread of affliction all the way to telling the story of redemption. Sukkot (Tabernacles) becomes the reenactment of the journey through the desert, the continuation of the Exodus. Shabbat becomes *zecher litziat mitzrayim*—once a week Jews live this day in memory (or, in actuality) of the Exodus. In the Tefillin (phylacteries), which are put on every weekday; in the tzitzit (fringe) worn everyday, in daily prayer, there is constant invocation of the Exodus. This confirms and strengthens the conviction that it happened. The implied claim of the religion is that in sacred time such as Shabbat, Passover, other holidays, the Jews literally re-experience the Exodus experience, i.e., the evidence which validates Jewish testimony. In sacred time and ritual, believers can step outside the stream of secular, normal history and are able to experience life in the Exodus itself. Thus in the words of the Haggadah, "In every generation a person is required to view himself as if he went out of Egypt." The personal experience of the Exodus, confirms the tension and sustains the ability to live with it. The taste of perfection in a Shabbat or Passover creates a dissatisfaction with everyday reality that prevents the Jew from slipping into equilibrium with the current reality which he inhabits.

Much of later Jewish theology and religious development is built into the very dynamics of this model of Revelation. God's mighty acts of redemption *are* in history and do not break loose from it. In taking this stand, Jewish tradition at once promises to move history forward. At the same time it leaves itself vulnerable to being shattered on the rock of that very history. It is an enormous wager of faith. It passes up the classical religious alternative: to remove religion from the realm of the contingent, i.e., history because that is the realm of the disprovable and to locate it primarily in the afterlife. Interestingly, medieval Christianity and medieval Judaism moved in this other direction—presumably because the reality appeared to be so irredeemable due to human limitations. Judaism also passed up other religious alternatives to resolving this tension, e.g., religion as the vehicle for taking humans out of history (the strategy of Buddhism and other Eastern religions); or by making religion and God timeless philosophical truths purified from the imperfections of historical accident and flawed human participation.

This is not to deny that over the course of human history there were Jewish theologians or Jewish communities that took up the option of removing Judaism from the contradictions. Such solutions are particularly appealing in times of great suffering or when Jews are in exile. It's very tempting to remove Judaism from history because the reality is getting so contradictory, the fundamental credibility begins to erode. However, even at the moment of greatest removal from life, there is the built-in tension—because the Biblical account and the rabbinic elaboration continue to influence thinking. Despite his own emphasis on philosophical purity and on the knowledge of God being ultimately beyond these adventitious historical facts, Maimonides is not able to escape the historical character of Jewish religion. Thus he ends up insisting that the Messianic Age is in history and is to be distinguished sharply from the world to come which would be an escape from history.

Built into this model is a much greater partnership between God and man from the very beginning. Despite the glorification of God and His Power built into the Biblical accounts, God, as it were, is dependent on human testimony for awareness of His presence. The ultimate locus of redemption is in a human setting and in the sight of humankind. The actual accessibility of God is subject to human behavior, especially that of the people of Israel. For this reason, tragedy and defeat in Israel cannot be ignored. Every major defeat or catastrophe of the Jewish people strikes at the credibility of the whole structure. It makes the Jewish testimony less credible to the rest of the world. What is even more threatening: it undermines Jewish ability or willingness to give testimony.

It follows from this that major tragedies have been turning points or development points in Jewish faith. The credibility of Jewish religion is so challenged by a tragedy which seems to indicate that the whole Exodus idea was a mistake and the whole notion of ultimate redemption is an illusion, that it is impossible to go on with Jewish faith as before. Unless the facts of suffering and defeat are reconciled with the claims of Exodus and redemption; the credibility of these claims, in fact the ability to make them, is overthrown. In the Biblical experience it is the "She-loves-me-she-loves-me-not" syndrome of Jewish history. Every time there is a tragedy, Jews question: Is the covenant still functioning? Does God still care? When the Jews are restored, this proves that God still loves Israel. Although this appears to make God and the covenant vulnerable to the vicissitudes of every change in Jewish history, there is no way of bypassing this issue. The commitment that redemption has taken place and will take place in history means that each time tragedy weakens the inherent credibility of the whole structure.

There have been three major strategies in Jewish history to cope with this problem. The first has been the emphasis that tragedy does not disprove claims about God and redemption because it was brought upon Israel by God. God is punishing Israel for its sins. (As the masochist said to the sadist, after receiving a beating, now I know you love me!") The Jewish people is confirmed in its faith each time a beating occurs, because the punishment proves God cares what this people does. It is the reproof of love and when the redemption comes, this is made manifest. This was the prophetic interpretation of the first destruction. We know from the prophetic record itself that many Jews were highly confident that the destruction would never take place. How could God allow his own Temple to be destroyed? In the conception of those times, if God is stronger than the other gods, He could not possibly "lose"; therefore Jerusalem was safe. The Temple was in fact destroyed; Jerusalem was overthrown. This plunged Israel into the crisis—did this prove that God was not The God? That other gods were God? Does it prove that the hope for redemption was mistaken? That the Exodus had no ultimate significance? Clearly, many Jews lost hope. But the prophetic interpretation that the destruction was proof that God cared won out. So it came about that Jews became more faithful to their God and religion in exile than they had been in their own country.

A variant of this understanding is found in the idea that the tragedy will be overcome by a redemption which will prove that the tragedy is only a fleeting, temporary departure from the long-term redemption which the Exodus model implies. An example of this is found in the second book of Isaiah. There the prophet insists that the magnitude of this redemption (bringing Israel back from its exile) will be the final confirmation that God is the God of the world and that the Covenant and the promises are true. Thus, the tragedy can be discounted because it represents only a temporary abberation. The redemption that will follow will make Israel forget this tragedy and will decisively confirm the hope and the promise in the eyes of mankind.

There is, of course, a difficulty in this solution. How long can Israel go without redemption before the promise turns hollow? This is why frequently in Jewish tradition the tendency has been to resort to the punishment-for-sins strategy in the short-run to cover the interim until the redemption comes.

The second major Jewish religious strategy for coping with tragedy has been to argue that the understanding of the nature of God, or of redemption, has been flawed hitherto. By the light of the tragedy, the new understanding emerges.

An example of this approach is the response to the destruction of the Second Temple. Again there was much the same attempt to answer that we are punished for our sins. Either because the magnitude of the disaster was greater or because the implications of the model had been spelled out further, this answer in itself was not adequate. Thus some Rabbis concluded that the understanding of God *per se* has to be modified. God was no longer going to be as available, as directly or dramatically involved in history, as He had been until then. Rather God has withdrawn and the human involvement in history, both in tragedy and redemption, was much greater than realized before. This is the dynamic behind the triumph of the halachic method and the conclusion that prophecy no longer existed. This is the validation of the rejection of heavenly voices as the decisor in legal disagreements.

A similar experience occurred in the rise of kabbalah and mysticism after the Expulsion from Spain. In this case, too, the mystery and the crisis of such overwhelming tragedy became so oppressive that, in essence, the Jewish religious strategy had to change too. The understanding of the nature of God had to change. Thus, in the kabbalistic development, we find that God is in captivity, as it were, in this world. There are built in structures that frustrate His purpose. The very structure of the world itself reflects a breakdown of God's ability to liberate the divine, to reunite the sparks with the source. The Jewish people are needed to achieve the liberation. Their suffering reflects the divine agony and their response will help achieve God's restoration and the perfection of the cosmic order as well. In this way the understanding of the Jewish role in history and of the inner content of religion is modified in order to overcome the tragedy and to live with it.

There is, of course, a third religious strategy: to agree that the tragedy proves it is all over. Probably the majority of Jews who ever lived adopted this strategy. They yielded their Jewishness because after catastrophe, exile or such experiences, they became convinced that the convenant never existed or that it was finished. In the words of the rabbi in Philadelphia, "Some of my best Jews are Friends." Ex-Jews stock almost every other majority religion. Ironically enough, the decision to check out may be seen as a Jewish religious response to the catastrophe. It accepts the event as normative and interprets its message as instruction to find new faith and covenant.

II   The Model Applied: The Case of the Destruction of the Second Temple*

The destruction of the Second Temple and the loss of Jewish sovereignty in Israel created a crisis which illuminates the dynamics of the model of history and revelation in Judaism. Until the twentieth century and the Holocaust, this cataclysm was unsurpassed for effect on Jewish religion. An exploration of Jewish response then can guide a projection of the future of Judaism after *the* major tragedy of Jewish history, the Holocaust.

The conclusion that the tradition was finished was adopted by many Jews. Among this group one can differentiate those who were carried away from Jewry by the shock wave of the destruction (including Jews driven into exile or sold into slavery, who were sundered from the body of Jewish people and culture and adopted the masters' or the other slaves' culture and religion); those who switched to the "winning side" (making the pragmatic religious judgement most practitioners make) and those who assimilated to Hellenism out of identification with its values. This last group mainly grew out of the intrinsic attraction of Greco-Roman culture. What the destruction did was to reduce the Jewish institutional re-

---

* The original core of this section was given in a lecture on "The Rise, Decline and __ of the Synagogue" given in 1971 at Temple Israel, Miami, Florida, and published privately by Temple Israel. However, in its present form I must express gratitude to Jacob Neusner whose essay "Four Responses to the Destruction of the Temple," reprinted in his *Essays in Rabbinic History* (Brill, 1975) has enriched my thinking and conceptualization of the issue.

sources that could reach the marginal Jews and to turn Jewish concern more deeply inward which weakened the resonance of its message among Jews in the main stream of universalism's culture and influence.

The other group of Jews who stand out in adopting this interpretation of the Destruction are the Christian Jews and here the dynamics of the historical revelation model are most striking. Up to the destruction of the Temple, Christian Jews had remained well within the structure of Jewish faith and Jewish community despite their insistence that the Messiah had come. Since they believed the Messiah had come, they had to confront the terrible problem: How does it happen that the world is still full of evil? That there is still suffering, including the suffering of the Jewish people themselves?

Classical Jewish tradition made clear that the model of redemption transcends the realities which contradict it. However, the conviction that the Messiah *had* come experienced by the early Christians brought the dialectical tension of model and reality to a much higher and painful level. The temptation to admit the unbroken reality and to deny that the Messiah actually had come was very great. As the New Testament hints, many initial Christians took this route. To this day, this is the main resolution of the Christian claim by most Jews.

Some Christians held on, choosing the second strategy—arguing that the contradiction is short run and temporary and will be overcome by an even more glorious final redemption. In Christian terms, this is expressed in the promise of the second coming which will imminently resolve the tension.

However, others resolved the conflict by reformulation of the concept (strategy two, above). After the Crucifixion, already some Christians began to distance themselves from the Jewish community. Out of faithfulness to the model that the Messiah's coming must bring drastic change and significant redemption but unwilling to repudiate the experience of the Messiah having come, the solution adopted by Christians was that the change *had* taken place *within.* Contrary to the anticipation that the Kingdom of God would be *visible,* politically, socially, economically, the Kingdom of God turned out to be *within*—invisible except through the eyes of faith and to those who experienced rebirth. Even this interpretation was possible within the framework of classical Jewish tradition—it is simply spelling out the model in a different way. But the destruction of the Temple brought the matter to a head. Both the Rabbis and the Christians saw this event as a touchstone of faith and response. This kind of understanding led Christians to leave Jerusalem shortly before the destruction (having distanced themselves from the Temple and Jewish sovereignty, there was no need to hang on) and to withdraw further and further from the Jewish people during the period from 70 to 135, when Jews desperately tried to revolt against the Romans, re-establish the Temple and accomplish the Jewish Messianic redemption in the political-social world.

The emotional polarization induced by the effort and struggle in 70 and again in the revolts of 115 and 131–135 combined with the threat 'o Jewish credibility implicit in the Jewish disaster led the Rabbis to draw a line—for or against— which excluded Christian Jews. By the same token, to Christian Jews, responding theologically as Jews, such a catastrophe would not be a neutral event. It confirmed that the Messiah was an internal liberator not a political savior. The repeated failure of the Jews to grasp this must be increasingly perceived as willful stubborness—even wickedness. The destruction (in 70 and 135) can then be interpreted as punishment for clinging to false notions of the Messianic redemption.

The same modes of response were adopted by those who stayed within the continuous Jewish faith convenant. Some Jews claim that the destruction was a temporary aberration soon to be overcome by a subsequent redemption—the restoration of sovereignty of the Temple, possibly in even more glorious form. Therefore the destruction carried no normative value or revelatory message. There was no need to reinterpret the tradition. The critical move was to win the political or military victory that would allow the rebuilding of the Temple. This would be the true resolution of the tension.

This interpretation, provided the historical-psychological dynamic behind the dominant thrust of the Jewish community for the next 70 years—the attempt to recapture Jerusalem and to re-establish the Temple. This also accounts for the internal Jewish messianic movements in the century that followed the destruction of the Temple. Rabbi Akiba supported the Bar Kochba rebellion, not merely as a political adventure but out of the conviction that this was the Messiah. It is the theological dynamic operating: when a tragedy all but destroys the credibility of the Exodus, the only thing that can overcome it is an equivalent redemption or even greater. After a minor tragedy, a minor redemption may solve the problem. After a tragedy of this scope, surely the Messiah must come! This is why Jews tend to have false messianic movements in generations shortly following great destructions. Or, as the Talmud puts it, on Tisha B'av (the day of the destruction of the Temple), the Messiah was born.

Another example of this dynamic operating can be found in the "Avaylay Zion" described in the Talmud. The Talmud speaks of these Mourners for Zion who were so faithful that they would eat no meat and drink no wine until the Temple was rebuilt. In another version, they would have no families until the Temple was rebuilt. What does it mean not to eat meat and not to drink wine? In the language of Jewish tradition this means that there will be no joy, no pleasure, no celebration. At every Jewish joyous event there is wine and meat, for these are the foods of celebration. What these mourners are really saying is: we are going to grieve and refuse to live normally until the Temple is rebuilt. Such mourning is a rather difficult thing to carry out indefinitely;

the position really assumes a speedy redemption is coming. To take the even more dramatic statement: not to have children until the Temple is rebuilt—this policy cannot last more than one generation. The underlying expectation is that redemption will occur well within that period of time. It is the same in the New Testament. The response to the challenge to Jesus' messiahship implicit in the crucifixion is that He is returning shortly. And we will have no marriage, no family life, no children until he returns. Again, it clearly shows the expectation of imminent redemption.

The third type of response to tragedy: reformulation of traditional understanding in light of the revelation in the event—is the one given by Rabbi Yochanan Ben Zakkai and the Rabbis. It became the dominant post-destruction form of Judaism. This way continues the tradition but reinterprets the nature of God and God's relationship to Israel and develops new channels of expression of the tradition. The crucial development is the shift from the revealed intervening God of the Biblical period to the relatively withdrawn Deity of the exilic period. God is close now as *presence,* as *Sheckinah,* not as the automatic intervener who brings victory to the deserving.

A number of Talmudic comments that have become staple cliches over the centuries of exilic existence leap into fresh life in the context of response to destruction. The Talmudic statement that after the destruction, prophecy ceased is not merely descriptive; it is normative. Prophecy ceases because God no longer intervenes overtly in the old mode. The old mode is credible in the context of the dominance of the Exodus model, not after a catastrophe.

What the Talmud is saying is that the catastrophe could not have occurred unless God, as it were, was withdrawing divine power from the world, allowing human effort and testimony to become more central, even decisive. The analogue in law, then, is that God no longer will send messages to resolve legal questions but the judgements of humans (the

Rabbis) will discover the divine will. It follows that the Temple where God is "visible" is no longer the key to divine presence. The family table at home becomes the altar; washing hands in preparation for the meal, use of salt at the table, not showing metal during the grace and blessings—all articulate the presence of a "hidden Temple"—parallel to the presence of the "hidden" God. By this model, prayer is the service of God analogue to sacrifices, even as acts of loving/kindness are the more hidden version of the atonement rituals.

The classic Rabbinic commentary on this reformulation is found in a later text. In Yoma 69b, the Talmud explicates a central Deuteronomic theological verse "the great, mighty and awesome God." (Deuteronomy 10, 17) This praise of the Lord has become the central praise as it opens the prayer which the Rabbis set at the center of the service, the silent, standing Shmoneh Esreh or Amidah prayer. Rabbi Joshua ben Levi says: this use of the verse is a restoration. The men of the Great Assembly who set up this prayer are called great because they restored the crown of God's praise to its ancient glory with this rehabilitation of the verse.

Moses had spoken of God as "great, mighty and awesome." Jeremiah—the prophet of destruction—declined to speak of God's might. If Gentiles cavort in His sanctuary where is His might? Daniel declined to speak of God as awesome. If Gentiles enslave and oppress His people, where is His awesomeness? The men of the Great Assembly restored this praise by *reinterpretation*. They answered: This is His might—that He controls His urges. When the wicked flourish (e.g., the Temple is destroyed) He is patient with them (e.g., He gives them time and freedom to act; He does not intervene and stop them). And this is God's awesomeness . . . Were it not for God's awe, how could this one people—the Jewish people—exist among all the other nations that are out to destroy it? How is it known that God is, in fact, present after the destruction? Only by a radical reinterpretation of His presence in the world: He controls himself. He is the hidden presence, not the intervening presence. The only other way we know His presence is that His people continue to exist in defiance of all logic and all force. This proves that behind it all there is a God who keeps the Jewish people alive.

The Talmud then responds to those who wish to act as if nothing has happened in the destruction. It asks: How could Jeremiah and Daniel change Moses' own language and leave out *gibor* (mighty) and *nora* ("awesome")? The answer given is: because they know that God is truthful and they refused to lie to Him. This is to say: to go on speaking of God as if nothing happened would be a lie. To go on with the same religious way of life would be a contradiction of the historical model of revelation which demands that catastrophe be taken seriously in order that Judaism make credible—not merely pious—statements.

It seems clear the authority to develop new institutional centrality for the synagogue, and to break from the sacramental dimension of the Temple and the power to turn Judaism into a much more personal religion of daily life came from the rabbinic understanding of God's nature after the destruction. This historical model of Revelation also explains the Rabbis' powerful sense of their own continuity with the Bible. Contemporary scholarship tends to make the Rabbis into cynics or liars, or at best simpletons, when they talk about continuity and/or the absolute authority of the Torah when in fact the Rabbis themselves clearly were changing the whole style and tone and development of Biblical religion. A classic rabbinic story tells that Moses came back to visit the *yeshiva* of Rabbi Akiba, and heard Akiba expounding the Torah—Moses' own teaching—and he didn't understand a word. Feeling very bad—*halsha daato*—he became faint from his own embarrassment and shame at not understanding. Then a student raised his hand and asked Rabbi Akiba, how he knew this law he was expounding. To which Rabbi Akiba answered, "It is *Halacha l'moshe misinai*—we know it from tradition from Moses at Sinai." At which point the rabbinical story assures us that Moses was greatly relieved and cheered. Either this story is the ultimate in cyncism or simple-mindedness or in it the Rabbis were trying to capture precisely the continuity described in this essay. It is not that the Rabbis failed to see that their own development has incorporated into the Torah rulings and practices that Moses himself did not understand—that is precisely the point of the story. However, the continuity which reassures Moses is in the model of historical revelation. We are doing what Moses has taught us, say the Rabbis, applying the Exodus model in our time as he applied it in his time. The unbroken tension between Exodus and reality is preserved in the rabbinic way. The continuity of hope and the promise of Exodus is truly identified with Moses—only God's presence is much less overt than it was at the Red Sea and Sinai. It is a much more self-controlled God who is experienced after the tragedy. The recognition means that the language of prayer, the types of practice and the policy assumptions must be modified accordingly. Simple loyalty to the inherited ways is not truthfulness; it fails to respond to the revelation of historical event.

As it turned out, a literal faithfulness would have spelled final catastrophe—for the Temple was not rebuilt nor was Jerusalem freed. The reinterpretation set in motion by Yochanan be Zakkai triumphed completely and became the main continuous form of Judaism. Indeed it became a renewal that flourished, brought forth many fruits and bore up under the repeated cataclysms of exilic history.

III   The Model Projected: The Case of the Holocaust

In the twentieth century the Jewish people has undergone the greatest catastrophe of its existence. The Holocaust not only struck at the very existence of the Jewry, it was carried out so as to destroy the sancta of the Jews along the way. The total denial of value to Jewish life (killing Jews cost less than half a cent in gas per person in 1944 yet children were burned alive to save that money); the deliberate scheduling of *aktionen* and liquidations for Sabbath and Jewish holy days; the trampling and mockery of Jewish religious practice and values—all constituted a massive assault on the credibility of the Exodus historical redemption faith. This suggests that a spiritual crisis of major proportions is underway and that a reformulation will be necessary to enable the Jewish testimony to go forward. Yet so influential is this paradigm in Jewish culture and history that we may anticipate just such a possibility—especially since the paradigm was not as deeply shaken by the preceding period of Emancipation/modernization as is widely believed.

Study of the Jewish-Christian response to the Destruction suggested that the Christians did not repudiate the Jewish model; rather they applied it to the development of Judaism. Accepting the life of Jesus as the fulfillment of the coming of the Messiah, they could see the Destruction as the confirmation that a new path of development was unfolding for Judaism. Thus the dominance of the historical events revelation model was so total that even those who "broke" from Judaism were operating by the dynamics of this pattern—applying it as they best understood it. The same can be said of the inroads of modernity into Jewry in the past two centuries. Modernity should be understood as the coming of the Messiah, e.g., of the expected redemption which would finally cast into a shadow all the previous tragedies and redemptions. As the modern era evoked a tremendous sense of a breakthrough in human relations and in social/political/economic redemption, good Jews revolted against continuation of the status quo in Judaism. They joined the messianic movements which promised to bring the redemption finally. As true Jews they understood that the new Messiah demands absolute authority. This is openly articulated in the famous statement of principles adopted by Reform rabbis at Pittsburgh in 1885. The fifth article of the declaration states:

> We recognize in the modern era of universal culture of heart and intellect the approach of the realization of Israel's great Messianic hope for the establishment of the Kingdom of Truth, Justice and Peace among all men. We consider ourselves no longer a nation but a religious com-

munity. Therefore we expect neither a return to Palestine, more sacrificial worship, nor restoration of any of the laws concerning the Jewish state.

The new Revelation incarnate in the unfolding historical event leads to reinterpretation of the past and recasting the observance pattern of Jews. It also follows that Jews must reduce their distinctiveness and turn more universal to help insure the Messiah's victory. "We acknowledge that the spirit of broad humanity of our age is our ally in the fulfillment of our mission." The ultimate resolution, and great task of Jews, is "to solve on the basis of justice and righteousness the problems presented by the contrasts and evils of the present organization of society." (*ibid.*)

This vision drove not just Reform rabbis but really all Jews in the modern period. Some decided the Messiah was Marxism and Socialism and acted accordingly; others decided the Messiah was Capitalism or Liberalism; still others accepted Democracy as their liberator. In all cases, acting out the historical model became the order of the day. The dominance of the modern redemption meant for some Jews secession and formulation of new religions; for others it meant reformulation from within; for still others it meant the conclusion that Judaism was finished.

The Jewish response to the Holocaust thus far can also be categorized as following the three strategies which have typically evolved in Jewish faith. Richard Rubenstein and his "death of God" theology represents the response that the covenant is finished and the claims of Exodus are no longer credible. And as Ruberstein has argued, many secular Jews are operating on this assumption even if they have not formulated their viewpoint into a formal theological statement. There has been a persistent strain within Orthodoxy especially its Yeshiva world that has upheld the classical "we-were-punished-for-our-sins" understanding. This insistence that inherited categories of meaning have not been shattered is a way of arguing that the destruction is not normative and

that religious life can go on as before. One can even differentiate various classical positions in this formulation. Thus the
disciples of Rabbi Kook, in effect, argue that the destruction
is brief and the redemption which follows immediately, e.g.,
the rebirth of Israel, overshadows it. Therefore, the redemption should be taken seriously as a commanding religious
presence but the Holocaust has no impact—unless it be that
it confirms the command that all Jews be in Israel. The Satmar Rabbi, Rabbi Joel Teitelbaum and some allied groups
have denied that Israel is redemption. They even identify
the Zionist enterprise as that sin which brought on the catastrophe. Thus the need for reformulation is not only denied;
it becomes the source of future sorrow and an unforgivable
departure from the prevailing pattern.

The beginnings of formal theological reformulation can be
discerned in works of Emil Fackenheim, Elieser Berkovitz
and, more significantly, Elie Wiesel. Fackenheim has profoundly and correctly argued that categories of secular and
religious mean very little in light of the Holocaust. Berkovitz
has deeply sensed the challenge to modernity that comes out
of the Holocaust as well as the new dimension it gives to
Jewish testimony of life and hope, particularly as incarnated
in the State of Israel. Analogy to past Jewish experience suggests that this is the most promising approach to the crisis of
meaning in this catastrophe. However, the weakness in both
may be the modest extent of the reformulation. A cataclysm
of this magnitude seems likely to evoke a reformulation more
drastic than that one which followed the destruction of the
Temple. This conviction is reinforced by the observation that
no small part of that event's impact was the new dominance
of the state of exilic existence, whereas now the reverse is
occurring. The center of gravity of Jewish existence is steadi-
ly being transferred to a state of sovereign Jewish existence,
Israel. The implication is that this is an age of birth pangs—
one of those rare periods in which a major metamorphosis of
Judaism is about to occur.

Three major facts argue that the new shape of Judaism will

be much more "secular" in form. One is that the reborn State of Israel occupies so much of Jewish activity, loyalty and spiritual energy. In historical interpretive terms this is a "call to secularity." Furthermore, in the Holocaust, the assault on Jews did not distinguish between secular and religious Jews. The existence of any Jew was perceived as denial of the absolute claims, e.g., the idolatry of Nazism. Finally, following the Talmudic statement that God's awesomeness is essentially known from the existence of his people after the catastrophe, the "secular" activity of building the Jewish state has been the key builder and guarantor of the life of the Jewish people and, *thereby, the most significant statement of God's awesomeness.* Just as the destruction of the Temple suggested that God's hiddenness was greater than anticipated, based on the Exodus model, so the Holocaust suggests a Divine presence far more subtle and elusive than hitherto estimated, based on the destruction and exile model.

As the Jewish way of life turns beyond the synagogue into a more radical secular setting, the question of the continued existence of the synagogue becomes a real one. (For a substantial fraction of the Jewish people, this question has already been answered in the negative.) Even as the Rabbi superceded the priests, as the Temple disappeared and guidance and mastery of learning became crucial, the Rabbis are likely to be succeeded by masters who can give Jewish guidance in secular activity. As halachic behavior is subtler, more naturalistically religious than the Temple's sacramental services, the new Jewish life style is likely to be concretized in subtler behavior, more anchored in the natural than current halacha. Every man his own Rabbi may be the analogous step to the democratization of access to God taken in the shift from priest to Rabbi. The emergence of a new leadership class is implicit in this and it is possible that the new dominance of laymen in Diaspora Jewry and politicians in Israel is the beginning of this process.

God's radical self-control vis-a-vis the wicked is profounder in the presence of Auschwitz and Bergen Belsen than in the destruction of the Temple. This suggests that the human role in redemption is more central and dramatic than that emphasized in the grandest speculations of Rabbinic tradition. The Vilna Gaon is supposed to have once said that atheism can be used in the service of God. When a poor man asks for help, one should not reply: God will help. Be an atheist and be completely responsible to the needy. A post Holocaust religious stance may demand an atheist position. Perhaps only secular Israelis who insist they are atheists but join the Israeli army fully understand the theological dynamics of Jewish life.

Why is this not simply a suggestion that Judaism is entering an atheist or purely naturalistic period? For one, the Holocaust has shattered the modern paradigm as deeply as it has the classical Jewish one. It challenges the credibility of humanism; the conviction that human liberation can be a purely human activity; the adequacy of the culture which made man sufficient and alone in the universe. Furthermore, there is the profound paradox that Jewish testimony is all the more awesome coming in the teeth of such genocide. And the redemption in the rebirth of Israel does speak (as Isaiah suggested) of redemption, purpose and fulfillment in history. The resolution would appear to be a holy secularism—activity in the world rooted at the core in the hidden presence of God and oriented toward bringing the final redemption.

The synagogue, the Halacha and other existing structures of observance and meaning face the dilemma of this gestation period. Their own existence is problematic and probably dependent on a successful, radical self-reinterpretation in the light of the Holocaust and Israel.

The extent to which the synagogue goes on with prayers as usual, the extent to which the existing lines—Orthodox, Conservative, Reform—still maintain themselves is the extent to which the synagogue is unlikely to be the vehicle of Jewish perpetuation. To rule halachically the same way as before is really to assume that God intervenes the same as before; this is likely to be the extent to which Jews will not live by *Halacha* at all. A good example is the question of "who is a Jew?" Many of the rulings in this area grow out of the assumption that the *Halacha* functions as it did before the Holocaust and that conscious acceptance and full observance of Judaism is central to being a Jew. This is in the face of a clearly contradictory Holocaust and Israeli experience. It should come as no surprise, then, that the Halachic answer has not been accepted in the State of Israel as fully adequate definition of who is a Jew. The resistance expresses the consciousness that the new norms were revealed in the historical event and they make any attempt to simply repeat past rulings inadequate. Only when Halachic redefinition takes place and takes into account the risk and sacrifice of being a Jew, which the Holocaust and Israel have shown is implicit in just existing as a Jew, will it be able to evoke the acceptance of the entire Jewish people. Similarly, the Halacha will have to give full religious weight to the new sensitivity to human dignity called forth as response to the total degradation inflicted in the Holocaust. This suggests new attitudes and responsibilities for women, Gentiles, and others. All areas need renewed consideration. Therefore, the community should consider the synagogue, and Jewish traditional life holding actions—ways to be guarded even as a major investiment is made in the unfolding of Jewish tradition in the light of the Holocaust and the rebirth of Israel.

To the extent that this policy is adopted Jews can anticipate that this is an age of major Jewish renewal and rebirth. Or, to put it another way, one should anticipate after such a major destruction that the Messiah is coming. It is the embarrassment and shame of this generation that Jews haven't had at least a *false* Messiah to show that they understand that in such a generation some major new development is likely to happen. At least those who followed a false Messiah know that they had the right anticipation; they only made a mistake in identifying the actual fulfillment. In this sense, those who have over-committed themselves to the State of Israel, the secular Zionists (so called), may have been the false—but therefore to be honored—messianic movement of our times. Indeed whether Israel will become the true messianic movement depends partly on the further unfolding of Jewish history and in good measure on the ability of Jews to again apply the historical events revelation model to their religious development. The past experience of Jewish history suggests it is a time to increase hope.

Prescription for Living

Introduction

The psychological value of a religion lies in its ability to satisfy basic human needs. According to Abraham Maslow, people need to feel safe, to be with others, to love and be loved, to feel self-worth and the esteem of others, and to grow in harmony with themselves and nature. By providing such experiencing, religion can play an important role in the life of the individual. The articles included in Part III explore various dimensions of Jewish ritual and observance, inquiring into their potential for helping the person live a more fulfilling and psychologically healthy existence.

In the first article "Psychological Wisdom in Jewish Law, Ritual and Observance," the editor highlights the unique aspects and structures of Judaism which make its "prescription for living" particularly useful. Beginning with the thesis that the principles underlying Judaism are grounded in sound psychological concepts and that its practice will lead the person in the direction of greater mental health, he goes on to detail five areas in which Judaism has incorporated important principles of a psychologically healthful lifestyle. These include: its all-encompassing, specific and consistent nature; its concern with all aspects of human functioning; its potential for providing true religious community; its ability to support the person through life's crises; and its sensitivity to changing times and the changing needs of the individual.

In reading this and the remaining essays in Part III, two important points should be kept in mind. First, analyzing a religious practice or ritual according to the psychological functions it serves does not in and of itself harm or threaten its vitality, as some would contend. Rather, it provides useful insights for those who value the psychological perspective to better understand the wisdom contained within their heritage. Such an analysis becomes insidious only when it carries the implication that all other ways of understanding and approaching the ritual or practice are ill-founded and misleading. To hold such a narrow conception of reality is to deny that Judaism can be as valuably understood and experienced from other intellectual as well as emotional and spiritual positions. Second, in understanding the usefulness of a specific practice or prescription, one must remember that proper intention or motivation is as necessary as actual behavior. Blind orthodoxy and rule-following do little to enhance the psychological life of the individual. Only by carrying out a ritual with clear understanding and sincere intent can anything of real value be derived.

One function of religion is personal expression, the venting of feelings and emotions which naturally arise in the course of human living. Whether it takes the form of a joyous "thank you" for something that has been received or the angry indictment of a seemingly uncaring and indifferent God, religion provides a vehicle for dialogue with the vastness that surrounds all people. This is the central theme of Zalman Schachter's article, "On Mystical-Empirical Jewish Prayer: A 'Rap.' " Reb Zalman, as he is called by his youthful followers, is a master of re-introducing alienated Jews to their heritage. Recognizing that prescription without understanding is the surest way to alienate interest, he begins by showing these highly assimilated Jews how religion was meant to function in the life of the individual—as a forum for personal expression and growth. He does this by first making them aware of their own religious needs. He teaches them to meditate in order to create a clearer perception of themselves and of their God. He challenges them to honestly and openly express themselves: their concerns, their frustrations, their fears. These become the building blocks for understanding Judaism. As each prayer and ritual is introduced, Schachter invites the student to recreate it for himself: to begin with the human emotions or processes which lie at its source and to personalize it, using language and material drawn from first-hand experience. In this way, he is able to make Judaism come alive and become real for these young people, introducing them to a side of religion lost to most in the contemporary world.

Religion also prepares people for and supports them during the critical moments of the life process. One is born, reaches puberty, chooses a mate, gives birth and raises children and eventually dies. Each of these events makes its own unique psychological demands on the person and those around him. Religion offers ritualized methods of dealing with these moments, ways of sharing the joy when appropriate and ways of cushioning the shock when necessary. At such times human beings are particularly vulnerable, aware of their own mortality and in need of the companionship of others. To the extent that these rituals bring people together, provide them with either celebration or solace and facilitate their movement through the natural processes related to each central human event, they are invaluable aids to the business of living. Judaism is unique in the detailed prescription and insight with which it approaches these events. The traditional Jewish practices surrounding death and grieving provide an excellent example. Only recently, with the monumental work of Elizabeth Kubler-Ross, have psychologists begun to study the previously taboo subjects of the phenomenology of dying and the process of grieving in survivors. As knowledge grows with each new piece of research, the wisdom and value of observing tradition Jewish practices become more evident. In "Death and Dying—Past, Present, and Future," Audrey Gordon, a former assistant to Kubler-Ross, reviews both the complex Jewish laws of mourning and recent discoveries in the psychology of death and then goes on to ponder some of the future problems in this area which may eventually confront Judaism and the individual Jew.

A third value in religious ritual is its ability to bring people into rhythm with the natural order in the universe. In the last article of Part III eminent psychologist Erich Fromm discusses the function of the Jewish Sabbath, seeing it as a way of temporarily instituting "a state of peace between man and nature" in anticipation of "messianic time." This view coincides with Fromm's more general interpretation of Judaism as a way of imitating God and His order in the life of each person. By observing the Sabbath laws which forbid any activities that disturb the natural or social equilibrium of the world, the Jew is placed in a state of God-like harmony and peace. This state of peace between man and nature is, unfortunately, sadly lacking in today's world. The overwhelming ethic of contemporary culture and technology is one of changing, improving and controlling the environment, rather than living in harmony with it. The result of continuing on such a path unabated appears to be the eventual depletion and contamination of all natural resources. Environmentalists are only now beginning to discover the frightening and, perhaps, irreversible consequences of the unrestricted consumption and pollution of the natural resource supply. Radical measures must be undertaken in order to reverse this process. Only by creating and adopting lifestyles whereby people live with and not at the expense of the environment is there any hope for future survival. In searching for ways of initiating such change the contemporary world might find it instructive to reacquaint itself with religion and religious rituals such as the Sabbath which serve a similar function.

Psychological Wisdom in Jewish Law, Ritual and Observance

Jerry V. Diller

Psychology has produced few comprehensive analyses of the practices of Judaism. This fact is doubly curious since Judaism as an intellectual tradition has played such a dominant role in the evolution of the study of human behavior, and individual Jews have participated disproportionately in its creation and development. (See Dov Peretz Elkins' article, "Judaism and Personal Growth," for a fuller discussion of this point.) The reason for this deficiency is, thus, not the lack of competent personnel capable of carrying out such a task. Rather, it lies in the basic view of human nature adopted by psychology in its first half-century of existence and the influence of its two major orientations: psychoanalysis and behaviorism. Both schools doubt the existence of higher-order functioning in the person. By doubting the usefulness of conceiving of the person as possessing consciousness, free will and the ability for transcendent experience, dimensions necessary for an understanding of religious experience, they de-value the institution of religion itself and its usefulness in human functioning. To the behaviorist religious belief functions merely as a reinforcer and source of social sanction and evolves through the process of superstitious behavior. To the psychoanalyst a belief in God functions only to satisfy our need for an all-powerful father-figure. Given these basic frameworks for studying human behavior, it is little wonder that neither school, together comprising the majority of past and contemporary psychologists, has generated any serious and unbiased investigations of religious experience, Judaism included.

This state is changing somewhat, however, with the growing popularization of a third perspective, humanism. To the humanistic psychologist religion is a uniquely human experience which serves important functions for the person as he moves through life. First, this view holds that man has periodic need for transcendent experience, for experiencing the world in a non-ego and non-conceptual way. This level of functioning, referred to as "peak experience" by Abraham Maslow, is the essence towards which religion strives. Second, the humanist sees religion serving other non-transcendent, but uniquely human needs as well. Included here are the needs for community, acceptance, personal expression and ethics and values. Only from such a perspective which values religion and religious experience in its own right can a fair assessment of the role which Judaism can play in the life of the person be made.

In the present essay I propose to explore Judaism from the perspective of the humanistic psychologist and assess its usefulness in helping the individual live a psychologically more satisfying and complete life. I will be arguing that there is great psychological wisdom inherent in the practice of Jewish Law, ritual and observance: that its approach to living is steeped in sound psychological theory and that its practice can channel the Jew in the direction of greater mental health. To accomplish this, I will focus on five different aspects of Jewish observance, each indicative of Judaism's psychological perceptiveness and utility. These include: its breadth of application, its concern with the full complement of modes of human functioning, its role as a religious community, its role in the growth of the individual and its sensitivity to the changing nature of the individual and society.

Breadth of Application

Unlike most other religions, Judaism represents an all-encompassing lifestyle, relevant to all spheres of human activity. As such, it deals with the secular and profane as well as the religious and sacred.

Donin in his book *To Be A Jew* describes this all-pervasive-ness of Judaism and Jewish Law, *Halakah,* as follows:

A person's eating habits, his sex life, his business ethics, his social activities, his entertainment, his artistic expression are all under the umbrella of religious law, of the religious values and spiritual guidelines of Judaism. Jewish religion does not dissociate itself from any aspect of life, and does not confine its concern only to ritual acts that have a mystical significance within a supernatural world. Fully and properly observed, the Jewish religion is life itself, and provides values to guide all of life. (pp. 29–30)

In order to grasp the extent of Jewish Law and clarify the nature of its prescriptive impact, various authors, both ancient and modern, have attempted to classify it. Maimonides, for example, in his *Guide For the Perplexed* lists fourteen areas of Jewish law including those dealing with: repentance and fasting; the prohibition of idolatry; the improvement of the moral condition of humanity; charity, loans and gifts; the prevention of wrong and violence; the prevention of theft, robbery and false witness; the regulation of business practices; the keeping of the Sabbath and holy days; religious rites and ceremonies; care of the Sanctuary; sacrifices; the regulation of things clean and unclean; the prohibition of certain foods; and the prohibition of certain forms of sexuality. In *Eight Questions People Ask About About Judaism* Prager and Teluskin break down *Halakah* into two categories: "laws between man and man" and "laws between man and God." They go on to enumerate the latter into laws that engender self-discipline and make for a more moral person, those that sanctify the everyday and those which bring about a more moral world. Finally, Donin distinguishes between laws which sanctify the person, those which sanctify time and those which sanctify place.

Thus, by addressing itself to the totality of human experience—to the intrapersonal and the question of how one should relate to himself; to the interpersonal and the question of how one should relate to others; and to the transpersonal and the question of how one should relate to God—Judaism provides a vehicle for total self-expression.

The directives of Jewish law are both specific and consistent. They are specific in their form of detailed, behavioral prescription. Being so well and clearly defined, they leave little room for misinterpretation or self-serving distortion as is true of more general precepts which leave specific interpretation and implementation to the individual. In this way confusion is reduced to a minimum, leaving the person with clear behavioral choices and thus a responsibility for his own actions. It is interesting to note that most contemporary psychotherapies see their goal as developing just such a sense of responsibility in their clients.

Jewish Law is consistent in that it reflects a single, all-pervasive theme. Maimonides believed that its purpose was to promote compassion, loving-kindness and peace in the world. Fromm in *You Shall Be As Gods* describes the whole of *Halakah* as a "value syndrome" consisting of several interrelated values: the affirmation of life, love, justice, freedom and truth. Irrespective of the specific arena of human concern addressed, Jewish Law embodies and promotes a more God-like order and a respect for His unique creations. Be it the laws of *kashrut* or keeping kosher which show us how to kill animals in the most humane manner, those of *hesed* which instruct us against slander and deceit, or those which require the employer to treat his employee fairly and with respect—all are cut from the same fabric and aim at creating harmony and a valuing of life. Thus, following *Halakah* leads one down a clear, consistent and humane path.

Modes of Functioning

A second source of psychological value inherent in the practice of Judaism resides in the diversity of experience it seeks to engender.

Psychologists are beginning to move toward a view of the person as multi-dimensional. By this I mean that the individual is seen as capable of experiencing life in several qualitatively different ways. Andrew Weil in *The Natural Mind* makes a distinction between what he calls "straight" and "stoned" thinking, referring to the general categories of rational vs. nonrational thinking. Robert Ornstein, in turn, in *The Psychology of Consciousness* calls these two facilities "right hemisphere" and "left hemisphere" functioning. In so doing, he alerts us to a growing body of proof which demonstrates that these two functions reside respectively in the right and left cortex of the brain. In my own work I distinguish between four levels of experiencing: rational and linguistic thought, emotional and connative reactivity, intuitive functioning and mystical experience.

Underlying such differentiations of consciousness is the assumption that each state fulfills particular and unique human functions and that only in conjunction can they account for the entire array of human potentials. In this view healthful functioning is defined as the ability of the person to move freely between these various states. To the extent that a given culture encourages such movement, it can be viewed as facilitating psychological health in its members.

Judaism does quite well on this dimension, acknowledging the existence of four different states of experiencing and providing means of access to each.

Rationality and non-rationality are equally balanced within the Jewish tradition. Rabbinic Judaism with its emphasis on rational understanding and interpretation of *Torah* and *Talmud* provides food for the left sides of our brains. Its methodology consists of confronting the student with seemingly incompatible commentaries and challenging him to discover some sort of creative synthesis between them. A lifetime spent pouring over such texts combined with endless hours engaged in argument over legalisms and *pilpul* serve to strengthen the critical and intellectual faculties of the student.

Juxtaposed against this form of activity are the mystical elements in Judaism, nourishment for the other side of the brain. The mystic seeks not to understand, but to directly experience God's Presence in the world. He calls upon his intuitive faculties to see beyond the surface and the obvious, to fathom hidden meanings and patterns in all things. The sourcebook for Jewish mysticism is the Kaballah, a collection of esoteric writings aimed at providing a glimpse of this other world as well as methods for reaching the state of consciousness where such glimpses are possible. Together these two elements, rabbinic and mystical, usher the person into the two very distinct worlds described by Weil and Ornstein.

Of equal importance within the Jewish tradition is that state of experiencing described by Martin Buber as "dialogue" or the "I-Thou relationship." By it he meant the total and unmediated contact between the individual and various aspects of his world: objects, other people and God Himself. To Buber holiness and spirituality reside in the complete meeting of two entities, a meeting in which each totally experiences the uniqueness of the other and does nothing to diminish it. Buber's fascination with the Hasidim stems largely from his realization that their lifestyle includes frequent sojourns into this plane of existence.

Last, but not least, is the centrality of emotion in Jewish life. Judaism is a religion of strong emotions. Its calendar chronicles a series of emotional highs and lows throughout the year. Festivals are days of great joy, celebration and abandon; serious observances are marked by great solemnity, tearfulness and grief. Jewish ritual orients itself to the most highly-charged moments of human existence: birth, the passage from childhood to adulthood and responsibility, marriage and death. The ceremonies surrounding these times not only highlight their importance but serve to help the individual fully experience and work through the emotions elicited by each. Emotion is, in addition, a significant part of the daily rituals observed by Jews. According to Zalman Schachter, the central purpose of prayer is the expression of emotion. Each blessing is a heart-felt "thank you;" each prayer is an emotional plea for help.

In these four ways Judaism provides access to the entire spectrum of human experiencing.

The Need for Religious Community

Judaism serves yet another important function in its capacity for satisfying man's growing need for religious community.

More than ever before the contemporary person must face his world alone and without the support of a primary group, community or belief in God. The family has crumbled. God is dead as a moving force in most people's lives. Young people are confronted with too many choices, too few opportunities for personal expression and even fewer ethical models. And these trends seem to be broadening, rather than diminishing.

Symptomatic of this problem is the growing popularity of psycho-religious cults in America today. We have witnessed in recent years an endless succession of religious and psychological gurus and movements, each offering "instant salvation" and a more satisfying lifestyle. The enormous and enthusiastic response to this phenomenon clearly reflects both a dissatisfaction with contemporary life and a void in an area of human experience previously satisfied by the religious community. As a lure, these groups promise happiness, a sense of peace and belonging, and a more meaningful existence. To the person involved, the price of allegiance, obedience and a rejection of personal past, friends and family does not seem too excessive in relation to what he might receive. Although the methods employed by these sects—brain-washing and the restriction of personal freedom—are repugnant to most of us, the psychological needs they promise to satisfy are real and urgent. As such, the lifestyle of these groups can provide valuable insights into functions that can be served by the religious community.

When asked what membership provides them, most "converts" speak in terms of meaning and belonging. Conversion and participation are described as filling existential voids and transforming meaningless lives into ones of happiness and bliss. When pushed for more specificity, they typically focus in on five particular dimensions, each representing a psychological need previously unsatisfied within their experience. Included are:

1) a dynamic, all-encompassing and all-involving, joyful and celebrative lifestyle;

2) a sense of purpose and meaning, a belief that what one is doing will ultimately make a difference;

3) a sense of belonging and community, membership in a collectivity which transcends the individual;

4) a coherent and comprehensive way of understanding and making sense out of the world; and

5) a set of clearly defined prescriptions for living one's life simply and without confusion.

These dimensions represent the potential positive consequences of membership in a vital religious-cultural group.

In turning attention back to the Jewish tradition one is struck by the great potential within it for satisfying these five needs. Judaism is, first of all, meant to be practiced as a joyous and celebrative lifestyle. To this end the present moment is valued over the future, and the flesh is given equal weight with the spirit. Man is alive not to repent for past sins or transgressions but to celebrate God and His Presence on this earth. According to Jewish mysticism, there are holy sparks in all things, and it is the task of the Jew to re-unite them with God by celebrating their holiness. This attitude is nowhere more evident than in the world of the Hasidim.

The idea of purpose and meaning is also central to the Jewish people. Historically, they see themselves as chosen by God, chosen to preserve and pass on the teachings of the *Torah* to all mankind. Whether interpreted literally or more symbolically as the passing on of a complete moral code, for example, this chosenness serves to define meaning for the Jew and to shape his life's activities. He is expected to play a significant role in making the world a more moral place.

Nothing is more vital to Judaism than the importance of community and belonging, the third dimension of a vital religious-cultural group. The Jew's "chosenness" has set him apart from the rest of the world, both in his own eyes and in the eyes of non-Jews. As a result, his need for belonging and community is critical. To be born a Jew is to inherit a guaranteed birthright of entry and acceptance into the community. With the rebirth of the State of Israel this inheritance has been translated into a guarantee of citizenship and sanctuary. The commitment to community is an integral part of Jewish Law and ritual as well. The Jew is held morally responsible for the welfare of his fellow men and women. Charity, for example, is seen as a responsibility on the part of the giver, not as a kindness. To follow the Law is to acknowledge the social, communal and interdependent nature of human life and to help in its flow. Even structurally, a subgroup of the community called a *minyan* is required to perform the most vital portions of the daily service. Without this quorum these functions cannot legally be performed.

The final two dimensions have already been discussed in an earlier section. It will be remembered that Jewish Law was described as both a detailed set of behavioral prescriptions dealing with all aspects of human life and as consistently portraying a unitary view or epistomology. Thus, we have two more instances demonstrating Judaism's ability to function as a vital and satisfying religious community.

Archetypes and Growth

Carl Jung, more than any other psychologist, seriously addressed the question of the function of religion. Critical to an understanding of his position is the concept of archetype. An archetype is an unconscious symbol relevent to some aspect of human experience. The archetype of the mask is the symbol for society; that of the Mother the symbol of nurturance; that of the shadow the symbol for evil; and so forth. By becoming aware of and acting upon the archetypes thrust into consciousness by the collective unconscious, the person is shown the path he must follow in order to reach self-actualization and wholeness. Religion, Jung believed, serves as an avenue to the wisdom of the archetypes. At the core of all religions are these very same symbols and through religious ritual the person is brought into direct contact with them.

A related route to the archetype is the myth. A myth is a metaphoric story which functions to either teach the individual something or empathically impart some experience to him. All religions have at their center a series of myths, and at the core of each is a single or several related archetypes. Joseph Campbell, for example, has written extensively of the hero myth, the hero being an archetype. All religions have their own hero myths in which a central figure —Jesus, Moses or Mohammed, for instance—undertakes a mystic journey in search of God. According to Campbell, the hero's journey is rooted in an archetype representing the person's striving for wholeness and actualization. By believing in and identifying with this myth, the devotee is encouraged to strive for wholeness in himself.

From Jung's perspective many ritualistic aspects of Judaism take on a new clarity. The festivals, for example, can be viewed as archetypically-centered. That is to say, each focuses on a particular critical issue basic to human existence.

Through the observance of these festivals, Jews are made to confront these basic human dimensions and their archetypes on a regular basis.

In certain instances the archetypal theme of a festival is obvious and close to its contemporary interpretation. The High Holidays, *Rosh Ha-Shanah* and *Yom Kippur,* for example, focus on the theme of self-renewal and rebirth. Once a year in this solemn time the Jew is invited to look inward and search his soul in an effort to better understand himself and his past behavior. Once done, the person is challenged to change, to grow, to begin again. *Rosh Ha-Shanah* is a celebration of the birth of the world which reminds us that all we possess has been given to us and can in the same manner be taken away and, concurrently, that change is always a possibility in human life. The ten days between *Rosh Ha-Shanah* and *Yom Kippur* are customarily a time of introspection and reconciliation. During this period the person is expected to seek forgiveness from those he has in any way injured in the past year. This setting of our intra- and interpersonal worlds in order is a means of preparation for *Yom Kippur,* when we seek to do the same on the transpersonal level. *Yom Kippur* invites us to return to God.

The festival of *Hanukah* provides an instance of a less obvious archetypal theme, one that is often missed or overlooked today. Beyond the historic drama of the Maccabees, *Hanukah* teaches us about the difference between the holy and the mundane, the special and the ordinary. Only a single container of consecrated oil was found in the Temple when liberated by the Maccabees. The rest had been destroyed by the Romans. While new and proper oil was sought, the one day's supply burned for eight. Ordinary, unconsecrated oil certainly could have been used, and some authorities hold that this was the intent behind the Roman's destruction of the Temple's special oil supply. The Romans were functionalists and could not abide with spiritual interpretations of the mundane. To them oil was oil, and they saw any other distinction as non-rational and archaic. In this miracle we are reminded of the vital importance of this distinction and are metaphorically invited to choose between the two types of oil in our own lives.

Similar archetypal meanings can be found underlying the daily and weekly Jewish rituals also. Often the ritual and festival interact to doubly remind us of something of which we have lost sight. Both the observance of the Sabbath and the celebration of *Succot* share the underlying theme of living in harmony with God's natural order and not unknowingly destroying it. On the Sabbath we stop our intrusion on the natural harmony and are invited to become a part of its flow. On *Succot* we actually live in the out-of-doors and are thus re-introduced to its meaning. In a similar vein the ritual of *leying teffilin* and the use of *mezuzahs* provide daily reinforcement of the Passover message which stresses the importance of freedom in human existence.

Sensitivity to Change

Finally, I would like to discuss Judaism's sensitivity to the changing nature of human society and the human condition itself. A tradition cannot long survive if it remains rigid and unresponsive to the changing needs of its members. Nor can it afford to be all-changing, a barometer of every movement and fad irrespective of its ultimate significance. A delicate balance between these extremes must be struck for optimal relevancy and survival value. It is my belief that Judaism possesses such a balance.

Judaism has changed radically over its long history, responding to major political and social forces at work in the world around it. (See Irving Greenberg's article "Judaism and History: Historical Events and Religious Change" for an enumeration of these changes.) Such change has been subject to certain constraints, however. First, being a social outcast with limited access to mainstream culture and, at the same time, a member of an all-encompassing group, the diaspora Jew retained a certain conservativeness and perspective on the ever-changing world around him. This attitude has been reflected in his religion, allowing it to retain a certain consistency, integrity and ability to differentiate between major and minor winds of change. Second, while change has certainly occurred, the basic themes of Judaism have not been altered or sacrificed, but have remained intact. Only their modes of expression have changed with time and place. By way of these two constraints Judaism has retained the balance described above.

Future change is also likely. Today, for example, Judaism is being challenged to redefine its role for women. This needed change will, however, progress in the same manner as all past change. Being conservative and slightly aloof, Judaism will wait to see the overall fate of the Women's Movement and borrow from it only those aspects which have proven themselves. Also, it will institute only those changes consonant with its own basic themes. In the end the amount of ritualistic change brought about by the Women's Movement in Judaism will depend on how closely their demands reflect the basic themes of the tradition.

Two phenomena are particularly reflective of Judaism's sensitivity to human change: its emphasis on deed rather than creed and its concept of *teshuvah* or returning.

Judaism differs radically from other Western religions in its emphasis on correct behavior rather than correct belief. One can, in fact, be a good Jew according to the *Talmud* without a firm belief in God or with varying conceptions of the nature of God. What is critical is the observance of Jewish Law.

In making this distinction between belief and action, Judaism demonstrates a keen awareness of human psychology. First, it reflects the realization that cognition and behavior do not always go hand-in-hand and that, when in conflict, behavior typically predominates. Everyone is aware of situations where behavior is motivated by nonrational processes, and where there is, as a consequence, little relationship between what one says and what one does. More unusual extremes are possible also. Social psychologists have demonstrated that under certain circumstances people will actually change their beliefs in order to be more congruent with their behavior. We are also aware, thanks to Freud, of the person's ability to distort, justify and rationalize all sorts of behaviors, irrespective of their original motives.

Second, the distinction between deed and creed is necessary in dealing with man's changing conception of God. The way in which God is conceived and understood varies greatly. This is true across generations, within the same generation and even within the life of a single individual. Requiring a single view of God would not only prove an extremely alienating practice—immediately rejecting those who do not at the moment truly belief and those who hold a contrary image—but would also lead to a regimentation and tyranny which is decidedly against basic Jewish values and principles. The Jewish emphasis on behavior also allows the doubting Jew to remain within the Jewish tradition and still confront his questions openly, without fear of rejection. Doubt is always a healthy reaction, and it is particularly normal in an age where God's existence is no longer a given.

Teshuvah is another important change-related concept in Judaism. *Teshuvah* means "to return," implying the return to God. The *baal-teshuvah* is one who is in the process of examining his relationship with God. The concept has meaning on two different levels. In a more traditional sense it refers both to the continued need for self-analysis and self-examination and the responsibility incumbent upon each Jew to keep Judaism alive. According to Donin:

> If he who saves a life is credited in our tradition with saving a world, it follows that he who destroys a life is guilty of destroying a world. If he who spiritually suffocates a Jewish life, be it his own or that of his own children, is accountable for the spiritual suffocation of a whole Jewish world, it also follows that he who spiritually re-

vives a Jewish life—be it only his own—is as though he spiritually revived a Jewish world. (p. 316)

More contemporarily, *teshuvah* denotes the process whereby the assimilated Jew returns to his tradition. It is an insightful religion which both recognizes the possibility of religious rejection and provides ritualistic methods for confronting it. The concept of *teshuvah* acknowledges both Judaism's relationship to the secular world and the fact that forces exist within people capable of pushing them away from their heritage. By valuing such an idea, Judaism also affirms the person's ability for free choice and personal growth. In short, *teshuvah* provides the individual Jew an opportunity to confront himself and his relationship to God. Recognizing the possibility of self-alienation, Judaism provides both a justification for and method of self-analysis and self-healing.

On Mystical-Empirical Jewish Prayer — A "Rap" *

Zalman M. Schachter

If I were to make a distinction between mystical and dogmatic elements in religion, the distinction would boil down to the issue of how much empirical stuff there is behind it. How much can be checked out as living reality. Mysticism says you can experience the Infinite right now, that beneath the surface of the obvious, there exists the Divine. The dogmatic approach, on the other hand, doubts the possibility of experiencing God on this plane and with our present consciousness tools and contents itself with belief in revealed principles, reasoned theology and outward observance and ritual. It sees little purpose in looking below the surface for hidden meanings and experiences.

People seem naturally drawn to one of these two positions, to the exoteric or the esoteric, using Frithjof Schuon's categories. This distinction underlies the old arguments of the Misnagdim against the Hassidim, of the Aristotelians against the Platonists. Some people are content to be the exoteric folk, to settle for a certain level of observance and insight and just leave it at that. Others cannot stay exclusively on this level. They feel it is just not enough and that they must move in search of the esoteric. They say: "I must know" and "I must get down to it." These are the people who come to mysticism. Since we have ways of making this kind of

---

* This essay is based on a taped interview with Zalman M. Schachter edited by Jerry V. Diller.

experience accessible to them, doing so is very exciting to me.

For many years now I have been introducing young Jews to the empirical experiences behind Jewish mysticism as well as more satisfying ways of relating to the exoteric elements in *Yiddishkeit.* Before going into my method per se, perhaps a little personal background and history may be useful in understanding how it evolved.

My introduction to Jewish mysticism came in 1939 through Lubavitch Hassidism. As a young man, I was angry, dispossessed and full of poison, like so many other Jews in Europe after the War. One day I found myself in an orthodox study house in Antwerp, challenging the teacher to answer the many questions and doubts I shared with everyone growing up in the chaos of those times. The teacher, a very understanding and well-educated man, let me get rid of all my poison without cutting me off. He then showed me that not only were my questions not stupid, but were in fact, legitimate ones raised by others before me. He suggested that if I could feel confidence in the way in which they raised these questions, perhaps I ought also feel confidence in the way they answered them. This was his approach, and he led me into a world which was very, very exciting. It turned out that he was a Lubavitcher Hasid. Because of him, I ended up going to Lubavitcher *yeshiva* and ultimately coming to America.

I was drawn to Habad Hassidism, especially Lubavitch, because of their promise that one could attain certain mystical experiences in this life time. The various tales told by the Hassidim about their Rebbes concern the attainment of such experiences. I also liked the nature of the relationship between the Rebbe and the individual hasid. Rather than saying that the person must allow the Rebbe to do the spiritual work and just hang at his coattails, Habad's basic notion was different. The Rebbe is just going to show you the way, but you have to do the work yourself.

I remember once bringing a group of young people to see the present Rebbe. When the Rebbe invited questions, one young man, the president of my Hillel group in Winnipeg, raised his hand and asked: "What is a Rebbe good for?" Instead of being put off, the Rebbe said: "It is a very good question. Let me tell you. It is written: 'You will be unto me a land of desire.' The Earth contains in herself all kinds of treasures, but you have to know where to dig. If you do not, you will hit either rock or mud or whatever. But, if you ask the geologist of the soul where to dig, you might find Silver, which is the love of God; gold, which is the fear of God; or diamonds, which is faith. All a Rebbe can do is show you where to dig. You must do the digging yourself." That was a beautiful answer and invited the young man to do further work.

I experimented with all these methods, having in mind the idea of bringing them out of the doors of Lubavich and into the camps, like Ramah, into the conservative and reform movements, and even into Orthodox circles. It is strange how so many Orthodox people are vaccinated against Hassidism. As long as there is dogma and specific behaviors to perform— as long as they put on *tefillin,* keep Kosher and all that—what more is there to want?

At this point in my life I had the good fortune to meet Howard Thurman, then Dean of the Chapel at Boston University. In our first meeting he floored me with the question: "Don't you believe in the Holy Spirit?" But he said it in Hebrew, *Ruach Hakodesh.* I left his office and spent three weeks living through hell, trying to figure out if I did indeed trust God. Or if I was a Jew because of my own needs, irrespective of what God wanted for me?

Because of his spiritual adroitness, I decided, after some deliberation, to take a course he taught in spiritual disciplines and resources. On the one hand, I wanted to see how all of the Lubavitch baggage I had picked up fit with other non-

Jewish approaches. On the other, I was unnerved by the prospect of trusting my soul to a non-Jew.

The course was marvelous, and I learned a great deal, especially from his use of labs. In his labs we experimented with various spiritual exercises. People seldom have the primary experiences in religion which William James, Aldous Huxley and others make reference to. Without this first-hand knowledge, the study of religion is poor in meaning. Such labs allow the student to understand what is being taught. This is now part of my method, providing these primary experiences. They turn out to be very, very important in the spiritual growth of the individual.

In time people started to ask me questions about these primary experiences, about what it is that we do in meditation. I started my first instructional group in Winnipeg which we called the Chapel Group for lack of a better name because we met in a chapel. In it I introduced the students to various Hasidic methods of meditation and inner exploration and awareness. As a result of the instructions that were given to the Chapel Group, I wrote the little booklet: "The First Step."* That was in the late fifties, before acid made the scene and before the whole consciousness explosion. I probably would not write it the same way today, given the changing needs of young people. But at the time it came almost as a result of automatic writing, as if I were merely a vehicle for the expression of Hassidic voices from the past.

Another aspect of my method came out of my previous work as a Rabbi in Fall River, Massachusetts. People would come to the synagogue to say *Kaddish*. When I would ask them to put on *tefillin,* they would say: "I don't believe in it." I wondered where they had learned not to believe in it. When visiting their homes while sitting *shivah,* I would again ask: "Do you have a pair of *tefillin:* let me show you how to

---

* "The First Step" appears as "A First Step: A Devotional Guide" in *The Jewish Catalogue,* edited by Richard Siegel, Michael Strassfeld and Sharon Strassfeld (Philadelphia: The Jewish Publication Society, 1973)

put them on, here in privacy." All of a sudden people started to believe in it. So I realized what they did not believe in was making an ass of themselves in public. What most people lack are basic skills in Judaism. So I showed them how to make *talaysim* and how to do *mezuzahs* and all that. I found that the more skills people could gain, the happier they were and the more they were able to relate to *Yiddishkeit.*

This attitude, together with the primary experiences, provide a perfect complement, a way of getting the outer and the inner parts, the exoteric and the esoteric elements, going at the same time.

Young people come to me most typically having first explored other non-Jewish avenues to mysticism. It is very seldom that I find a spiritual virgin saying I would like to get more into *Yiddishkeit* or learn about Judaism or learn about spiritual things. A lot of the people have smoked dope which means they have experienced certain expansions of the mind —certain openings. They come looking for a map to help them make sense out of these experiences. Others come who have had Transcendental Meditation. They say: "I am happy doing TM; it is really great. I have gotten many benefits from it. But it is a little too foreign for me, not Jewish enough. What can I do about it? Can you give me a Jewish mantra?"

Still others come a more circuitous route, beginning at a place where they are very suspicious of anything having to do with religion, especially with Judaism. Not only Judaism, but all Western religions are suffering from having become over-verbalized and under-experienced. Eastern religions, so popular today, come on with this fabulous propaganda that they have a "high" you will never come down from and so forth, and find a receptive audience. So, for many a Jew it happens that he has to come to us via Eastern religion. It is in the nature of the situation that people will turn away from something which is not satisfying to them. When I am being manipulated by my religion and do not like that manipulation; when I am not being given decent answers to my questions; when the people who teach me at my Bar Mitzvah do not know; when my teachers do not speak from first-hand experience; when they really do not know who God is and can only tell me what others have said about Him; I will surely turn away. On the other hand, there is this Zen master who says: "Come and sit and experience for yourself." So I go there and I find out.

But paradoxically, once I go and sit and mediate for a while, I find that a lot of Jewish stuff starts coming through—*Bubbeh, Zayde, Torah, Shabbes;* all kinds of stuff buried deep inside that both resistance and the normal pressures of everyday life does not allow to come out. But, if I do Zazen it all starts. The pressure is off; it starts coming out and has to be dealt with. So many young Jews involved in other movements which call for Sunyata, the void, for psychological emptying, find themselves in this crazy position, confronted once again with their Jewishness. They may want to cut off this Jewish stuff, but in order to do this, they have to choke off the Eastern goodies as well. What happens is that these Jewish elements take on a different perspectives when viewed from this Eastern viewpoint. They realize that what they so despised before as *schmaltz,* they now like when seen as nectar in Hinduism, for example. They begin to ask questions and eventually turn to things Jewish.

I am not upset by the fact that many young people come back to *Yiddishkeit* through Eastern religions. I do not believe that anyone has the exclusive Truth. What we have is a good approximation, for Jews, of how to get there. But even that is inexact. Each person in his own life has to create the exactness that fits his situation. While there are differences between Jewish and non-Jewish approaches to mysticism on the exoteric level of methods, there are none on the esoteric, in regards to the experiences themselves. When it comes down to what I call the "heart stuff," all approaches overlap.

In fact, I find these comparisons and parallels interesting

and useful in communicating with the young people who come to me. Let me describe a particularly exciting example. Psychologist-guru John Lilly in his *Center of the Cyclone* talks about a number of spaces—inner spaces borrowed from Sufi mysticism—that he calls 48, 24, 12, 6 and 3. These descriptions are amazingly parallel to the Kabbalistic teachings concerning ways of experiencing God. Level 48, called physical *Assiah* in the Kabbalah, is the designation for this physical world. Level 24 or *Assiah* is a place of spiritual action or the spiritual ground upon which we stand. The inner experience of feeling or deep emotion is *Y'zirah* or 12. The world of thought or contemplation where we want to understand the blueprint of the universe, what it all means and what its significance is, is 6 or *B'riya*. Finally, 3 or *Azilut* is a deep or divine intuition that participates in the thing it intuits about. Within Jewish mysticism these inner spaces are represented by both parts of the body and letter in the holy name of God, *YHVH*. My head (3) is the Y; my arms and shoulders (6) are the H; my spine (12) is the V; and my pelvis and legs (24) are the lower H. Spiritual man is thus made in the image of God. Each of these inner spaces has different laws and potentialities, each related to its particular symbolic location.

Now, if you have this schema, a whole bunch of things will start making sense. Many religious rituals, for example, are really journeys through these inner spaces. In Hinduism the various yogas each relate to a different and higher inner state. Hatha yoga is body yoga; karma yoga is 24 stuff; bhakti yoga is oriented toward #12 experience; Jnana yoga is 6 stuff; and raja yoga is #3.

The *davening* or daily prayer in Judaism is also built that way, as a journey up through these spaces and down again. In order to heighten this realization I often combine *davening* with other spiritual practices, some Jewish and others non-Jewish. The *davening* begins with various *b'rakhot* or blessings oriented towards the physical body. With this in mind they unfold naturally: "Blessed are you Lord God, King of the Universe, who takes those who are bent and straightens them out, Who opens the eyes of the blind, Who gives me firm ground to stand on, Who girds me with strength." I accompany these blessings with appropriate yoga postures, and they serve to bring the *b'rakhot* into sharp focus. Another *b'rakhah* says: "O God, the soul you give me is pure." But in Hebrew the word for soul in this context means breathe, so I do some breathing exercises in conjunction with it. I particularly like an exercise I found in the writings of Rabbi Joseph Ibn Gikatilla. All of the breath expelled, the sound of the Y; breathing in, the sound of H; holding the breath, the V; and exhaling, the sound of the other H. So I have the rhythm and awareness of *YHVH* as I breathe.

The second part of the *davening* is called the sacrifice of the *Korbannot* and is focused on the plane of 24. This part of the service encourages me to begin exploring inner spiritual spaces, to make sure that the places from which my psychic energies come are still alive. I must be sure that there are coals burning on the inner altar. Sometimes I just feel what is going on in my body; other times I add to that energy through yoga breathing exercises. Reb Nachman of Brazlav said that if you want to know God, you need only listen to His voice within, the pulse. One need never be lonely for Him or out of touch with His inner spirit; you can always touch your pulse and say: "Oh, there You are."

The person moves from this place into the world of V or 12. That is what the *Halleluyas* and the *Ashrei* are about. They focus me on the feeling and emotional side of my being. So it begins with an emotional plea: "God, what good will it be if I go down to the pit? Will the dust praise You?" And so forth. "I praise you God for all the good that You have done . . ."

Then I go still higher into the place where the *Shema* is located. This is an invitation for meditation, for the H or 6 space is a level of contemplation of God and His Universe. At this point my prayer is less loud, more gentle; the melodies become more head melodies.

After this I move into the highest point of the service and get in touch with a level of deep intuition with God. This calls for a different kind of meditation, one in which I try to become one with Him. It begins: "Lord, open Thou my lips and my mouth shall show forth Thy praise." Rather than seeing myself as a supplicant before God, I try to visualize myself as seen by Him saying these prayers. I become object and He subject, rather than remaining a subject opposite and apart from him. This merging with Him is what the Y level of consciousness entails.

Finally, after the *Sh'moneh Essray,* I do all my private praying, for all the needs that I have. "God, I need this today; I need that today." And then coming down again, I bring back all of the spaces I visited on the way up. Periodically throughout the day I reflect back on each of these, as a means of keeping myself spiritually alive and focused. Now you have a sense of the journey up and down that the *davening* was meant to be and how the schema I described above makes this process clear and understandable.

I believe that much of *Yiddishkeit* has become elite religion: highly prescriptive, over-verbalized and intellectualized, and under-experienced. In order to overcome these trends I first introduce young people to the meaning and experiences underlying Jewish rituals and observance, to their psychological and emotional intent rather than to their outward manifestations. People must realize that religious acts are no more than natural unfoldings of the human condition. In order to do this I show the person how to re-create these acts, beginning with his own experiences in living. By replicating the process, he moves naturally closer and closer to the ritual itself, becoming aware that the ritual is a tried and true means of accomplishing the same human ends.

Let me give you several different examples to make this point clear. First, let us look at the blessings or the *b'rakhot.*

Traditional expectations hold that the person repeat those *b'rakhot* which the Rabbis prescribe. According to the *Gemara:* "Everything of the world belongs to God—the earth is the Lord's and the fullness thereof." But He has given the earth to man. The *b'rakhah* is a means of re-striking this bargain, of feeding coins of the realm into the permission machine to secure something from God. Now this is a nice legal move, but it is not a heart move. Ultimately, this approach cannot help but turn many people off.

If a person wants to learn how to say the *b'rakhot* and what they are really about, I say to him: "Everytime you feel something good happening to you or even something tough or painful say: *Barukh attah Adonai . . .* You make the sun shine. *Barukh attah Adonai . . .* it is a beautiful day out today. *Barukh attah Adonai . . .* the air is so polluted it is amazing that I am still alive." Each time a person focuses in this way, *b'rakhot* become a reality, and the person really begins to learn about prayer and life.

In a similar vein, when a person asks me how to start *davening,* I suggest he not use the *siddur* for a while. When you come to the *Sh'moneh Essray,* for example, let the meaning of this unfold itself within you. First, recognize the chain that connects you to God through your ancestors. Make a *b'rakhah* and thank God for that. Then recognize the chain that connects you to life and make a *b'rakhah* over that. Then recognize the chain that connects you with holiness. Now, begin asking for the things you need. The first thing you need is to have the good sense to know what to ask for. Ask for *sekhel.* You get some common sense; the next thing comes in: "Who the hell am I to ask anything of God?" Why? Because I am so far away from Him. OK, now pray to get closer. The next thing you realize: "Did I do this? Did I do that?" So pray for forgiveness. "It is such a struggle to live." So pray over the struggle. "I have got so many things that are sick inside of me." Pray for them. "I have got to make a living." Pray for that. So, as you watch the *Sh'moneh Essray* unfold, you see it is a very natural unravelling of the human being and the human situation. Once a person learns how to make a request and seal it with: "Thank you God," he gets closer to the design of the prayer. Once he replicates the process underlying the prayer, he will be appreciative of having the *siddur* as a guide.

Now, the *siddur* or prayer book has come to be highly misunderstood today in most Jewish circles. As a result, many people have become alienated from it and what it represents. The problem goes back to the 19th Century and its over-emphasis on rationality. The 19th Century was so smart it was stupid. It outsmarted itself. To many Jews of that time period, as is now true today, the prayer book became a book of information. Whenever it said: "Say this three times," they did not want to do it. One time is enough they reasoned; for information, one time is enough. But the prayer book is not a book for information. Approaching it as such cannot help but turn you off and distort the experience it is meant to convey.

Let me give you an example. I am settling down to sit and read in the synagogue, to sit and read a book of information. My body goes into the posture I would assume if I want to read a novel. I look in the front of the book to find out what committee worked on it. I look in the back to see who the contributors were. Very quickly I become bored; I do not know what to do with it anymore.

Now, if I relate to it in a slightly different manner, the whole thing changes. I sit more grounded, with a kind of body eagerness. I hold the *siddur* in the left hand and begin to look at it only with one eye. I do not *daven* into the *siddur*. Rather, I pick out a phrase, look away from the book, focus toward the Presence, and repeat it. Everytime I look in the *siddur* I do not talk; everytime I repeat the phrase I do not look in. I project a bit. I try to get into the feeling of the phrase. I breathe in a particular way; I *shuckle* with my body, make gestures and try to give the feeling a total scene to develop in.

In this way I can say the same stuff I said last week. I can say it again. It is like when a husband says to his wife: "I love you." What is he talking about? He is not giving her new information. If she sees it as information, she says: "Stop, you told me already, enough." But he says: "I am not telling you this for information. I have a feeling and this is the best way I can express it. We are not in a place where I can kiss you or make love to you. But I can say: 'Dear, I love you so much.' " And when he does this it is not a vehicle for information. It is a vehicle for feeling. *Davening* and the *siddur* are vehicles for creating these feelings and not for information. How many times can you say: "I love you?" As many times as I have the feeling and energy to put into it.

Even the prayer language chosen by those of the 19th Century reflects their bias against feeling words. Sanctuary is for the head; holy place is for the heart. I encourage young people to make their own translation of texts, into a language which they understand and to which they can relate. When they can pick language from the Zeitgeist and at the same time retain a faithful translation to what the Hebrew says, people can get off on it, and the process will have real significance for them.

The *Q'riyath Shema,* the traditional prayer said before retiring at night provides yet another example of how Jewish ritual can function in one's life. The problem of how one lives deliberately underlies the intention behind the *Q'riyath Shema.*

Most of us have trouble distinguishing between living for ourselves and living for others. While a lot of people think that they know how to live, in reality they are being lived. They are being lived by their parents, by the school, by the draft board, by everyone else. They are consistently ripped apart trying to live up to each demand made upon them and never get a chance to live deliberately, for they are too busy living up to someone else's expectations. The first move toward living deliberately entails assessing where you are each day and initiating whatever changes necessary, re-programming for tomorrow.

But having an insight is not enough in itself, I must also spend some time erasing all the other tapes that do not connect with the new insight. If, for example, I have been over-eating for many years and get the insight that it is not good for me, I have only begun the process. Now I have to learn something more about why and where it came from. I may find out that when I over-eat, I am hungry, but not for food. I may be hungry for meaning, or love or knowledge. I learn that I have lost the ability to discriminate between hungers, that my appestat is not working. I may be able to trace it back to my mother. She may have said to me repeatedly: "Eat for your father; for mama eat a spoon; one for *bubbeh,* one for *zayde,* one for your teddy bear." And I did not even feel like eating. In this way my appestat was over-ridden, and I can no longer make the distinction between different kinds of hunger. But with this awareness I can begin the change process, the re-programming necessary so I can once again be able to make the distinction between what I need and what others wish for me. If I do not take the time out to learn to make these discriminations, I will eventually need a shrink.

Late evenings, before going to bed, provide an excellent time to do this work, to develop such awarenesses and to set up strong anticipations for changes in my behavior for the next day. And this is what the reading of the *Shema* before retiring at night is all about, a time to insure deliberate living in our lives.

I also encourage my students to develop a more personal interaction with God. Good communication is based upon giving clear and honest messages and receiving in return good feedback on how well we are being understood. Only by making our needs, expectations and feelings clear to another person, can we avoid misunderstanding and miscommunication.

I remember once coming to a session after spending a whole night working on a crisis. I began by asking the people present to tell me if they felt I was in touch with them. Some wanted reinforcement and said: "Of course." The majority, however, said: "We really do not feel you are totally here now." I thanked them and told them they were right; that I was not quite there and was working with a depleted energy source. I went on. "I do not know what else to tell you. You and I are contracted to spend this time together. Let's spend it in the most profitable way, but I cannot give you the best performance possible. I haven't got it." Now, what I did, instead of confusing them, was to try to communicate clearly about my emotional and energy state at the time. I did not want them misinterpreting my behavior or their own reactions to it. I did not want them wondering why they were not getting off on Zalman; because everyone is supposed to get off on him. I did not want them misreading the situation and taking it to be their fault, rather than mine.

Now, if I can get my communication straightened out on the interpersonal plane, I can begin to do the same on the intrapersonal plane (with myself) and on the transpersonal (with God). A lot of people are blocked in any relationship to God because they have never been able to tell Him how angry they are with Him for the lousy trick of creating them. "You did not ask me if I wanted to be born, You know, what kind of stupid thing was that to create me?" If I cannot rail at God, I will not be able to pray to Him either, because the good stuff cannot come through with all the bad stuff in the way.

So people have to be able to get angry at Him on occasion. Unfortunately, most religions do not allow for the "freak-out." But if I have mad spaces inside of me, and those are closer to God than my saintly spaces, not getting in touch with the mad spaces blocks me from getting in touch with God in any manner. When I can bring the shadow side of me (to borrow a concept from Jung) to God, when I can be angry with Him and mourn and cry; only then can I also dance and laugh. That is why the whole thing about giving and receiving straight signals is so important.

I cannot hear prophesy or read Bible for instruction if I cannot learn how to take them as straight signals. If I expect a prophet always to reinforce my behavior, and if I get angry and turn away every time he does not, I am in bad shape. I am in better shape if I can say: "Thank you, your feedback really helps me to understand and to learn." If I can do this with people and with myself, I can also do this with God.

Thus, I encourage people to begin the Jewish re-awakening process with primary experiences rather than formal prescription, by getting them to discover the process which underlies the ritual and by personalizing that process. That is the way of lesser resistance for most young people today. When there is a strong commitment created by these primary experiences and personal discoveries, the resistance to prescription tends to disappear. I am confident that sooner or later people come to some for of *Halakah,* or traditional observance, once they start on the spiritual path. Lubavitch and others take the notion that you do not teach anyone anything about the spiritual path until you have gotten them into *Halakah.* They see *Halakah* as the *only* payoff. I see the organic relationship of the soul to God, of a human being to God as the payoff. In this context what difference does it make which one comes first?

Death and Dying—Past, Present and Future

Audrey Gordon

—The Past

The Bible portrays the concept of death and dying in various ways. The aetiological question as to why death exists is answered by the Adamic myth of sin and punishment in the Garden of Eden with death as one of the punishments meted out by God.

> "The man has become like one of us knowing good and evil; what if he now reaches out his hand and takes fruit from the tree of life also, eats it and lives forever." (Gen. 3:19 NEB)

> "So the Lord God drove him out of the Garden of Eden to tell the ground from which he had been taken." (Gen. 3: 22–23)

The form which the dead take is poetic justice as well as reality.

> "You shall gain your bread by the sweat of your brow until you return to the ground; for from it you were taken. Dust, you are, to dust you shall return." (Gen. 3:19 NEB)

From this citation comes the Jewish tradition of using only organic materials in which to encapsulate the corpse (wooden coffin, linen shroud, etc.) for its burial so as to ensure the speediest decomposition to its natural "dust" state and the consequent prohibition of any materials which might preserve the body from its natural disintegration (metal coffin, preservative fluids, hermetically-sealed vaults, etc.). Death, the Biblical writer of Genesis seems to say, is divinely ordained, final, total and part of the natural process of growth and decay.

The Psalmist reports another view of death. Among many ancient peoples death was seen as a weakening of the energy level *(nefesh)* necessary to sustain life. If you were too weak to live, you went down to Sheol where you existed in a faded, listless dimension which still required minimum sustenance. (Johnson, *The Vitality of the Individual in the Thought of Ancient Israel,* pp 15–16.)

It was a custom in Ancient Mesopotamia for the graves of the dead to have hollow tubes near the headstone into which the family of the deceased poured foodsfuffs in order to sustain the deceased in the Netherworld. This concept of death as a diminution of energy is found in Psalm 6:

Be merciful to me, O Lord for I am weak; Heal me, my very bones are shaken; My soul quivers in dismay, And thou, O Lord—how long?

Come back, O Lord; set my soul free Deliver me for thy love's sake. None talk of thee among the dead; Who praises thee in Sheol? (6: 2–5)

If he died, the ailing psalmist will go to the abode of the dead where none praise God. " . . . the normal Israelite view, which dominates the conception of man in the Old Testament, is that to be in sickness of body or weakness of circumstance, is to experience the disintegrating power of death, and to be brought by Yahweh to the gates of Sheol; but to enjoy good health and material prosperity is to be allowed to walk with Him in fullness of life." (Johnson, *The Vitality of the Individual in the Thought of Ancient Israel,* p. 107). His argument for restoration hinges on the rationale that God requires praise from man and cannot be praised too abundantly. Through references such as these in Psalms, Proverbs and other Biblical writings, we gather a picture of death as residence in a cheerless, dispirited realm to which all must inevitably go. However, if the corpse is not securely and safely interred (protected from wild animals, grave robbers, etc.) then the spirit of the dead would continue to haunt the family until the body is safely underground in its appointed place. From this configuration of ideas arises the Jewish traditions concerning the duties of the *onen* with the *mitzvah* of burying the dead before actual mourning may begin, as well as the memorial *Yahrzeit* remembrances (i.e. probably surrogates for yearly offerings of sustenance at the grave sites).

The Halachah forbids mutilation of the body at death. This prohibits autopsy and organ donation in many cases, but with the development of heart transplants, Halachah was interpreted to allow the donation of a critical organ (such as the heart) in order to save a *specific* life. Specificity is the key concept in permitting the organ donation. There must be a specific person threatened by death and needing that organ in order to live. Jewish law pre-eminently maintains the importance of saving a life over any other legal requirement. However, this interpretation does not permit the random donation of kidneys, corneas, bone, etc. to organ banks where the specific recipient is not known at the time of the donations. Biblical and post-Biblical ideas which originate and reinforce this prohibition against scattering, amputation and mutilation of bodily parts are the concepts of bodily resurrection (Ezekiel 37) and Jewish taboos against the ancient belief in *mana* (magical powers) which pagan peoples perceived as possessed by the dead body but not the living. Some common later examples of this belief in *mana* can be found in the founding of Greek cities in the vicinity of the tombs of its heroes so the heroes in death can continue to protect the city, and the religious devotion in some parts of Christianity to the bodily "relics" of saints. Ancient Israelite religion said (and Judaism continues to say) that the person is gone when death occurs and that the body is but a shell that now must be immediately and reverently buried so as to avoid any misuse.

The theology of bodily resurrection also plays an important role in Jewish laws concerning the treatment of the body. In Orthodox and Conservative Judaism (not Reform) a belief exists in a personal Messiah who will raise the dead for the World-To-Come *(Olam-Ha-Ba)*. The physical bodies of the dead will rise so it is important to preserve the body and all its parts (including previous amputations) in its gravesite to await the coming of the Messiah. Autopsy (wherein parts of the body are removed for examination) and embalming (removal of blood from the body replaced by temporary preservative) are strictly forbidden in order to ensure the intactness of the body. The custom of burying Jews with sticks in their hands to dig themselves out of their graves when the Messiah came developed over the centuries but is now rarely seen.

—The Present

Where does all this lead? The Bible reflects the life and customs of ancient times—the Halachah the wisdom of rabbis meeting needs and situations over the ages with interpretations that reinforced the identity and cohesiveness of the Jewish community. How does the Twentieth Century respond to the prescriptions from the past?

It was not (we believe) an accident that Freud was a Jew (See David Bakan, *Sigmund Freud and the Jewish Mystical Tradition*). The penchant for introspection, self-analysis, observation of human nature, and understanding the dynamics of relationship seems intrinsically Jewish. Though the birth of psychology as a social science came after the Nineteenth Century, many of the laws, customs and folk wisdom of Judaism is rooted in sound psychological practice.

The Jewish rituals of death and dying have much evidence of this psychological wisdom.

The Halachah commands us not to abandon the dying in their final hours. Psychologically the greatest fears of death are not of death itself, but of dying. We fear abandonment, loneliness and separation. Death means a loss of relationships. Judaism enjoins us to accompany the dying to their final minutes—not to desert them for even one moment until they have reached the security of the grave and the attention of God. That which we fear most we are commanded to alleviate. It is humanly impossible to predict the exact hour of death. The command for the Jewish community to be present at all times relieves the family of guilt feelings they might have if they were not able to be with the dying constantly and fulfills the religious commandment of recitation of the Sh'ma at the moment before death, either by the dying or a member of the community. Confession of sins *(vidui)* prior to death is a rite of passage from one stage of life to another (from this life to life with God) just as the bride and groom undergo a confessional before the wedding day as they prepare for a new stage of life together. Fears of death as mutilation and castration are spoken to in the prohibitions against the desecration of the body as mentioned earlier.

When the loss that death represents overwhelms us, many times we wish to die also. Not only do we identify with the dead, we can also see the death state as an escape from the pain of grief and the reality of life without the loved one. Here the duties of the *onen* function as an important psychological deterrent. The definition of an *onen* is the status of the mourner (father, mother, sister, brother, husband, wife, son or daughter) before the burial has taken place. It is the duty of the *onen* to make whatever arrangements are necessary for the funeral suspending all other religious obligations to perform these tasks. Mourning (here, distinguished as attention to one's own grief and the ritual comforting by the Jewish community) may not properly begin until after the funeral. This activity of the *onen* reaffirms that the bereaved is alive, has responsibilities to fulfill, and may not sink into the numbness and oblivion of depression and self-negation. At a time when we might wish most to be dead to join our dead loved one, the tradition insists upon life and familial responsibility.

The grief process is painful. Sometimes, in kindness, friends or more distant relatives attempt to shield the mourners from making personal decisions about the conduct of the funeral service or disposal of the body. Psychologically painful though it may be, it is more therapeutic for the mourners to be involved in these decisions directly than to experience the funeral service and burial as an impersonalized decisionless ritual. This direct involvement fosters a sense of continuing care for the deceased as well as the recognition of the finality of death which is so necessary for healthy grieving. Sedation for the mourners is not advised. (I remember one well-meaning family who sedated their elderly mother, when their father died, for the funeral and *shivah* week. When she emerged from her semi-comatose state ten days later, her first questions were, "What happened?" and "Where is my husband?" She had to face her painful feelings alone without the comforting community.)

Much has been written about funeral directors in past years so as to leave the impression that they are too commercially-minded, callous or ignorant of the Jewish traditions of burial. We, as consumers, are largely responsible for the direction that the Jewish funeral has taken because we have abdicated our rights as persons to make decisions and to express *our* wishes in keeping with the traditions. Let us lay a popular myth to rest: Embalming is *not* required by any law (state, city or federal) unless the person has died of an exotic disease that is potentially dangerous to others (typhoid, cholera, etc.).

The Jewish tradition in its "dust to dust" approach to body disposal forbids embalming because it draws the blood of life from the body leaving it incomplete, not "whole", as it must be for the Messianic restoration in the World-To-Come. The lack of artifice and simplicity of the traditional Jewish funeral serves many good purposes psychologically. The reality of the death is not denied if the dead are not cosmeticized to appear as if they are "sleeping". The ritual washing of the body *(taharah)* by the Chevrah Kadishah is a loving act by the

Jewish community for one of its members reaffirming that, even in death, the Jew is safe from strangers. The natural state in which the body must be kept speaks to and reassures our deepest psychic fears of mutilation which we all share in some measure. The shroud *(tachrich)*, the Rabbis said, reminds us of our equality before God—that we appear before God with no external coverings to distinguish us as to status or wealth, only that we are Jews. The immediacy of burial not only provides therapeutic activity for the mourners, but also shifts the focus to the mourners as quickly as possible (rather than the emphasis on viewing the body of the deceased as in a wake) so that the mourners may begin grieving and return to living fully that much sooner.

The demand for simplicity in the Jewish burial averts the misuse of guilt which is another common psychological dynamic of grieving. When someone we love dies, we feel guilty. We feel guilty because they are dead and we are not—or we are angry at them for dying and we feel guilt over that anger—or we remember times when we did not behave lovingly toward the dead—or their death is a relief to us—or we did not love them (and we think we should). These are some of the reasons for the many experiences of guilt and anger that most people feel at some time after the death. Frequently a way of defending against these feelings of guilt and anger is to lavish funds on expensive funeral arrangements to convince the world (and ourselves) of our loving feelings for the dead. Recognition of these feelings and working them through with counseling is extremely important to personal health in order to avoid later psychosomatic damage. Recent studies corroborate the theory that unresolved grief can cause later mental and bodily malfunctioning (heart attack, colitis, ulcers, etc.) as well as death. (Parkes, *Bereavement*, 1973; Shneidman, *Deaths of Man*, 1973)

"The most striking Jewish expression of grief is the rending of garments by the mourner prior to the funeral service. The rending is an opportunity for psychological relief. It allows the mourner to give vent to his pent-up anger and anguish by means of a highly controlled, religiously sanctioned act of destruction." (Lamm, *The Jewish Way in Death & Mourning,* p. 38)

The tearing of clothes, *Keriah,* or its more abbreviated form, the tearing of a black ribbon, signifies the internal anguish at the tearing away (separation) of a loved one. The fabric of life has been torn by the death. Modern society tends to trivialize the rituals and symbols of death in an effort to deny the death. The American funeral ritual "is constructed in such a way as to deny all of its most obvious implications." (Rakoff, "Psychiatric Aspects of Death in America", *Death in American Experience,* p. 158)

When we do not wear these outward symbols of mourning, we participate in this death-denial by not permitting society to comfort or respond to us as vulnerable persons in need of care (as we are). Symbols of mourning, such as the torn ribbon, mark us as wounded persons. They signify the need for a helping response from the community. When we deny our vulnerability, we deny the fact of the death and the reality of our pain. These torn garments may be mended after the *shivah,* but never so completely that the tear is not visible. The separation is not mended, the loved one has still been torn away, nevertheless the hurt and pain will heal.

The funeral service itself contains several spurs to the open expressions of grieving. The purpose of the eulogy *(hesped)* is, through praise of the dead, to make the mourner aware of the magnitude of the loss suffered and thereby bring tears. *El Malay Rachamim,* heard many times before, for the first time now is heard with the name of the beloved. The recitation of the *Kaddish* at the cemetery with the mourners standing at the gravesite re-emphasizes the reality of the death and reaffirms the community's bond to each other as they collectively remember and re-experience their own times of mourning with the newly-bereaved.

The *Kaddish,* extolling the greatness and inscrutability of

God's ways, sanctions the outpouring of anguish by controlling it within a prayer praising God at a time when we are
most likely to want to curse God for the death. It protects us
from our own desire to vilify God—an action that we would
later feel guilty about or regret.

The work of the burial itself is to be done, at least in part,
by the mourners. This is the final act of "putting to rest" that
again helps the mourner confirm the reality of the death and
fulfills the *mitzvah* of safe burial for loved ones. Artifice here
also should be shunned. Artificial grass covering the dirt from
the grave-opening is obscene. The raw earth is reality—"dust
to dust" the tradition demands. A word of warning: A few
cemeteries are so crass and unfeeling as to have a bull-dozer
visible and waiting at the gravesite. Ask the funeral director
IN ADVANCE for hand burial in the Jewish tradition and shov-
el the dirt yourself and ask other willing members of the
community to help if they are able. If a bull-dozer must finish
the task, at least it can wait until the mourners have left the
cemetery grounds.

After the burial, the mourners return to the house of *shivah* to find the "Meal of Recuperation" *(seudat havra'ah)*
prepared for them to eat. Hard-boiled eggs are a symbol of
the fullness and completeness of life in their round shape.
They also signify the ancient sacrifice in the Jerusalem Temple as well as the implicit fertility of new life. An egg represents life, just as the meal provided by the caring community
also carries the message of life to the mourners. The act of
eating also carries other messages. Mourners are not permitted to ignore physical needs or abuse health—the mourners
must go on living even though at that moment they may wish
to be dead. The community says "We are here to feed you
though your loved one is no longer here to answer your
needs. You are not alone—we can help care for you now
when you feel weak." This first mandatory meal is a resocial-
izing experience, reinstating the mourner within the realm
of the living and within the patterns of health.

"Mourning is essentially a process of unlearning the expected presence of the deceased." (Rakoff, "Psychiatric Aspects of Death in America" in *Death in American Experience,* p. 159) The most important task of the week of *shivah* that now begins is telling the "story of the death" so that the death is verified and placed into the perspective of the family's history. Only when the family can assimilate and thereby cope with the details and events surrounding the death will they then be able to talk of the meaning of the life of the person who is now dead. When we can recapture the memories of the dead, their significance for our lives, their feelings of love for us, then their positive contributions to us as persons continues forward with us into our future. It is when we cannot (or will not) remember the dead that their life truly ceases. It is important to note that within important emotional relationships there are always negative as well as positive feelings. Recalling these negative aspects of the person and our feelings about them is a therapeutic part of the healing process of mourning. When we overlook this aspect of our relationship with the deceased and elevate their memory to unwarranted sainthood we again deny the reality of the life that has been lived and the loss that is experienced.

Many people experience discomfort when visiting the newly bereaved. This arises out of a sense of inadequacy in feeling unable to comfort the mourners in the face of the severity of their loss and also a subconscious feeling of relief that they are not in the same situation (a universal human response). The wisdom of the Jewish tradition rescues the uncomfortable comforter by decreeing that the *mourner* makes the first conversational overtures and the visitor listens. In this way the comforter comforts by sharing what the mourner wants to share, and by not intruding into areas that the mourner does not wish to go. Silence is very often a warm, participatory, caring experience when it is understood that no conversational burdens are necessary. The custom of bringing sweet foodstuffs to the house of mourning symbolizes the Jewish belief that life is sweet and worth living. Judaism recognizes that there are different levels and stages of grief and organizes the requisite year of mourning into four parts: the first three days of deep grief within seven days of *shivah* and abstention from normal social functioning, thirty days of gradual reabsorption *(shloshim)* into the community, and eleven months of remembrance and recovery. The mourner is slowly drawn back from the numbing isolation of loss toward responsibility and concern for the living so that at the conclusion of the year of mourning the loss has been felt, worked through and accepted, though not forgotten. The Jewish custom of lighting a memorial candle on the anniversary of a death *(Yahrzeit)* structures a bounded time situation in which the feelings of grief may be permitted to re-emerge for expression and examination. Feelings of continuing grief thus are sanctioned and limited within a religiously-controlled framework, reinforcing the Jewish view that joy is the essence of God's presence and sorrow is unavoidable but should not be the pervasive element of life.

Too often the modern pace of life seeks to shorten or abrogate ritual. Mourning rituals provide the wayside markers for open and appropriate expressions of grief. They say, "Now, it's all right to cry"; they identify "Here is someone who's hurting"; they comfort with "God is in control of this situation even if I am not." When we deny rituals, we cheat ourselves of time-tested and sanctioned avenues for the healthy expression of intense emotions that arise when a death occurs. A death causes a painful bleeding internal wound for the bereaved, mourning rituals advance the healing process.

The Future

The wisdom of the Jewish traditions about death and dying from the past centuries have been shown to be consonant with the best psychological knowledge about healthy grieving and humane treatment of the dying. Judaism survives as a way of life because it has built within it the answers to constantly emerging social problems and religious questions. We must look into the future in an attempt to see what social forces and concerns might be cause for creative religious thinking and liturgical and ritual refreshment so as to meet the needs and identity of the Jew of the future.

I offer the following problems and prescriptions for the future as a way of initiating dialogue in the Jewish community in areas that have been overlooked or "buried":

1. The women's movement is a fact of modern life. Women's movements within Judaism are struggling—they gain basic recognition from one another, official (and token) recognition from Reform Jewish organizations, half-hearted ambivalence from Conservative citadels and silence from Orthodox bastions. Specifically, concerning the rituals of death and dying, Jewish women *must* be allowed to recite the Kaddish for a loved one, conduct and be part of a *minyan,* be official pallbearers, and fully participate in all the religious rituals of mourning so that their grief is also given its fullest dimension and focus.

2. Inflationary trends could make funeral costs taxing to all but the most affluent families. A return to the simplicity and dignity of the Jewish funeral can include the use of a pall (cloth covering) to cover the casket so that the plainest, least expensive casket may be chosen. This pall can be the property of the synagogue or the funeral director, simply woven, perhaps with significant Jewish symbols. If the funeral service is returned to the province and grounds of the synagogue, the need for elaborate funeral establishments (with their high overhead costs) will also decrease. The funeral director provides an important and necessary service to the Jewish community—it is the material purchases adjunct to these services that must be re-evaluated and limited, not the services themselves. Most funeral directors will say (and rightly) that they provide what people demand. Therefore we must change our notions of what constitutes an appropriate Jewish funeral before the funeral industry will change to meet our needs. Reinstating the Jewish traditions of equality of all persons in dress, simplicity of casket and burial, and

natural dignified treatment of the body will restore the Jewish funeral to its appropriate place in Jewish ritual rather than the now often slavish imitation of the American culture-at-large.

3. Ecological concerns and the utilization of urban land will continue as important questions into the future. Jewish tradition calls for earthen burial, yet this may become impossible (or illegal) in the urban areas in which most Jews live. Cremation may become the preferred method of body disposal for the future. We cannot, as Jews, ignore this reality and alternative funeral choice. Those Jews who now choose to be cremated (Reform Judaism permits cremation) find themselves without appropriate rituals to bridge the gap between the funeral service and the Shivah. The finality of the graveside service (and the inner expectation of the mourner from past experiences that the burial is where the finality of the death is made evident) is lost—the mourner is left psychologically adrift, not able to go to from Ritual A to Ritual C unless Ritual B follows in its due course. (The comfort of structure, of course, is that we can follow it automatically without additional effort.) What is needed in Judaism is the development of liturgical and ritual approaches for cremation. At what point should the Kaddish be said when the family arrives at the crematorium with the body? What prayers can be recited when the urn of ashes is delivered to them? What prayers and rituals are appropriate for interring the urn either in the ground under a family marker or in a columbarium? What practices must be discouraged as being un-Jewish (display of the ashes, ostentation of the urn, etc.)? These and other questions are neither confronted nor answered so that the Jew, who turns to cremation, finds himself a religious outcast forced to adapt to Christian or secular styles.

4. With the advance of medical technologies, questions of the prolongation of life and the "right to die" will become commonplace and we must have Jewish answers to preserve the quality of life as we understand it. The concern for the

preservation of health for "life" is at the bedrock of most Jewish law. Judaism has always permitted passive euthanasia. When Rabbi Judah the Prince was lingering and suffering in his dying, his servant-woman went outside to the rabbis praying and threw a jar from the roof into their midst so that they would cease their prayers for his remaining on earth. They did so, and he died, ending his suffering. *Sefer Chasidim* (#315–318 Frankfurt Edition) commenting on *Ecclesiastes* "There is a time to live and a time to die", says: "If a man is dying, we do not pray too hard that his soul return and that he revive from the coma; he can at best live only a few days and in those days will endure great suffering; so 'there is a time to die'."

When the path to death is clear, the Jew may not interfere with the death. Active euthanasia (intervention in the dying process so as to hasten the death) has clear-cut Jewish prohibitions against it although there has been much discussion of it. The physician may not do anything to hasten the death, but he may remove the causes of the delay of death. (Moses Isserles in the *Shulchan Aruch* and others). Some Reform Jewish groups have given support to the concept of the Living Will as being within the Jewish ethical framework for death & dying. The Living Will requests that there be no prolongation of life if suffering and death are inevitable, and, that narcotics that may hasten the death be administered to alleviate pain. Although the Living Will is only legal in the State of California in 1977, more whole-hearted support from religious groups will help it to become the law of the land. As a people who knows and condemns suffering, how can we abdicate our responsibilities toward those who suffer to no avail and look to us to relieve them? We must have a firm modern Jewish position on this problem.

These are some thoughts and problems on the course of future Judaism. There may be others that must be considered. The purpose in exploring sensitive and frequently painful issues in death and dying is to enable us to live richer, happier, more meaningful lives within a community of sup-

port. Death and loss are inevitable—happiness and growth
are not. To view death only as a biological end is to deny the
ultimate reality of God's love and will for us as Jews. What is
life without the boundedness of death to give it value? God
says:

> "I offer you the choice of life or death, blessing or curse.
> Choose life and then you and your descendents will live;
> love the Lord your God, obey him and hold fast to him: that
> is life for you . . . "

Deuteronomy 30: 19–20 (NEB)

References

1. Bakan, David. *Sigmund Freud and the Jewish Mystical Tradition.* New York: Schocken Books, 1965.

2. Johnson, Aubrey Rodway. *The Vitality of the Individual in the Thought of Ancient Israel.* 2nd Edition, Cardiff: University of Wales Press, 1964.

3. Lamm, Maurice. *The Jewish Way in Death and Mourning.* New York: Jonathan David Publ. Co., 1969.

4. Parkes, Colin M. *Bereavement.* London: Tavistock Publ. Ltd., 1973.

5. Rakoff, Vivien. "Psychiatric Aspects of Death in America" in *Death in the American Experience,* New York: Schocken Books, 1974.

6. Shneidman, Edwin. *Deaths of Man.* New York: Quadrangle Books, 1973.

The Sabbath

Erich Fromm

Most of the biblical and rabbinical laws are understandable in their ethical and human significance (aside from those which have a pure ritualistic and usually archaic meaning); one law, however, which has a central position within the whole system, has often not been adequately understood, and hence needs a more detailed interpretation: the law concerning the Sabbath.

There can be no doubt of the fact that the Sabbath is a, or perhaps *the,* central institution of biblical and rabbinical religion. It is commanded in the Decalogue; it is one of the few religious laws emphasized by the great reforming Prophets; it has a central place in rabbinical thought, and as long as Judaism exists in its traditional customs, it was and is the most outstanding phenomenon of Jewish religious practice. It is no exaggeration to say that the spiritual and moral survival of the Jews during two thousand years of persecution and humiliation would hardly have been possible without the one day in the week when even the poorest and most wretched Jew was transformed into a man of dignity and pride, when the beggar was changed into a king. But in order not to think that this statement is a crude exaggeration, one must have witnessed the traditional practice of the Sabbath in its authentic form. Whoever thinks that he knows what the Sabbath is because he has seen the candles lit has little idea of the atmosphere the traditional Sabbath creates.

The reason why the Sabbath has so central a place within Jewish law lies in the fact that the Sabbath is the expression of the central idea of Judaism: the idea of freedom; the idea of complete harmony between man and nature, man and man; the idea of the anticipation of the messianic time and of man's defeat of time, sadness, and death.*

The modern mind does not see much of a problem in the Sabbath institution. That man should rest from his work one day every week sounds to us like a self-evident, social-hygienic measure intended to give him the physical and spiritual rest and relaxation he needs in order not to be swallowed up by his daily work, and to enable him to work better during the six working days. No doubt this explanation is true as far as it goes, but it does not answer some questions that arise if we pay closer attention to the Sabbath law of the Bible and particularly to the Sabbath ritual as it developed in the post-biblical tradition.

Why is this social-hygienic law so important that it was placed among the Ten Commandments, which otherwise stipulate only the fundamental religious and ethical principles? Why is it explained by equating it with God's rest on the seventh day, and what does this "rest" mean? Is God pictured in such anthropomorphic terms as to need a rest after six days of hard work? Why is the Sabbath explained in the second version of the Ten Commandments in terms of freedom rather than in terms of God's rest? What is the common denominator of the two explanations? Moreover—and this is perhaps the most important question—how can we understand the intricacies of the Sabbath ritual in the light of the social-hygienic interpretation of rest? In the Old Testament a man who "gathers sticks" (Num. 4:32 ff.) is considered a violator of the Sabbath law and punished by death. In the later development, not only work in our modern sense is forbidden, but activities such as the following: making any

---

* In the following pages I draw upon the ideas and the material of a paper on "The Sabbath Ritual," in E. Fromm, *The Forgotten Language* (New York: Holt, Rinehart and Winston, 1951), pp. 241 ff. In the same year (1951) a book entitled *The Sabbath* was published by Abraham J. Heschel, which contains a beautiful and profound analysis of the Sabbath (New York: Farrar, Straus & Giroux).

kind of fire, even if it is for the sake of convenience and does not require any physical effort; pulling a single blade of grass from the soil; carrying anything, even something as light as a handkerchief, on one's person. All this is not work in the sense of physical effort; its avoidance is often more of an inconvenience and discomfort than its execution would be. Are we dealing here with extravagant and compulsive exaggerations of an originally "sensible" ritual, or is our understanding of the ritual perhaps faulty and in need of revision?

A more detailed analysis of the symbolic meaning of the Sabbath ritual will show that we are dealing not with obsessive overstrictness but with a concept of work and rest that is different from our modern concept.

To begin with, the concept of work underlying the biblical and later Talmudic concepts is not one of physical effort, but it can be defined thus: *"Work" is any interference by man, be it constructive or destructive, with the physical world. "Rest" is a state of peace between man and nature.* Man must leave nature untouched, not change it in any way, either by building or by destroying anything. Even the smallest change made by man in the natural process is a violation of rest. The Sabbath is the day of complete harmony between man and nature. "Work" is any kind of disturbance of the man-nature equilibrium. On the basis of this general definition, we can understand the Sabbath ritual.

Any heavy work, like plowing or building, is work in this, as well as in our modern, sense. But lighting a match and pulling a blade of grass, while not requiring any effort, are symbols of human interference with the natural process, are a breach of peace between man and nature. On the basis of this principle, we can understand the Talmudic prohibition of carrying anything, even of little weight, on one's person. In fact, the carrying of something, as such is not forbidden. I can carry a heavy load within my house or my estate without violating the Sabbath law. But I must not carry even a handkerchief from one domain to another—for instance, from the private domain of the house to the public domain of the street. This law is an extension of the idea of peace from the social to the natural realm. A man must not interfere with or change the natural equilibrium and he must refrain from changing the social equilibrium. That means not only not to do business but also to avoid the most primitive form of transference of property, namely, its local transference from one domain to another.

The Sabbath symbolizes a state of union between man and nature and between man and man. By not working—that is to say, by not participating in the process of natural and social change—man is free from the chains of time, although only for one day a week.

The full significance of this idea can be understood only in the context of the biblical philosophy of the relationship between man and nature and the concept of the messianic time. The Sabbath is the anticipation of the messianic time, which is sometimes called "the time of the perpetual Sabbath"; but it is not purely the *symbolic* anticipation of the messianic time—it is its real precursor. As the Talmud puts it, "If all of Israel observed two Sabbaths (consecutively) fully only once, the messiah would be here" (Shabbat 118a). The Sabbath is the anticipation of the messianic time, not through a magic ritual, but through a form of practice which puts man in a real situation of harmony and peace. The different practice of life transforms man. This transformation has been expressed in the Talmud in the following way: "R. Simeon b. Lakish said: 'On the eve of the Sabbath, the Holy One Blessed Be He, gives to man an additional soul, and at the close of the Sabbath he withdraws it from him' " (Beitzah 16a).

"Rest" in the sense of the traditional Sabbath concept is quite different from "rest" being defined as not working, or not making an effort (just as "peace"—*shalom*—in the prophetic tradition is more than merely the absence of war; it expresses harmony, wholeness).* On the Sabbath, man ceases completely to be an animal whose main occupation is to fight for survival and to sustain his biological life. On the Sabbath, man is fully man, with no task other than to be human. In the Jewish tradition it is not work which is a supreme value, but rest, the state that has no other purpose than that of being human.

There is one other aspect of the Sabbath which is relevant to its full understanding. The Sabbath seems to have been an old Babylonian holiday, celebrated every seventh day *(Shapatu)* of a moon month. But its meaning was quite different from that of the biblical Sabbath. The Babylonian *Shapatu* was a day of mourning and self-castigation. It was a somber day, dedicated to the planet Saturn (our "Saturday" is still in its name devoted to Saturn), whose wrath one wanted to placate by self-castigation and self-punishment. But in the Bible, the holy day lost the character of self-castigation and mourning; it is no longer an "evil" day but a good one; the Sabbath becomes the very opposite of the sinister *Shapatu.* It becomes the day of joy and pleasure. Eating, drinking, sexual love, in addition to studying the Scriptures and religious writings, have characterized the Jewish celebration of the Sabbath throughout the last two thousand years. From a day of submission to the evil powers of Saturn, Sabbath has become a day of freedom and joy.

This change in mood and meaning can be fully understood only if we consider the meaning of Saturn. Saturn (in the old astrological and metaphysical tradition) symbolizes time. He is the god of time and hence the god of death. Inasmuch as man is like God, gifted with a soul, with reason, love, and freedom, he is not subject to time or death. But inasmuch as man is an animal with a body subject to the laws of nature, he is a slave of time and death. The Babylonians sought to appease the lord of time by self-castigation. The Bible, in its

* Cf. E. Fromm, "The Prophetic Concept of Peace," in *The Dogma of Christ.*

Sabbath concept, makes an entirely new attempt to solve the problem: by stopping interference with nature for one day, time is eliminated; where there is no change, no work, no human interference, there is no time. Instead of a Sabbath on which man bows down to the lord of time, the biblical Sabbath symbolizes man's victory over time. Time is suspended; Saturn is dethroned on his very day, Saturn's-day. Death is suspended and life rules on the Sabbath day.*

---

* It is interesting to speculate whether the basic principle of the Jewish Sabbath might not be practiced on a day of rest (Saturday) different from the day of recreation constituted by our present Sunday, which is devoted to sport, excursions, and so on. Considering the increasing custom of having two free days, such an idea does not seem to be impractical in industrialized countries. When I speak of the principle of the Jewish Sabbath, I am not referring to all the details of the Jewish Sabbath law, such as not carrying even a book or a handkerchief or not lighting a fire. Although I believe that even these details are important to create the full atmosphere of rest, I do not think that—except perhaps for a small minority—one could expect people to follow such cumbersome practices. But I do believe that the principle of the Sabbath rest might be adopted by a much larger number of people— Christians, Jews, and people outside of any religion. The Sabbath day, for them would be a day of contemplation, reading, meaningful conversation, a day of rest and joy, completely free from all practical and mundane concerns.

PART IV

Purpose and Meaning

Introduction

Finding purpose and meaning in one's Jewish identity presents two related problems, one of looking back and one of looking ahead. In looking back the person must confront, first of all, his feelings about his own Jewishness. In the Twentieth Century this process cannot help but be bound-up with the reality of the Holocaust and two thousand years of senseless anti-Semitism and hatred. No person of Jewish heritage can hope to come to any sort of peace or resolution about personal identity without facing this sobering side of his birthright. The haunting realization—"But for a slight accident in time, it could so easily have been me in the camps and not them"—cannot be laid to rest in any other manner: not through denial; not through repression; not through escape. To confront the Holocaust does not mean to justify it. How could anyone justify such an atrocity? Rather, it means to find some kind of personal answer which allows one to go on and to look to the future. For some it is the birth of the State of Israel. For others a realization of man's true nature. For still others it represents a renewed challenge to spread the light of Jewish moral teachings. According to psychiatrist and concentration camp survivor Viktor Frankl, this search for meaning, especially in the face of such senselessness, is life's ultimate challenge to the human being.

The religious theology of Richard Rubenstein, the author of the first article of Part IV, provides an example of just such a confrontation. Unable to reconcile the horrors of the Holocaust with the traditional Jewish concepts of an historic God and a chosen people, Rubenstein's personal answer took the form of a radical re-interpretation of what Judaism means. In his response to *Commentary* Magazine's "Symposium on Jewish Belief" he summarizes this reformulation. A former pulpit rabbi and Hillel director, Rubenstein chose to separate himself from the established Jewish community. In a later autobiographical work, *Power Struggle,* he traces the roots of both the Holocaust and his own disillusionment with contemporary Judaism back two millennia to the Fall of Jerusalem. At the time of the second destruction of the Temple, Israel was faced with the problem of coming to terms with its Roman conquerors. Two very different strategies evolved: one symbolized by Yochanan ben Zakkai and the other by Eleazar ben Yair. As leader of a sizable segment of Israel, Yochanan chose to submit to the Romans, trading political autonomy and independence for the right to study and worship freely. Eleazar, unhappy with such a choice, retreated with a small band of followers to Masada and fought, preferring death to submission. Yochanan's approach prevailed, and, according to Rubenstein, his "bargain" shaped the nature of Jewish history and the Jewish mentality for the next 1850 years. Ultimately, this choice set the stage for the Holocaust and culminated in the ultimate form of submission— Auschwitz. Rubenstein found Yochanan' bargain still in effect in many segments of the present Jewish community and, therefore, turned away from it. He urges contemporary Jew to never forget this historic lesson and to choose Masada, and not Jabneh (the site of Yochanan's rabbinic academy), as their symbol for the future.

In looking toward the future many Jews are finding yet another kind of purpose and meaning in their Jewishness, one derived through the creation of significant social change. Throughout its history Judaism has served as a ready forum for the expression of dissatisfaction with the status quo as well as a receptive medium in which to actually experiment with change. In a similar manner today Jews are speaking out against the injustices and destruction in contemporary life. In so doing, they are continuing an age-old tradition within Judaism of being responsible for the plight of all living creatures: whether human or sub-human, whether Jewish or Gentile. Others are developing alternative lifestyles and cultural forms, forms which are both consistent with Jewish values and aimed at alleviating some of the most pressing maladies in modern society. The remaining articles in Part

IV offer three very different examples of how Jews are meaningfully confronting the present in order to improve the
quality of life for the future: political activism, the Women's
Movement in Judaism and alternative communities.

American Jewish activists have had a stormy, but colorful
history, confronting at various times the American establishment, various segments of the Jewish community and, most
recently, the more "hawkish" elements in Israel. Some are
Jewish radicals, committed to Judaism's values but not its
religious practices. Others, radical Jews who find it impossible to separate the two, take their mandate for change from
religious concepts such as the Exodus, the Sabbath and messianism. Arthur I. Waskow is a central figure in this latter
group. In his work and prolific writings one can discern the
beginnings of a new form of politics, derived largely from
religious sources and lessons. In *The Freedom Seder* he uses
an ancient Jewish form, the Passover *Haggadah,* as a means
of piquing contemporary social and political awareness. In
The Bush Is Burning! he describes a new role for the diaspora
Jew after the establishment of Israel, that of creating a new
sense of community and *Halakah* aimed at achieving world
peace and social justice. In his article presented here, "The
Making of a Jewish Politics," he carries this idea further,
proposing an alternative form of politics called "God-Wres-
tling," drawn from the model of Genesis. The commitment
to such concepts by Waskow and a number of other well-
known American Jews has led to the formation of Breira,
probably the most controversial Jewish organization in the
world today. Breira is committed to achieving a lasting
security in the Middle East through recognizing the mutual
rights of both the Israeli and Palestinian peoples to self-deter-
mination and living in peace. Its attempts to bring about real
dialogue between the two sides have enraged various segments of the world Jewish community: the Jewish Defense
League, more conservative elements of American Jewry and
various groups in Israeli society.

There is a growing Women's Movement in Judaism.

Sharing many similarities and concerns with its larger sister organization, it aims at transforming and broadening the role and status of women in Judaism. Traditional Judaism has always prescribed very different and unequal roles and duties for men and for women. In general, men are held responsible for conducting the majority of the important religious rituals, especially in the synagogue, while women are relegated the tasks of caring for the home and raising the children. Specifically, women are not counted as part of the *minyan,* are not called to the *Torah,* are denied many other *Halakhic* responsibilities, are severely discriminated against in Jewish divorce, are denied access to advanced Jewish education, and are noticeably absent on synagogue boards, in community leadership positions and in rabbinical seminaries. And this list only scratches the surface. Although women's demands for equality are consistent with the highest values of Judaism, their fight is not an easy one. Not only do Jewish feminists have to overcome and alter chauvinistic attitudes in men and women alike, they have to bring about the re-interpretation of those Jewish Laws which institutionalize these attitudes. To do this they must confront the knotty problem of separating specific Talmudic prescription from the social customs and interpretations which have been incorporated along the way. The latter are much more susceptible to change than are the former. To truly understand the concerns of participants in the Jewish Women's movement, one must look beyond specific problem areas and inquire into the actual experience of being a woman in Jewish culture. In her thought-provoking article "On Being a Religious Jewish Woman," Rita Gross zeroes in on the central issue motivating contemporary Jewish women to speak out.

Many Jews today are dissatisfied with the nature of the Jewish religious community itself, especially with its synagogue. They feel it is, in many instances, a mockery of what it once was. No longer a forum for perpetuating Jewish values or enhancing the spiritual life of the individual, it has become, in their view, a handmaiden of the status quo: fearful of change and of alienating the Gentile segment of society, highly assimilated and acculturated, a social phenomenon rather than a religious one. Unlike their brothers and sisters of previous American generations, these critics are not turning away from Judaism in response, however. Rather, they are seeking to create alternative communities of their own, ones more in keeping with the spirit and essence of Jewish Law, tradition and morality. Jewish history, both recent and past, is replete with models for this task: the *shtetl,* the Hasidic community, the kibbutz. Blending old values and themes with contemporary modes more in keeping with the lifestyle and needs of today, their experiments have taken many different forms including group living, alternative religious communities and alternative educational systems. This is the topic of the final article of this section, David M. Szonyi's "Alternative Jewish Communities: An Overview". Only time will tell the outcome of these radical ventures. They may prove to be only passing phenomena, momentary efforts which will leave no lasting mark on Jewish history. Or they may hold far greater significance. Perhaps they anticipate a new stage of Jewish evolution, the consequence of the Holocaust, the reverberations of which Irving Greenberg suggests are only now beginning to be felt in the Jewish world. In either case, participation in such important social experiments cannot help but imbue these Jews with a real sense of purpose and meaning.

Symposium on Jewish Belief *

Richard L. Rubenstein

The Questions

1. In what sense do you believe the Torah to be divine revelation? Are all 613 commandments equally binding on the believing Jew? If not, how is he to decide which to observe? What status would you accord to ritual commandments lacking in ethical or doctrinal content (e.g., the prohibition against clothing made of linen and wool)?

2. In what sense do you believe that the Jews are the chosen people of God? How do you answer the charge that this doctrine is the model from which various theories of national and racial superiority have been derived?

3. Is Judaism the one true religion, or is it one of several true religions? Does Judaism still have something distinctive —as it once had monotheism—to contribute to the world? In the ethical sphere, the sphere of *ben adam lachavero,* what distinguishes the believing Jew from the believing Christian, Moslem, or Buddhist—or, for that matter, from the unbelieving Jew and the secular humanist?

4. Does Judaism as a religion entail any particular political

* This essay contains Richard L. Rubenstein's response to *Commentary's* Symposium, *The State of Jewish Belief* which appeared in the August, 1966 issue. It also appeared in Richard L. Rubenstein, *After Auschwitz: Radical Theology and Contemporary Judaism* (Indianapolis: Bobbs-Merrill, 1966).

viewpoints? Can a man be a good Jew and yet, say, support racial segregation? Can a man be a good Jew and be a Communist? A Fascist?

5. Does the so-called "God is dead" question which has been agitating Christian theologians have any relevance to Judaism? What aspects of modern thought do you think pose the most serious challenge to Jewish belief?

The Answers

(1) I believe the entire Torah to be sacred but not divinely revealed. It is the authoritative document out of which the inherited corpus of Jewish religious myth and ritual is ultimately derived. I find it impossible to accept any literal conception of divine revelation. I do not believe that a divine-human encounter took place at Sinai nor do I believe that the norms of Jewish religious life possess any superordinate validation.

Nevertheless, I do not regard the tradition of divine revelation as meaningless. It has psychological truth rather than literal historical truth. Something happened at Sinai and in the experience of the Jewish people. Somehow the Jewish people structured their personal and group norms by objectifying the parental image, projecting it into the cosmic sphere, and interpreting these norms as deriving from the objectified group-parent. I believe religion to be the way we share the decisive times and crises of life through the inherited experiences and norms of our community. The Torah is the repository of those norms. Because of its origins in the psychological strivings of the Jewish people, it is largely appropriate to its function.

All 613 commandments are equally binding, but our existential situation is one of total freedom to accept or reject any or all of them. There is no agency, human or divine, which can compel our response. I suspect that, in our times, the response to a large proportion of the commandments will be negative. I am, however, opposed to any contemporary Jewish group's legislating its historically circumscribed reaction to the 613 commandments for generations to come. I hope it will be possible for subsequent generations to confront all 613 commandments in the light of the insights of their time in order to decide what sector is meaningful for them. I seriously doubt that they will respond as we have. They may very well be ritually more compliant. Since we are totally free before the commandments, no two people will respond in the same way. I suspect that all attempts to construct a set of guiding principles to determine what type of commandments remain meaningful are doomed to failure. I think it is wisest, both theologically and practically, to recognize *both* the binding character of all the commandments and our total freedom before them.

I believe some of the commandments lacking ethical or doctrinal content are among the most meaningful. We must distinguish between the *latent* and *manifest* content of the commandments. By proclaiming the continuing relevance of only those rituals which have an explicit ethical content, we tend to ignore rituals which dramatize our feelings concerning enormously important areas of life. At the manifest level, a ceremony such as *bar mitzvah* has little ethical significance. Nevertheless, something very important takes place. The young man passes through a puberty rite. He is confirmed as a male and a Jew at a crucial moment in the timetable of his life. The real question we must ask about ritual is how it *functions* in the life of the individual and the group. Vast areas of Jewish ritual are deeply rooted in our psychological needs. Religion's primary function is priestly rather than prophetic, insofar as we can separate the two categories. It is excessively difficult to effect ethical improvement through religious instrumentalities. Most rabbis function largely as priests. Their role is to help the individual pass through the crises of life with appropriate rituals which have the power to alleviate the conflicts inherent in the worst moments and heighten the joys of the happier times. People aren't going to change much. Moralizing rituals have a severely limited potency. Rituals which help us pass through such crises as birth, puberty, marriage, sickness, the changing seasons, and death are indispensable.

(2) I believe that my Jewish identity is an absurd given. It is the way I have been thrust into the world. This identity involves having been born into a community with an inherited mythic tradition. That *mythos* includes the doctrine of the election of Israel.

I find it impossible to believe in the doctrine of the chosen people, yet I know of no way in which Jews can be entirely quit of this myth. The Jewish people made a fantastic claim for themselves, that their traditions and destiny were peculiarly the object of God's concern. Ironically, the Gentile world took them seriously, so seriously that the Christian Church to this day asserts the election has passed from the "old" Israel to the Church, the "New" Israel. Too frequently, Judaism is criticized for its "chauvinistic" chosen-people doctrine, as if Jews were the only ones with such a doctrine. In actual fact, Christianity cannot be understood apart from its chosen-people doctrine, the claim that the Church has replaced the Synagogue as the New Israel. The real problem implicit in the chosen-people doctrine is not Jewish ethnocentricism but the two-thousand-year-old sibling rivalry of Jew and Christian over who is the Father's beloved child.

When I recite the prayer "Praise be Thou O Lord our God . . . who has chosen us from among all peoples and given us the Torah," I assert the appropriateness and sufficiency of the Torah as the authoritative document of Jewish religion in the face of the continuing claim of the Church that my religion remains an imperfect anticipation of and preparation for Christianity. I do not see how a believing Christian can avoid claiming that he is a member of the New Israel, the truly elect of God. Even Jewish and Christian death-of-God theologians cannot avoid this Law-Gospel conflict. It has an

Antigone-like quality. There is no way out, save moral and psychological modesty in recognizing that the Christian has been thrust into his religious identity as absurdly as the Jew into his.

I see no inner resemblance between the chosen-people doctrine and modern doctrines of racial superiority. The chosen-people doctrine has been the source of millennia of pathetic and unrealistic self-criticism by Jews. Because Jews felt under special obligation to fulfill God's covenant, they have been convinced since the prophets that their religious performance was never good enough. They have interpreted every Jewish disaster from the destruction of Jerusalem in 586 B. C. E.* to the hideous disasters of the twentieth century as God's attempt to punish His errant children in the hope that they would be restored to perfect fidelity to Him. This contrasts with modern ideologies of racial superiority. The racial doctrines are totally devoid of any shred of self-criticism or the feeling of unworthiness before God. On the contrary, these ideologies lend respectability to the most vicious kinds of self-aggrandizement by the nations involved at the expense of their neighbors. The bitter irony of the Jewish doctrine was that its effect was to magnify beyond all realism Jewish guilt-feelings before God. There can be no comparison between the chosen-people doctrine and modern ideologies of racial or national superiority.

(3) I believe that all the major religions are psychologically true for their believers. As such, they are deeply congruent with the needs and identities of their participants. In terms of psychological function, Judaism is no "truer" than any other religion.

I believe that Judaism continues to make a unique contribution to the world, more in terms of the quality of its men and women than in terms of any special insight absent from other religions. Judaism will continue to make a distinctive

---

* Before the Christian era.

contribution so long as it develops men and women who function as an element of creative discontent before the regnant idolatries of any given time or community. I also believe that Judaism possesses a peculiar sanity which ought never to be overlooked. Judaism is largely a this-worldly religion. It focuses attention upon the requirements of I and Thou in here and now. In this context, the old Law-Gospel controversy retains enormous contemporary relevance. Two thousand years ago, the Christian Church claimed that some of the tragic inevitabilities of the human condition had been overcome through the career of Jesus. Before this claim the rabbis preferred their sad wisdom that the human condition had not been altered. They focused Jewish attention on those norms which could make life's limitations more viable, rather than on a savior who promised to overcome the limitations. The fundamental Jewish posture is one of realism before existence rather than one of seeking an escape from the world's necessities.

There is a sense in which I am forced to assert that Judaism is "truer" than Christianity. The Christian Church makes certain claims about the way the career of Jesus changed the meaning of the Synagogue and its traditions. Christianity does not assert that it is an entirely different religion from Judaism. It claims that the full meaning of Israel is finally revealed through the Christ. That is why Vatican II could only go so far in resolving the Church-Synagogue conflict. I regard the claim of the Church vis-à-vis Judaism as inherently mistaken. Insofar as Christianity is compelled to define the ultimate meaning of my religious community in its own special perspectives, I must be a dissenting partisan. I find myself in the paradoxical position of asserting that Christianity is as psychologically true for Christians as Judaism is for Jews, while maintaining that the manifest claims of the Church concerning Israel and Israel's Messiah are without foundation.

I find your question about the distinction in the ethical sphere between the believing Jew and the believing Christian the most difficult to answer. I honestly don't know. As a this-worldly religion, Judaism stresses the ethical more insistently than does Christianity, the only realistic alternative in our culture. I might almost be caught saying that a truly believing Jew would be more fully committed within the sphere of I-Thou than others. I find that I have to pull back. I wish it were so. Certainly, Jewish ethical standards are no worse than others. I doubt very much that one could demonstrate that unbelievers have a lower standard in behavioral matters than believers. I am convinced that any attempt to establish the current uniqueness of Judaism on the basis of the special virtues of its believers is doomed to failure.

Finally, I would caution against the tendency in contemporary Judaism to overstress the moral and the ethical. Admittedly, Judaism seeks to inculcate high ethical standards, but one of the most important functions of a religious community is the *sharing of failure,* especially moral failure. We turn to the sanctuary less to be admonished to pursue virtue than out of the need to express and share our inevitable shortcomings in that pursuit.

(4) In the absence of a biblically ordained theocracy—which few contemporary Jews desire—Judaism has much to say about justice but very little about politics. It would make little difference whether a practicing Jew was a Republican or a Democrat provided the area of disagreement concerned the political means whereby an equitable society could be achieved. However, the problem of Judaism and politics cannot be divorce from the historic experience of the Jewish people. I do not see how Jews could possibly feel at home in right-wing groups or parties. Their underlying appeal is for the supremacy of a particular racial or ethnic community. Inevitably, such groups turn anti-Semitic or at the very least yearn to "put the Jews in their place." That is why Jewish opposition to the Goldwater campaign was so overwhelming. Jews understood instinctively that the half-Jew Goldwater was seeking to harness the irrational forces in American

political life which were striving to assure white supremacy. They knew instinctively that the Goldwater campaign, if successful, would ultimately become anti-Semitic. Jews have fared best in multiethnic communities in which the ties between citizens were rational and contractual, rather than emotional and based on real or imagined membership in a primary group. For that reason, Jews will usually favor that party which fosters a rational, contractual conception of citizenship and is neutral in religious and ethnic matters.

I do not believe a religious Jew can support racial injustice or enforced segregation. Nevertheless, Jews do believe in a measure of religious separateness. We do not favor intermarriage. Hence we tend to be cautious about a host of social arrangements which can lead to it. I am convinced that the Jewish community will continue to be an ally of the Negro community in its quest for political justice. There are, however, important areas of conflict between the two communities. The Negro community's goal seems to be the ultimate obliteration of the voluntary as well as the involuntary kinds of segregation in America. The Jewish community is not prepared to heed that call. To do so would be to destroy the religious and communal basis of Jewish uniqueness.

I see no impediment to a believing Jew's being a Marxist, but he cannot, I think, be a Communist. As a Communist, a believing Jew would have to endure an insupportable conflict between party discipline and loyalty to his religious community. I can never forget the way in which Communists of Jewish origin insisted that Hitler's war was of no concern to them until the Nazi attack on the Soviet Union on June 22, 1941. These people were indifferent so long as Hitler was murdering Jews, but not when he attacked the Soviet Union. After the Hitler experience, I fail to see how any believing Jew could be a Fascist.

(5) I am convinced that the problems implicit in death-of-God theology concern Judaism as much as Christianity.

Technically, death-of-God theology reflects the Christian tradition of the passion of the Christ. As such, the terminology of the movement gives Jewish theologians some very obvious problems. Nevertheless, I have, almost against my will, come to the conclusion that the terminology is unavoidable. The death-of-God theologians have brought into the open a conviction which has led a very potent underground existence for decades. Death-of-God theology is no fad. It is a contemporary expression of issues which have, in one way or another, appeared in embryo in scholastic philosophy, medieval mysticism, nineteenth-century German philosophy, and in the religious existentialism of Martin Buber and Paul Tillich.

No man can really say that God is dead. How can we know this? Nevertheless, I am compelled to say that we live in the time of the "death of God." This is more a statement about man and his culture than about God. The death of God is a cultural fact. Buber felt this. He spoke of the eclipse of God. I can understand his reluctance to use the more explicitly Christian terminology. I am compelled to utilize it because of my conviction that the time which Nietzsche's madman said was too far off has come upon us. There is no way around Nietzsche. Had I lived in another time or another culture, I might have found some other vocabulary to express my meanings. I am, however, a religious existentialist after Nietzsche and after Auschwitz. When I say we live in the time of the death of God, I mean that the thread uniting God and man, heaven and earth has been broken. We stand in a cold, silent, unfeeling cosmos, unaided by any purposeful power beyond our own resources. After Auschwitz, what else can a Jew say about God?

When Professor William Hamilton associated my theological writings with the death-of-God movement in his article on radical theology in *The Christian Scholar,* I was somewhat dubious about his designation. After reflection, I concluded that Professor Hamilton was correct. There is a definite style in religious thought which can be designated death-of-God theology. I have struggled to escape the term. I have been embarrassed by it. I realize its inadequacy and its Christian origin. I have, nevertheless, concluded that it is inescapable. I see no other way of expressing the void which confronts man where once God stood.

I am acutely aware of the fact that Christian death-of-God theologians remain fully committed Christians, as I remain a committed Jew. As Professor Hamilton has suggested, Christian death-of-God theologians have no God, but they do have a Messiah. Christian death-of-God theology remains Christocentric. I affirm the final authority of Torah and reject the Christian Messiah, as Jews have for two thousand years. Professor Thomas J. J. Altizer welcomes the death of God. He sees it as an apocalyptic event in which the freedom of the Gospels is finally realized and the true Christian is liberated from every restraint of the Law. I do not see that awful event as a cosmic liberation. I am saddened by it. I believe that in a world devoid of God we need Torah, tradition, and the religious community far more than in a world where God's presence was meaningfully experienced. The death of God leads Altizer to a sense of apocalyptic liberation; it leads me to a sad determination to enhance the religious norms and the community without which the slender fabric of human decency might well disappear. In the time of the death of God, Christian theologians still proclaim the Gospel of the Christ; Jewish theologians proclaim the indispensability of Torah.

I believe the greatest single challenge to modern Judaism arises out of the question of God and the death camps. I am amazed at the silence of contemporary Jewish theologians on this most crucial and agonizing of all Jewish issues. How can Jews believe in an omnipotent, beneficent God after Auschwitz? Traditional Jewish theology maintains that God is the ultimate, omnipotent actor in the historical drama. It has interpreted every major catastrophe in Jewish history as God's punishment of a sinful Israel. I fail to see how this position can be maintained without regarding Hitler and the SS as instruments of God's will. The agony of European Jewry cannot be likened to the testing of Job. To see any purpose in the death camps, the traditional believer is forced to regard the most demonic, antihuman explosion in all history as a meaningful expression of God's purposes. The idea is simply too obscene for me to accept. I do not think that the full impact of Auschwitz has yet been felt in Jewish theology or Jewish life. Great religious revolutions have their periods of gestation. No man knows the hour when the full impact of Auschwitz will be felt, but no religious community can endure so hideous a wounding without vast inner disorders.

Though I believe that a void stands where once we experienced God's presence, I do not think Judaism has lost its meaning or power. I do not believe that a theistic God is necessary for Jewish religious life. Dietrich Bonhoeffer has written that our problem is how to speak of God in an age of no religion. I believe that our problem is how to speak of religion in an age of no God. I have suggested that Judaism is the way we share the decisive times and crises of life through the traditions of our inherited community. The need for that sharing is not diminished in the time of the death of God. We no longer believe in the God who has the power to annul the tragic necessities of existence; the need religiously to share that existence remains.

Finally, the time of the death of God does not mean the end of all gods. It means the demise of the God who was the ultimate actor in history. I believe in God, the Holy Nothingness, known to mystics of all ages, out of which we have come and to which we shall ultimately return. I concur with atheistic existentialists such as Sartre and Camus in much of their analysis of the broken condition of human finitude. We must endure that condition without illusion or hope. I do not part company with them on their analysis of the human predicament. I part company on the issue of the necessity of religion as the way we share that predicament. Their analysis of human hopelessness leads me to look to the religious community as the institution in which that condition can be shared in depth. The condition of finitude can only be overcome when we return to the Nothingness out of which we have been thrust. In the final analysis, omnipotent Nothingness is Lord of all creation.

The Making of a Jewish Politics *

Arthur I. Waskow

In this generation as in the past, an authentically Jewish politics would have to spring from both of two deeply inter-twined roots: Jewish peoplehood and Jewish tradition.

First of all, let's look at the situation of Jewish peoplehood and what that would lead us to, for a Jewish politics in this generation.

We are not a great power. We are a small people.

We're a people that is still dispersed, as it has been for a very long time, since before the destruction of the Second Temple. In this generation we are something remarkably strange: we are a people that both has dominant power in a nation-state and does not, and is conscious of itself as a people even in the places where it does not have dominant power in a nation-state. We were strange enough in the diaspora, but we are even stranger now because we are both a diaspora and a nation. That makes it extraordinarily difficult to ex-plain to anybody. We thought a generation ago it was hard to explain how we were a people when we did not own a nation-state. Now that part of us do and part of us don't, it is still harder. Yet, I think that's one of the aspects, one of the roots from which a Jewish politics has to spring . . . that both of those facts are true.

---

* This paper was given at the first national convention of Breira, near Washington, D.C. in February, 1977.

We are also embedded in what people have been calling this past generation the first, second, and the third world. That also makes us very difficult to cope with, because we're embedded within the capitalist west, with its urgings toward democracy, and the state-bureaucratic east with its urgings toward socialism, and the third world. Yet, we are *of* none of them, as we have been not quite *of* any of the societies we have been embedded in. And what we are now attempting, out of the last generation of Jewish history, and what I think Breira is all about, is to understand what it means to be embedded *in,* but not quite *of,* the three major divisions of world political culture.

One political conclusion that I draw from our situation as a people is that as small peoples have traditionally recognized, militarization is not useful for us—from whatever direction it comes in the world. Militarization has been useful to great powers, at least in the short run, even in the middle run. But it is not useful to us. It may have seemed useful for the briefest moment of our history, from 1956 to 1973, but the fact is that we are a small people and militarization cannot help but benefit great powers. It may benefit the great powers of the Arab nation, the great powers of the Soviet Union, the great powers of the United States of North America, but not us. That fact I think should be leading us to explore again what our tradition has always said, that militarization is not good for us as it is not good for the rest of humanity either, and we ought to be examining what in this generation that means in the toughest, realest, concretest form, what it means for us to be struggling toward.

We have already seen that militarization in the Middle East was of terribly brief benefit to Israel and to the Jewish people, that it is already draining resources and energy and morale from the Jewish people.

In the USSR it is clear that militarization strengthens the enemies of the Jewish people. It strengthens police institutions, it strengthens the central bureaucratic institutions, it weakens the possibilities of a renewed, vital and free Jewish culture, it weakens the possibilities of the willingness of Soviet society to let Jews be Jews, either in the Soviet Union or to leave it to be Jews outside.

In the United States, militarization weakens the Jewish middle class, it weakens the Jewish poor in the cities, it weakens all the elements of American civilian life of which the Jews are extraordinarily a part, it pits the society internally against itself, it puts the Jews in the classic position of being the in-betweens in a society more and more prepared to be at war with itself because it continues to spend its best energies, its greatest chunks of money on the military.

And the militarization of the US also puts the US Government on the side of at least two governments in the third world where sizeable numbers of Jews live and where those alliances forbode deep, deep trouble fcr the Jewish community—that is, the alliance between the American government and South Africa, and the alliance between the American government and Argentina. A racist government in one case and a fascist government in the other. A government in Argentina which is increasingly taking on the tones of classic fascism, including the explicit anti-Semitic tones of it; a government where in the other case, at best, the Jews will find themselves an incredibly thin tissue between the white and black communities of South Africa as they come closer and closer to civil war. The militarization of the United States has moved in the direction of supporting both those governments as against possible non-violent change in those two societies—possible with great difficulty, with great hesitancy, with overwhelming difficulties—but still possible.

In Western Europe, too, the militarization of the world has weakened the possibilities of democratic capitalism or democratic socialism, has indeed weakened the whole parliamentary experiment in western European society, and thus has damaged the future of the Jewish communities in France and Britain.

So, I would suggest that as a world people, certainly in the protection of Israel, certainly in the protection of American and Soviet Jewry, we ought to be looking toward the devolution of the arms race and the devolution of the increasingly military definition of how societies in the Middle East, in Eastern Europe, and in the West protect themselves. That is a very crucial part of a Jewish politics.

Secondly, very briefly, I think that the situation of the Jewish people is such that our politics needs to be one of decentralization, one of locality. Both in the Soviet Union and in the United States, the ability of Jewish communities to develop their own lives could only come if those communities had far more power, far more authority over their own lives than we now do. We are not the great power in American society. In order to shape the lives of our communities in ways that Jews would want to, the communities themselves, the localities themselves, would have to be far more able to do that. Again, very briefly I would say, it seems to me stemming from the present situation of Jewish peoplehood in the world, locality, decentralization are a crucial part of what that politics should be, just as demilitarization is.

Now I want to turn to what the other root, the intertwined root of Jewish politics would be. There I think it has to be the Jewish tradition, in the broadest sense, beginning with Chumash and going down to Buber and Rosenzweig, Dubnow and Achad Ha'Am, secularist and religious, Zionist and Diasporanist, and into our own generation.

What does it mean to continue to be Jewish? I would say that the deepest definition of our being is Yisrael, the God-Wrestler. I would say that to be Godwrestler means in one of its aspects wrestling with all those elements of Jewish tradition. *Wrestling* in the sense that wrestling is that strangest of fusions, a fusion of making war and making love; wrestling is neither just fighting nor just making love—it is both, and that what we need to do with the Jewish tradition is both.

That's not all Godwrestling is. In its deepest root, the wrestling of Jacob was a wrestle that fused the political and the spiritual, as well as fusing making love and war. Jacob wrestled, says the Torah, with men and with God. Jacob wrestled, to begin with, with a *man,* not an angel—the one thing the text *doesn't* say is that it is an angel, it says that it was a man, who appears and with whom he wrestles. He wrestled out of fear and guilt over his preparation to meet next day with his brother Esau, from whom he had stolen the birthright and the blessing, but not only out of fear and guilt. What made his struggle a Godwrestle was that he wrestled also out of the kind of existential challenge to a world in which it was only *possible* to get to be Jacob by stealing from Esau, in which it was only *possible* to get to be what he needed to be and what he was intended to be and who he dreamed of being by cheating and lying and stealing to and from his father and his brother. The struggle that night that gave us our name, was one that began with a struggle with a human being, with his brother and himself, and then became a struggle with God because Jacob pierced the guilt and fear to even a deeper level, to the level of the question why does it have to be this way. How do I turn the world as it was given—a world of conflict, of cheating, of stealing—into a world of comradeship?

That is what he was able to do by wrestling, perhaps because wrestling, despite Buber, is a more crucial way of being with God than talking. Since wrestling does combine fighting with making love, wrestling alone can teach us how to turn fighting into making love. It teaches us how to turn the world as it is given us—in which to be brothers means to be Cain and Abel—into the world in which Jacob and Esau were able to kiss and embrace the next morning.

So the Godwrestling is not only the synthesis of fighting and making love. It is also the synthesis of political and spiritual struggle, not dividing the two, struggling with human beings and finding *in that struggle* the spiritual struggle with God.

And wrestling is the synthesis of our love of Jewish tradition and our anger and bafflement at the tradition. For by wrestling we come to the tradition with the problems that we face, we come not just to ask what Rashi said, but to ask what did Rashi say in Rashi's time, that we may learn better what to say in our time. We come to the tradition not just to obey it, and not to reject it, but to wrestle with it and to create something new out of that wrestling. But the something new that we create is still Jewish because it is that tradition with which we are wrestling. And so it is this wrestle which creates a *Jewish* politics.

I want to say something about what the content as well as the process of that is. This is only a piece of that content. It's a piece that I have been wrestling with during the past several years, that I am just beginning to get down on paper . . . That is the piece of the tradition that encompasses both the Jacob/Esau struggle and all the other brother struggles in the book of Genesis. I want to suggest that the book of Genesis should be viewed by us as an important alternative model to the Exodus model of how you win justice. The Exodus model is one of overwhelming oppression, resistance, destruction, and separation. It's the model that has formed much of the West's liberation theory from then till now. It's the model we still, I think, carry in our heads when we say the word "liberation." I want to suggest that the book of Genesis carries a different model which is one we need to be wrestling with now, even more than the other. The model of Genesis is useful in a world where it is not possible ultimately to separate, not even to separate as much as it was possible for Am Yisrael to leave Egypt and go to Eretz Yisrael.

What happens in Genesis from Isaac and Ishmael down to Menasseh and Ephraim is that brothers struggle until their relationship is transformed in the direction of justice and freedom for the weaker brother, the one who starts weaker, the younger brother. But these struggles end with reconciliation and the ability to live together, as well.

Genesis begins the brother struggles with a kind of quick note as to what flat, normal history is; flat normal history is that the older brother is more powerful and kills the younger one. That's Cain and Abel, and that is the standard, that is "normal." What is then to *become* the norm is described through the book. I think it is instructive that it doesn't end until Menasseh and Ephraim have had their strange blessing. Generation after generation of the Jewish people is an attempt to answer Cain and Abel. It is an attempt to say that the younger brother is supposed to win or to prevail or—to use the Hebrew that's usually translated as "prevail" in the Jacob struggle with God—to *be able,* that's all. That the younger brother is to become able to do that and then to win reconciliation.

The first case is the struggle of Isaac and Ishmael. The younger brother wins, the elder is cast out into the wilderness, but the prophesy tells us that one day Ishmael is to dwell in the face of all his brothers. Then the text tells us that when Abraham dies, it is possible for the two of them to come together. I want to come back to that one, because I think that when we are facing a Jewish politics of how Jews and Arabs, Israelis and Palestinians, deal with each other, we should pay special attention to that one since our tradition tells us that Ishmael is the forebear of the Arab peoples, and their tradition tells them that too.

The second case is the Jacob/Esau case where, again, the younger brother wins the birthright and the blessing, struggles deeply with what it means to have done that, and then is able to win reconciliation with his brother.

The third case is that of Joseph and his brothers where not the elder brother, not even the several elder brothers, but a younger one wins. Having won, he is able to win reconciliation and finally able to achieve peoplehood, twelve brothers working together able to create the Jewish people.

The last of the brother stories is this very strange moment

in which Jacob, who stole the birthright as the younger son and who remembers that very powerfully, demands to bless his grandchildren, Ephraim and Menasseh. Joseph brings them, tries to arrange them so that the older brother will get the older son's birthright. Jacob crosses his hands, turns his hands around so that the younger one gets the older one's birthright and the older one gets the younger one's birthright. When Joseph says, wait a minute, you've got it all wrong, Jacob says, no, I know what I'm doing. He indeed does know what he is doing, he is the one who knows what it means to have this criss-cross of older/younger brother. He blesses them at the same moment, the first time that this older/younger business has been asserted and dissolved at the same instant. What he does by blessing them both by crossing over is to assert, I know that I am criss-crossing the older and younger birthright, but I am doing it in such a way as to reach beyond my own history and to carry on to you the blessing that the older and the younger can be equal. And even beyond you, to the future of the Jewish people, because we are to be blessed throughout the generations that we shall be as Menasseh and Ephraim, that we be the brothers who do not forget that the younger brother has to win but remember it in such a way that the conflict is simultaneously resolved, transcended, reconciled.

The model of Genesis teaches that the powerful are not to be allowed to continue to be more powerful—the less powerful must win in order that justice be established. But must win without destruction, without the drowning of Pharaohs and armies, because even an elder brother was not Pharaoh. Genesis teaches us that winning can happen in such a fashion that reconciliation can follow it.

I think we are now caught in a world in which that model is by far the most useful model. It is not simply Christian nonviolence, not simply loving your neighbor, because those are very tough conflicts if you look back at them, they are rebellions, they are insistences on winning, they are insistences on transforming the situation so that the weaker becomes the stronger in such a way that the stronger can then reach out and the weaker not be ashamed to respond to the stronger. But look at our world. Look, for example. at the struggles of women to transform the situation in which they have been the powerless throughout our history, where they have been in the situation that Genesis describes as that of the younger brother, in which the sister has been the weaker element in Jewish history, in human history. That women's struggle is one in which the end result is not going to be and ought not to be an utter separation as in Exodus and a destruction as in Exodus. It is one in which the struggle is intended to be one of transformation, not simply revolution in the sense of "revolving." It is one in which the result is to be reconciliation on a new basis of justice. I think we also find ourselves now clearly in a situation where all the great national conflicts which once would have been solved by withdrawal and destruction, the building of a new society alone, can't be done in the world we live in. The world has become too closely drawn for that.

Surely we can see that most clearly of all in the brother-conflict we live out in agony—the struggle of Israelis versus Palestinians. Israel was born as a midrash on the Exodus. For Zionism was a kind of secularist midrash on the Prophetic vision of the Messianic redemption, and that vision is built on the Departure from Egypt. The Jews depart from their exile, cross the sea of troubles that surround them, and reunite in Eretz Yisrael. So have we done!—and yet the redemption is not complete. Why?

I would suggest that in our world we must learn from the model of Genesis as well as Exodus. Hitler (yemach shmo!) was Pharaoh, but the Palestinians are not Pharaoh—they are Ishmael. It was necessary for the remnants of our people to have an Exodus, but now we confront an adversary who is not to be destroyed but who must learn to live with us—as we with them.

This does not mean that we abandon who we are. Let us

hear the story in the Torah—hear it carefully. The key knowledge, the key turning of the Ishmael/Isaac story is that Isaac, "Yitzchak," means laughing boy, and Yishmael mitza-chek, Ishmael laughed at the laughing boy. The root of what he did that Sara found impossible to deal with is that he mocked the root of Isaac's being, the laughing root. He laughed at the laughter, he turned inside out the other's identity. They were too much like each other, not identical, but too much like each other for the two of them to grow up together. It was precisely the similarity of their identity which made it *necessary* for them to separate and *important* for them, again, someday, to dwell in each other's presence.

The war we have seen this last generation is born from the deep similarities between the people that loves Eretz Yisrael and the people that loves Palestine. These similarities, and the love of those two peoples for the same land, has been what has made it impossible for us to deal with each other. Look at the similarities of the Palestinian diaspora and the Jewish diaspora (with the single exception of the Holocaust). The Jewish diaspora has been a mixture of making-it and pogrom, as the Palestinian diaspora has been a mixture of making-it and massacre. As the story says, Ishmael has become the wild jack-ass in the desert, his hand lifted against everyone, and everyone's hand lifted against him. But there remains for us the fourth portion of the prophecy, "and he shall dwell in the face of all his brothers," not *fused with* all his brothers but also not seen in the cloudy mirror of a confused identity. Different, but face to face.

That, I think, is where we need to be drawing a Jewish politics from the brother stories for the Middle East, as I think we need to be drawing a Jewish politics from the brother stories in all the rest of Genesis as well. We need to draw out a Jewish politics that says:

—We were the weaker brother and yet we prevailed against the power of Ishmael. Now we can face him, recognize him, live face to face with him. Not in one country but in two—for our identities, though similar, are different—and indeed are defined as different by their very similarity.

—We drew the sword, but we must never depend upon the sword. We became a power because we had to, but we are not a great power and we cannot live by the sword—and do not want to.

—*We are the Wrestlers who know how to turn our wrestling from a way of making war into a way of making love.*

Thus, it seems to me, our sociology as a modern people and our history as a people wrestling with Torah intertwine. I have described a process, wrestling with humans and with the Tradition and with God, that can make for us a Jewish politics. I have suggested what content it seems to me that process might bring us to, if we used it facing the most urgent of the issues that the Jewish people faces.

Learning *both* to wrestle that we may prevail and then to turn our wrestle into an embrace of love—that is Yisrael, that is what it means to be the Jewish people and create a Jewish politics.

On Being a Religious Jewish Woman *

Rita M. Gross

In the midst of current claims and counterclaims about the position of women in Judaism, it is useful to step back from the data about women's role and the debate about women's position in Judaism. One steps back, not because the facts are unpleasant and the debate useless or unimportant, but because it is more important to *analyze why* significant numbers of Jewish women are angered and alienated by their present role and position. In this essay, I will assume some knowledge about the role of women in Judaism, as well as a certain amount of anger about that role. Instead of rehashing those facts, I will demonstrate *why* women must respond so ambiguously to the Jewish vision-quest. Then I will propose changes in Jewish practice in the light of that analysis.

Before I analyze the causes of Jewish women's anger, let me delineate my identities, since they clearly shape and color my interpretations of the role of women in Judaism. Ranked in order of descending comprehensiveness, though not necessarily in order of decreasing importance, I think of myself as female human being, scholar of religions, religious, and Jewish. To be self-consciously a female human being is at the same time so obvious as not to be worth mentioning and yet one of the most difficult discoveries that one can make. Despite biology and rhetoric, few people really comprehend the implications of the conjunction of the terms

* This essay was first presented in a program on "Women and Spiritual Judaism," at the First Jewish Feminists' Conference in New York City in April, 1973. An earlier version appeared in *Anima*, Vol. I, No. 1, Fall, 1974.

female and *human being.* Therefore, despite its superficial obviousness, I consider that this element of my identity is fundamental and cannot be denied or shortchanged by other elements of my identity. The identity of *scholar of religions* is less ambiguous, but its impact on my interpretations of Jewish problems is overwhelmingly important. I am trained in the history of religions and spend much of my time analyzing and interpreting the data of mankind's religious expressions. I utilize these same tools in understanding my own religious identity. Both by training and conviction, I reflect on Judaism within the larger context of religion. The identities *religious human being* and *Jewish* seem less complex to me. They are simply there, important aspects of my being. I strive then to put all these identities together into a consistent pattern. That is to say, my being religious and my being Jewish cannot undercut my being a female human being nor can they be contradictory to what I know as a scholar of religions.

Out of this perspective, after significant involvement in several Jewish religious settings, I have begun to develop a framework for interpreting and understanding both the woman's role in Judaism and my frustration with that role. This framework also serves as a rationale for changes in Jewish practice. My analysis of anger and rationale for change proceed by means of five interlocking propositions about women's role in society and in Jewish life.

The first proposition states that when one thinks analytically and critically about the various ways in which human beings conceive of themselves and talk about themselves, one discovers two distinctly different modes of self-concept. These two modes of self-concept, which point toward two fundamental dimensions of human life, can be called the relational and the essential modes of human existence.

The relational mode emphasizes one's existence in the midst of others, one's connections with them. When one is in the relational mode, one exists because of, and for, the sake of others. The most obvious example of relational language is found in family and kin terminology—one simply cannot be a mother without offspring, or a husband without a wife, or a cousin in the absence of cousins. Other realms in which relational language predominate include some aspects of education—one is not a teacher without students and vice versa—and any other enterprise in which nurture and caring for others is the major purpose of the endeavor. These situations all have a crucial common characteristic: another person with whom one is in relationship is logically necessary to one's own existence. However, there is minimal attention to one's core, to one's self; this is the major difference between the relational mode and the essential mode of being.

In the essential mode the stress is more on what one is in one's own right, irrespective of the communal setting in which one exercises one's talents. When one answers the question "Who or what am I?" in the essential rather than in the relational mode, that answer does not logically require the existence of another human being, as is the case with relational language. Instead, one points to one's own core, one's own center. One says, "I am an intellectual, or a carpenter, or a lawyer, or whatever," thus defining oneself without special reference to others. The fact that usually there is an audience or a community which acknowledges one's being does not materially alter the analysis. The relationship of an intellectual or a carpenter or a lawyer to her/his audience or community is logically very different from that of a parent to his/her child. The fact that no one exists in a vacuum does not change the fact that there is a mode of self-understanding that primarily asks who one is and what one can do, not what relationships one is engaged in.

Before going on to the second proposition in this analysis, it is important to note that neither mode is more desirable nor more important than the other. I am not trying to assign values at this point, but simply to point out, separate, and clarify aspects of self-concept that usually are somewhat hazy and not well sorted out.

The second proposition correlates the kind of language used to discuss the woman's role and position with the analysis of modes of self-concept. Basically, woman-language is in the relational mode. Women are almost always talked about and thought about as if they consist only of their relationships. They are taken as nothing more than relational ciphers whose purpose is to link people with one another. Furthermore, the language of the essential mode is thought to refer primarily to males. This is so much the case that if a woman does happen to develop an identity in the essential mode, the terms used to refer to her essential identity are usually modified in some way to point out her femaleness. In *her own right,* a woman is and has nothing, for her total existence is bound up in being *for* someone rather than in *being* someone.

Although examples of this way of talking about women could be multiplied endlessly, two will suffice. Erich Neumann's book *The Great Mother* (Bollingen, 1963) is one of the most ambitious attempts to date to pull together, interpret, and analyze symbols, myths, and artistic representations of women from a wide variety of times and places. He concludes that the central symbolism of the feminine is that of the vessel. He contends that this is the basic and primordial image of womanhood because it accurately and powerfully portrays what it means to be female—to take substances into one's self, transform them, and send them out again. The purpose and meaning of a vessel, of course, is to contain something. It would not exist otherwise. Appropriately, a vessel is hollow; it contains no core, no center. Not only does it exist for the sake of something else—the primary characteristic of the relational mode—but it lacks the primary characteristic of the essential mode having a central reality. Neumann's theory is not untypical of a great deal of speculation about, and investigation into, the role and position of women.

Within the Jewish realm one can see this same tendency to think of women as purely relational beings in popular interpretations of the role of women in Biblical literature. The great Biblical female heroes are most often interpreted as mothers, not as people, not as Jews, not as participants in the revelatory narrative of Israel's history. Their characters are not explored. In fact, they are hardly treated as individuals, and their own independent role in the Biblical narrative is ignored. They are all lumped together into the category "mother" and viewed basically as links between the various male Biblical heroes. An exegesis that was not based on the presupposition that women exist only in the relational mode would reveal another dimension of the Bible's female heroes.

Once we understand that most woman-language is relational and that almost none is in the essential mode, we can solve a problem that keeps cropping up in the debates about the role of women in Judaism. It is often asserted that women have a high position in Jewish culture and that such an assessment is strengthened when one compares the role of women in Judaism to their role in other religions and cultures. Both the relative protection of women's rights in Jewish law and the glorification of women in segments of Jewish lore and literature are cited. That all these things are true does not change the fact that women are lauded and glorified as relational beings only. They are praised for being kindly and efficient in relation with other human beings, but are not encouraged or expected to have an identity apart from those relationships. This is the sum and substance of the idea that women have a high position in Judaism.

It should be noted in passing, that the language used to talk about men's lives contains a much more even balance between the relational mode and the essential mode. No one would ever think of defining a man's identity primarily or exclusively as husband and father, as a father in Israel, but neither are men cut off from the relational mode of being. For example, in discussions of male heroes in the Bible, there is usually emphasis both on their family positions as fathers and on their contributions to the overall Biblical narrative.

They emerge *with faces,* as characters and individuals. They are not merely relational ciphers.

The third proposition in the analysis is the assertion that for maximum realization of human potential both the relational and the essential mode must be available to everyone. To create a life style or a religion that makes it difficult or impossible for significant elements within the community to realize both modes of existence is to create frustrated, destructive people, one might even say half-human people. Either mode by itself simply is not enough to sustain meaningful life over a full lifetime. Neither of the two modes is ultimately more valuable or worthwhile than the other, but either one by itself becomes meaningless. Put more simply, having a chance to be a "mother in Israel" is simply not enough. Having a chance to be a scholar—a rabbi or teacher —and a saint is also necessary and essential.

The analysis thus far, though applicable to the Jewish situation, has been on a general level. The fourth and fifth propositions deal specifically with Jewish practice in light of the assertions already made. The fourth proposition recapitulates in Jewish terms the first and second propositions, and the fifth proposition specifies the third for the Jewish situation.

The fourth proposition is that in the practice of Judaism, only the relational mode is fully available to women and the essential mode is totally unavailable. This assertion is based on complex analytic interpretations of the Jewish materials. There are two interpenetrating elements in this interpretation. One of them is the definition of Judaism as a *ritual covenant community* in which women have only an auxiliary role. The other is the statement that Judaism, as a ritual covenant community, is maintained and expressed through two institutions, the home and the synagogue, one in the relational and the other in the essential mode, one available to women in a tangential way, and the other not available at all. Let us analyze these statements one by one.

First, it is necessary to know precisely what is meant by *Judaism,* for the label can cover a multitude of possibilities. Though a Jewish identity can develop for many different reasons, the primary definition of Jewishness must remain that of membership in the ritual covenant community of Israel. None of the other Jewish identities would exist were it not for the possibility of Jewishness, *per se,* and that possibility began with the ritual covenant community and continues to make sense only in that context. If Judaism is not to survive as a ritual covenant community, then there seems little meaning left in the label or the identity, and if to be Jewish is not to be a member of that ritual covenant community, then there is little reason to be Jewish. Furthermore, the definition *ritual covenant community* is carefully constructed to express the central realities of Judaism. *Community* indicates primacy of obligation and interrelations between all Jews, but *covenant* indicates that, however it may be conceived, that community does not exist for merely human, natural, or historical reasons. *Ritual* indicates that the primary means of demonstrating that we are a *covenant* community, both to ourselves and to others, is through a myriad of gestures, large and small, that informs our lives with a particular and peculiar style. This, then, is the central meaning of being Jewish, and other aspects of a Jewish identity, such as ethnic or national identity, are secondary and derivative.

The statement that the major institutions of the Jewish community are the home and the synagogue needs little explication. It is also unnecessary to demonstrate that women participate to some extent in the ritual dimensions of the Jewish home but not at all in the worship and study that go on in the synagogue. The correlations between the relational mode and the family institution are somewhat more complex.

If the relational mode involves focusing on interdependence, on what happens *between* oneself and another, then the correlation between that mode and the home-family institution in Judaism is not hard to make. In fact, family relationships can serve as a primary model for the relational mode, since they logically imply the existence of others and are primarily concerned with obligations and expectations *between* people. It is important to realize one of the implications of this correlation, for it means that however great the values and virtues of the Jewish home may be, existence in the essential mode is not available in that institution. Within the Jewish family, as in the relational mode itself, there are no identities to be found which point toward, and focus on, one's own core and central reality, irrespective of one's surrounding network of ties. This is important because we need to know precisely the possibilities of the Jewish home for developing a meaningful Jewish identity. For while all cf those who talk about the meaningfulness of the Jewish home are certainly right, and we should not underestimate its possibilities, we should also know its limits and not over-estimate its potential for meaning. *By itself, it does not provide a full Jewish identity or an adequate method of expressing one's Jewishness.* We should also realize that, just as there is a much better balance of the relational and essential modes in language about men than about women, so in Jewish practice, the home, unlike the synagogue, is available to both sexes. *Only* the home institution of Judaism is available to the women, but it is not available *only* to them.

In Judaism, the essential mode is primarily experienced through the synagogue. However, one must understand that the term *synagogue* does not denote the distant and meaningless institution that the organized congregation has often become today. Instead, I have in mind that institution in and through which prayer and study take place in a profoundly meaningful way. It is necessary to understand how these activities are the Jewish expression of the essential mode. Despite the profoundly communal, and hence relational, style of prayer and study that characterize Jewish ritual practice, the stress is on who or what *one* is, even if one is in the midst of community. Though in practice Jewish study and prayer are often communal, they are not logically so, as is the case regarding the relational nature of the Jewish family. Furthermore, the stress in prayer and study is on the improvement and perfection of *one's self* in the community of Israel. One wants to understand better the resources of the Jewish tradition, and one wants to engage in truly meaningful prayer activity. In study and in prayer, one looks to one's core and central reality, to who and what one is in the face of the ultimate, and that is activity in the essential mode. However, unlike the family institution which is available to both sexes, the synagogue is really available only to men. There is no need to document this statement, for although women are sometimes permitted to pray and study, they are not encouraged to do so, and they are not defined, by themselves or by men, as people who pray and study. They are defined primarily as wives and mothers, and any invasion into the realms of prayer and study is tokenism—even in liberal Judaism.

There remains the question of the degree to which each of the major Jewish institutions—the home and the synagogue —fosters participation in the Jewish ritual covenant community. Since those aspects of Jewish life and practice that make it a ritual covenant community are the crucial aspects of Judaism, this is an important question. There can be no doubt that both institutions are integral to the functioning of the ritual covenant community, and that central ritual expressions of the covenanted nature of the Jewish community occur in each institution.

However, the major expressions of the ritual covenant community involve the life and prayer and study, which stems from and centers in the synagogue-school. It is true that study and prayer do not constitute the totality of Jewish religious practice, but on the other hand no one would make a case that genuine full participation in the covenant is possible without them. It is also true that the life of prayer and study can be carried on without a synagogue and school, but one rarely finds the original commitment or the life-long practice of that life style without encouragement from and participation in the synagogue-school. Thus, not only is the synagogue-school the major Jewish expression of the essential mode but also a crucial vehicle for participation in the ritual covenant community. This makes the exclusion of women from this institution exceedingly serious and problematic, given the centrality of membership in the ritual covenant community to the Jewish identity.

Furthermore, when one looks closely at those elements of the ritual covenant community that do occur in the home, one discovers that most of them are primarily available to men. In the ritual meals this is clearly the case. While candle lighting gives women some involvement in the ritual covenant community in their own right, from then on the rest (and major portion) of the ritual is conducted by males. The ritual meals give women their clearest and most direct entry into the ritual covenant community. The other major expressions of the ritual covenant community occurring in the home (handling of food and conduct of family relationships) are really the responsibility of the men, who need the cooperation of women to fulfill their ritual obligations in the covenant community.[1] Thus, even their activities within the family, which are women's major resources for Jewish identity and meaning, give women only a marginal participation in the ritual covenant community. Even here, women are basically adjuncts to the men's participation in the ritual covenant community, not participants in their own right.

This, then, is the overall situation pointed to in the fourth proposition, the proposition that in the practice of Judaism the relational mode is available to women but not the essential mode. This is true simply on grounds that the synagogue-school, the major vehicle to the essential mode of being in Jewish culture, is closed to women. It is doubly true when one realizes that although the central realities of Judaism are expressed through both the family and the synagogue (rela-

---

[1] See Rachel Adler's perceptive essay, "The Jew Who Wasn't There: Halacha and the Jewish Woman," in *The Jewish Woman: An Anthology,* Summer 1973 issue of *Response: Contemporary Jewish Review.*

tional and essential modes), the covenanted aspects and activities of *both* institutions are primarily available to and applicable to men. Women can have a Jewish identity in the relational mode via the family institution, but not in the essential mode via the synagogue institution. Nor can they really participate in the ritual covenant community of Israel, whether expressions of that participation occur in the synagogue or the home. In that situation, one may well question whether women are Jews in any meaningful sense. *The painful realization that we are Jews only in a technical sense is the simplest way of explaining why Jewish women must be angered and alienated.*

Thus having isolated and analyzed the fundamental cause of the anger and ambivalence experienced by Jewish women in the quest for a meaningful Jewish identity, the fifth proposition delineates the only appropriate response. It is a specification in Jewish terms of the third proposition that one mode is not enough for meaningful human life. For meaningful Jewish life, women must exercise their right to *full* and *genuine* participation in every aspect of the ritual covenant community, especially in the activities of the school and synagogue. Women must be able to live out their Jewishness in the essential mode as well as in the relational mode by being Jews *in their own right, not vicariously and not as links between male Jews.*

Having finished the analysis of anger and its attendant rationale for change, one arrives at the task of explicating what this argument means for Jewish tradition. That task requires a second paper rather than a postscript and can only be outlined here. The basic problem is to show that the changes required in Jewish practice will not destroy the fabric of Judaism and in fact may be necessitated by some of the threads woven into that fabric.

First one might suggest that, instead of being detrimental to the stability of Judaism such changes actually are required if Judaism is to survive. For Judaism, like any other religious symbol system, is a set of constructed meanings growing out of experience and changing with changing experience. Only by incorporating changing experience into itself can it survive. Those that cannot do so either disappear or lose themselves in irrelevancy. Therefore, the fear of change rampant in some quarters is probably more dangerous to Judaism than any required changes in ritual.

Furthermore, incorporating the required changes into its fabric is really nothing new in Judaism. Despite the myth of Judaism as a finished product, the history of Judaism reveals a continual and continuing evolution of values, norms, and practices, some of which involved much more total change than anything required at present. Another fear, related to the fear of change, is the fear that if some groups adopt the proposed changes into their practice, there will be further fragmentation in the Jewish community. Implicit in this argument is the notion that fragmentation is undesirable and recent. However, the myth of Judaism as a monolith seems about as accurate as the myth of Judaism as a finished product. As there has always been change in Judaism, so there have always been various ways of being Jewish.

These two myths can powerfully inhibit the utilization of the total Jewish tradition as a resource in the current situation. Those who propose changes in Jewish practice to incorporate women fully into the ritual covenant community are made to feel, on the basis of these two myths, that they are engaged in dangerous unprecedented changes. However, that is an interpretation of Jewish history, not Jewish history itself. There are other, at least equally valid, interpretations of Jewish history as a continual incorporation of changing experience which always includes radically different Judaisms. Following that interpretation of Jewish history, those who advocate the full participation of women in the Jewish ritual covenant community are fully in the mainstream of developing Jewish history rather than in some deviant position. Not only is this a more pleasant place to be; it is where we are.

Following this method of interpreting Jewish history, one can understand past utilization of gender rather than more relevant criteria for distributing membership in the ritual covenant community of Israel as a problem in the evolution of Jewish thought and practice. We can explicate the reasons why it was done and also recognize that in the continual and continuing evolution of the Jewish tradition it must be surpassed, since we now know that sex is an irrelevant and inhuman criterion for distributing membership in the ritual covenant community of Israel.

We also contend that in a fundamental sense, not only Jewish history but Jewish values serve as a resource for justifying and requiring the proposed changes. The strongest argument against the participation of women in the ritual covenant community is that some of the required changes violate current legal rulings. Implicit in this argument is the notion that the Jewish law is the sum total of Judaism, which seems to me an ill-chosen and ill-fated definition of Judaism. There are other elements of Judaism that may well conflict with Jewish legal structure but are richer, more meaningful and *more normative.*

For instance, if one thinks about the central reality of Judaism as a search for a certain quality of relationship between human beings and God, then sex is a totally irrelevant basis for determining entry into the ritual covenant community that specifies such a relationship. One's sex has nothing to do with whether or not one has an intense experience of the meaningfulness of the Jewish vision-quest, or a compelling desire to express that meaningfulness through participation in the ritual covenant community, or an overwhelming curiosity about the Jewish religious heritage. All of these are much more relevant bases for determining who should fulfill roles and perform rituals than an accident of anatomy. One can interpret Judaism as being more *primordially* concerned with the quality of the relationship between human beings and God than with the legal rulings that attempt imperfectly to guide, structure and specify that relationship. A ruling that constricts that relationship for some Jews conflicts with deeper values of Judaism. The more normative nature of those deeper values must be taken seriously by all Jews, for any legal system is in deep trouble when the values that it seeks to foster are undercut by specific legal rulings. In that situation the legal rulings, not the values, must change.

In sum, those of us who are frustrated by the orthodox interpretations of Jewish history and by the strictures of Jewish law should reclaim the totality of the Jewish heritage and utilize its resources in forging a meaningful Jewish identity—rather than let ourselves be defined out of "normative Judaism." For normative Judaism is an opaque resource rather than an unambiguous given. It is important always to remember that there are good Jewish reasons for women to do and demand what they are now doing and demanding. The demand for change, for inclusion and participation in our own right in the ritual covenant community of Israel arises out of strong experience of the meaningfulness of the Jewish vision-quest. That we experience that meaning in spite of systematic exclusion from the central realities of the ritual covenant community indicates something of its power and attractiveness. So does the assertion that, if I am to be Jewish, then I will be a fully participating member of the ritual covenant community. For I can see no other reason to be Jewish. Therefore, either I will be a fully participating member of the ritual covenant community or . . .

Alternative Jewish Communities: An Overview

David M. Szonyi

Havurot

In the past decade, "alternative Jewish communities" have added a new dimension to Jewish life outside of synagogues and Jewish community centers. The core of these communities are *havurot,* relatively small (usually 10-35 people) circles of friends who are striving for an authentic and integrated Jewish lifestyle, one which is responsive both to the Tradition and to modernity. Meaning? That's not clear—the *havurah* (singular) movement is still fairly new, evolving and, within certain limits, eclectic. This essay will offer only an overview of the movement, its origins and some of its institutions and experiments.[1]

The basic commitment of *havurah* members is to Jewish learning, personal inter-action and religious living via both ritual and social action. How much emphasis should be given to each of these is an ongoing point of discussion and debate within each *havurah*—and one which is never resolved.

Most *havurot* members are college graduates in their 20's, 30's and 40's. (An increasing number of synagogues in the Reform, Conservative and Reconstructionist movements have formed *havurot.* For the purpose of this essay, however, I'll be referring to non-synagogue *havurot.*) In contrast to a synagogue population, a significant percentage of the members tend to be single. Religiously, members are what has been called "traditional non-Orthodox". While violating some areas of *halacha* (traditional Jewish law), they often observe such laws as *kashrut* (Jewish dietary laws) and are (more or less) *shomer Shabbat* (observing the prescriptions against such Sabbath activities as riding and spending money). And while religiously observant in varying degrees, most *havurah* members share a keen interest in and openess to the Jewish religious tradition. (Were they asked whether they observe certain of the more strenuous *mitzvoth*—religious commandments—many would answer with the great German-Jewish philosopher Franz Rosenzweig, "not yet.")

In terms of Jewish background, *havurah* members are a diverse lot. Some are lapsed Orthodox Jews educated in *yeshivot* (Jewish schools focusing on the study of Talmud, Torah and the commentaries thereon) or Jewish day schools. Others have good Jewish backgrounds having spent one or more summers in such Jewish camps as Ramah (a series of camps sponsored by the Conservative movement) or the Brandeis Camp Institute in California, or having lived for a year or more in Israel. Not a few, however, come from relatively assimilationist backrounds, having only recently "discovered" their Jewishness. (But then even Rabbi Akiva didn't become literate in Hebrew and learn the rudiments of Torah until age 40.) And as there are "lapsed Orthodox" Jews in the movement, so are there more than one *ba'al teshuvah* (formerly non-observant Jews who have recently taken on the "yolk" of Halacha), as well as converts from other religions.

What Havurot Do

The average *havurah* meets once a week, either on *Shabbat* (the Sabbath) or on a regular weekday meeting night. Activities include prayer, the study and discussion of the *parshah* (weekly Torah portion), discussion of some classical text or work of modern Jewish literature, often in relation to some theme or contemporary issue, as well as discussions on political, social and inter-personal questions and purely festive and social get-togethers. Usually any, if not all, of these activities include, and sometimes are centered around, that great Jewish pasttime—food.

Both in order to "get away from the city" and for their members to get to know each other better, most *havurot* go on a retreat anywhere from two or three times a year to (in the case of the New York *Havurah*) once a month. As well, since 1974, *havurot* on the East Coast have gone on a joint retreat three times a year at Weiss' Farm, New Jersey. (Weiss' Farm is not really a farm, but a large house which until recently doubled as a kind of hostel/hotel for numerous Jewish groups.) Often, these retreats coincide with the *Hagim* (Jewish holidays). In my *havurah,* Derech Reut (the "way of fellowship") in New York, a particularly important, intense and exhilirating retreat takes place over *Shavuous,* when the group participates in the traditional *tikkun,* an all-night study session in "preparation" for "receiving" the Torah. Traditionally, the *tikkun* consists almost entirely of Torah and Talmud study but ours features classical texts, a study of and discussion of some themes in the Book of Ruth (customarily read on *Shavuous*) and possibly a short story by Schmuel Yosef Agnon or I.B. Singer.

Like most synagogues, most *havurot* have classes for their members, some in the same areas a rabbinical seminary might offer: courses on Hebrew language and literature, classic texts, etc. (For that matter, the first two *havurot*—Havurat Shalom in Somerville, Massachusetts and the New York Havurah—started out in part as alternative rabbinical seminaries.) A *havurah* might also offer a course in "The Jewish Radical Tradition" as well as in such practical skills as *laining* (chanting the *parshah* using the centuries-old cantillation).

Havurah-Style Davaning

The *havurah* movement has developed a style of *davaning* (prayer) which combines elements of hassidism (with its emphasis on joy, spontaneity and community), the Conservative tradition, and the cultural ambiance of the 1960's and 70's.

In many ways, a typical *havurah*-style Sabbath morning service resembles its Conservative counterpart. It is mostly in Hebrew, is quite long (2-3 hours) and has a fairly set order centered around the Torah reading. However, services in most *havurot* and *minyanim* (prayer communities) include a number of significant differences from Conservative (as well as Orthodox and Reform) services:

—*The lack of a rabbi:* Because *havurah*-style *davaning* encourages participation by as many people as possible, and because many people are willing and capable of leading services, services are led by a rotating *Sheliach* (or *Shlehah* in the feminine) *Zibbur,* literally a "messenger of the community."

—*Full equality of women with men:* For the past few years, the Reform and Reconstructionist movements in Judaism have ordained women rabbis and the Conservative movement has left it up to individual congregations to decide whether women should be counted in the *minyan* (quorum of ten necessary for communal prayer). More than any of the four denominations within Judaism, however, *havurah*-style *davaning* involves full ritual equality between men and women. Women read from the Torah and receive *aliyot* (the honors of being called up to say blessings before and after a section of the weekly *parshah* is read) as regularly as men do. The reason has to do both with the movement's interpretation of *Halachah,* which has unquestionably been influenced by the feminist movement, and by the practical consideration that successful *davaning* depends on whatever spiritual leaders—male or female—are willing and able to serve the community.

—*Seating and Demeanor:* In *havurah*-style *davaning,* the congregation generally sits in a square or circle as opposed to the rows of most synagogues. This reversion to the pre-Emancipation synagogue structure, where the rabbi and the cantor were on the same level as and in the middle of the congregation, has the effect of making of the congregation more of a community, "in touch with" and responsive to itself.

As well, dress is informal, in part also to encourage a sense of community, in part because the Jewish, like the general, "counter-culture" is prone to informality and the celebration of diversity.

Taking its cue from the *shtiebel* (small Orthodox neighborhood synagogue) or the Hassidic *Fabrengen* (gathering for prayer, celebration and to hear an address by the *rebbe*), *havurah*-style *davaning* puts greater emphasis on group and individual expression, exuberance, and concentrated intention (all of which are implied by the Hebrew word *kavannah*) than on the ordered decorum found in most Conservative and Reform synagogues.

—*Torah Discussion:* While only part of each Shabbat's *parshah* (Torah portion) is *lained* (chanted), it is discussed at length. (In most *havurot* and *minyanim* with a discussion leader; in a few, such as the Fabrengen in Washington D.C., without.) The discussion attempts to develop some theme or explore some problem in the *parshah,* to make of Torah a teaching which reverberates into our lives and experience.

Why the Havurah Movement

The *havurah* movement has come into being for a wide variety of reasons, an adequate analysis of which would comprise a lengthy essay in itself. At the very least, it represents a response to at least three major factors:

(1) the fact that large numbers of Jewish adults go through extended periods of singlehood or marriage without children in communities apart from those of their families. For many of their members, then, the *havurah* serves as their Jewish family;

(2) a dissatisfaction with most traditional synagogues, which *havurah* members tend to see as too large and imper-

sonal, too rabbi- and cantor-centered with, concomitantly, too passive congregations and, finally, providing an inadequate ritual role for women;

(3) perhaps most importantly, the political, cultural and psychological climate of the 1960's, particularly the decade's emphasis on community and ethnicity. As Alan Mintz has written, the *havurah* is an attempt to overcome the atomization of modern urban life, in which Jewishness is less *lived* in an integrated way than is one shard of a fragmented whole:

> . . . the young Jew today . . . cannot expect to exist in a milieu in which his full person can be actualized and exposed, but must accept the realities of fragmentation and compartmentalization. He chooses one group for his political involvement, another for his intellectual growth, another for his religious practice, still another for his spiritual search, and so on . . . To each group, he presents an encapsulated aspect of himself to be shared; nowhere must he expect fully to reveal himself.

> The emerging concept of decentralized fellowship seeks not to avoid the tension of living in secular society but rather to create a milieu in which Jews can grapple together with a shared appreciation of struggle, a base from which to look outward on the world. That is, a setting where personal relations can be formed, based on the full knowledge of the full person, where being rather than performance is encouraged. Here, hopefully, the sparks of self-integration and group trust might begin to be regathered.[2]

Problems and Successes

The *havurah* movement is now a decade old (Havurat Shalom was founded in 1967), but whether it will have a lasting impact on American Jewish life remains to be seen.

Perhaps the movement's major problem in its efforts to

forge communities is the hyper-mobility of its members. Most *havurot* have a high "turnover": over one-half of the members of the *havurah* to which I belong were not members of the group when I joined two and a half years ago; many of the members at that time have moved and some have left the *havurah* because of personal reasons.

Havurot also continually face the "creative tension" of setting priorities. While members share an intense commitment to Jewish community, some put more emphasis on the "Jewish" (prayer, study, Sabbath and holiday activity), some on the "community" (discussion, social activity) half.

Finally, a number of the movement's own members have criticized it for being too insular in terms of interaction with local synagogues and other facets of the "established" Jewish community. With varying degrees of legitimacy, *havurot* have also been criticized for being too Diaspora-oriented and, in general, apolitical.

Unquestionably, the *havurah* movement has many flaws, for it is still quite small and new. (Perhaps a 1000 American Jews belong to non-synagogue *havurot, batim*—Jewish houses or communes— and American-style *kibbutzim.*) Yet the successes outnumber these flaws. For one thing, a *havurah,* in providing a satisfying and friendly setting for Jewish communal living, has undoubtedly made its members far more "Jewishly active" than they would be without it. Further, the movement has produced or contributed to a number of institutions, projects and experiments which have already had an impact in revitalizing American-Jewish life.

The Heder

In the past three years, two *havurot*—the Fabrengen and the New York Havurah—have each developed a *heder,* a small, alternative Jewish school, usually meeting one or two afternoons a week. The *heder* attempts to make Jewish learning more enjoyable and creative than is the case in many Sunday and Hebrew schools.

The *hederim* are open not only to children of havurah members, but to children of parents living in the havurah's neighborhood. As opposed to most Hebrew and Sunday schools, *heder* teachers and parents meet regularly, so that parents, in contributing to the development of a curriculum, are continually involved in their children's education.

Heder and other *havurah* members helped initiate and lead the Conference on Alternatives in Jewish Education, the first nation-wide meeting of Jewish educators (held at Brown University in August-September, 1976) since World War II.

Tzedakah Collectives

In the past two years, groups of individuals both within and without *havurot* have formed *tzedakah* collectives. (*Tzedakah*, a word usually translated as "charity," means "righteousness." In the Jewish tradition, aiding the disadvantaged is an obligation, without any of the condescension that "charity" frequently implies.) These collectives exist both to encourage the giving of *tzedakah*—most require that their members commit a minimum percentage of their incomes to the collective—and to learn about and investigate the effectiveness of possible beneficiaries. Many *tzedakah* collectives give a significant portion of their funds to small institutions not normally covered by the large American Jewish philanthropic organizations such as the United Jewish Appeal.

Unlike UJA donors, *tzedakah* collective members decide how their money is allocated. Further, by measuring contributions to the collective as a percentage of income, rather than in absolute numerical terms, the collectives avoid plutocratic control by one or several members.

Projects for the Elderly

In a number of cities, young Jews have developed projects for the Jewish elderly, especially the indigent among them. The oldest and best known of these is "Project Ezra," a volunteer home visitation project on a one-to-one basis in the Lower East Side of New York. (Once the home to a thriving Jewish community of 500,000, the Lower East Side now has only 50,000 Jews, the majority elderly and indigent.) Project Ezra also helps clean and renovate old and neglected synagogues and sponsors outings and other special events for senior citizens, for whom it also provides a medical outreach service.

Dorot ("Generations") offers a similar service on Manhattan's Upper West Side. Its monthly Sunday afternoon "Havurah Neighbors Project" is a get-together of elderly and young Jews—to see and discuss a film, celebrate a holiday, hear a speaker or simply to socialize and bring the "generations" closer together. *Dorot* also sponsors *Succot* and Passover food projects, bringing food packages provided by suburban synagogues as gifts to the indigent, homebound Jewish elderly.

In Chevy Chase, Maryland, the Kosher Kitchen, a kosher restaurant initiated and run collectively by young Jews, operates a "kosher meals-on-wheels" program for the homebound Jewish elderly in the Washington D.C. area.

Women's Groups and Rituals

The influence of modern feminism on the *havurah* movement led to the formation of *Ezrat Nashim* (named after the women's section of the Temple) in 1971. Ezrat Nashim is a group which attempts to study *halachahic* questions and other areas of Jewish life affecting traditional (but non-Orthodox) Jewish women, and also attempts to influence rabbinical organizations such as the Rabbinical Assembly to reconsider sexist elements of the Tradition in light of the position of modern Jewish women.[3]

In New York and at Brown University in Providence, among other places, women's *minyanim* have been formed. Jewish feminists have also started a new quarterly periodical, *Lilith.*

A number of *havurah*-oriented Jews, including Daniel and Myra Leifer in Chicago and Michael and Sharon Strassfeld in New York, have developed a new *Brit Milah,* a ceremony welcoming the Jewish baby girl to the community. (At present, there is no ritual for the Jewish baby girl which corresponds to the elaborate celebration that occurs at the time of the *Brit,* or circumcision, for the baby boy.) Other Jewish feminists have developed special services and rituals for *Rosh Hodesh,* the first day of a new Hebrew month.

Periodicals and Publications

Members of *havurot,* Jewish artists and others have contributed to *The Jewish Catalog* (edited by Richard Siegel, Michael Strassfeld and Sharon Strassfeld, Jewish Publication Society, 1973) and *The Second Jewish Catalog* (edited by Michael and Sharon Strassfeld, JPS, 1976). They also contribute to two excellent quarterly periodicals: *Response* and *Davka,* published in New York and Los Angeles, respectively. Two special issues of *Response,* which has appeared since 1967, have been published as books: *Living After the Holocaust: Reflections by the Post-War Generation in America* (edited by Lucy Y. Seinitz and David M. Szonyi, Bloch, 1976) and *The Jewish Woman: New Perspectives* (edited by Elizabeth Koltun, Schocken, 1977).

The best, although slightly outdated, book on "the new Jews" is an anthology with that title (edited by James A. Sleeper and Alan L. Mintz, Vintage, 1971). Several members of the *havurah* community have also contributed to the anthology *Jewish Radicalism* (edited by Peter Dreier and Jack Nusan Porter, Grove, 1972).

Finally, members of East Coast *havurot* publish—if sporadically—a newsletter called *Kesher,* which focuses on themes discussed at Weiss' Farm retreats and on questions on "new *Halacha*" in general.

Learning By Experiencing

There is no way to generalize or come to an "objective conclusion" about the *havurah* movement. One should experience a *havurah* or *minyan* him- or herself. Many *havurah* activities—and almost all *havurah* and *minyan* services and observances—are open to members of the community.[4] Only by experiencing a *havurah* or *minyan* service or activity can one really get a feel for the movement's special *ruach* (spirit) and learn whether this dimension of what has been called "the Jewish renaissance" in America (which also includes growing interest in Jewish studies on the college campus and the growth of Jewish day schools) meets one's spiritual and communal needs.

Footnotes

1. For more on the movement, see some of the books and periodicals listed at the end of this essay.

2. Alan L. Mintz, "Along the Path to Religious Community" in James A. Sleeper and Alan L. Mintz, *The New Jews* (New York: Vintage, 1971), p. 27.

3. On Ezrat Nashim, see Alan Silverstein, "The Evolution of Ezrat Nashim," *Conservative Judaism,* Fall, 1975, pp. 41-51.

4. Some *havurot, minyanim* and related groups are listed in "Guide to Jewish Student Groups," published by the North American Jewish Students Network, 15 E. 26th St., New York, 10010.

About the Authors

Jerry V. Diller is Assistant Professor of Psychology at Wilson College, Chambersburg, Pennsylvania. He received his Ph.D. from the University of Colorado in social psychology where he specialized in race relations and small group dynamics. He has also taught at Thomas Jefferson College and the University of Colorado. He is a trained group facilitator and counselor, a psychological consultant and has written in the areas of innovative education, humanistic psychology, personality theory and race relations and minority psychology.

Dov Peretz Elkins is a rabbi, educator, human relations consultant and counselor. Dr. Elkins served in several major pulpits before becoming Director of Growth Associates, a human relations consulting and publishing firm based in Rochester, New York. In this position he does lectures, workshops and training events for various Jewish agencies. He has written fifteen books including: *Glad To Be Me: Building Self-Esteem in Yourself and Others* and *Teaching People to Love Themselves,* as well as those mentioned in his article.

Maurice Friedman, Ph.D. is professor of Religious Studies, Philosophy, and Comparative Literature at San Diego State University. He is the author of *Martin Buber: The Life of Dialogue; Problematic Rebel: Melville, Dostoevsky, Kafka, Camus; The Worlds of Existentialism: A Critical Reader; To Deny Our Nothingness: Contemporary Images of Man; Touchstones of Reality: Existential Trust and the Community of Peace; The Hidden Human Image;* and *Encounter on the Narrow Ridge: Milestones in the Life of Martin Buber,* to be published by E. P. Dutton in the Spring of 1978.

Erich Fromm is a psychoanalyst, social philosopher and author. A founder of the William Alonson White Institute of Psychiatry, Psychoanalysis and Psychology, he has also taught at Yale, New York University, Bennington College, Michigan State University and the National Autonomous University. He is the author of *The Art of Loving, Escape From Freedom, The Sane Society, Man For Him-*

self, *The Forgotten Language, You Shall Be As Gods, The Crises of Psychoanalysis* and *The Anatomy of Human Destructiveness.*

Audrey Gordon is an author, psychotherapist and lecturer. She is a member of the faculty of Oakton Community College, Morton Grove, Illinois, and former High School Director at Beth Emet Synagogue, Evanston, Illinois. She served as Chaplain at Billings Hospital in Chicago where she assisted Dr. Elisabeth Kubler-Ross in "The Death and Dying Seminar." She also teaches courses and gives workshops on "Death & Dying" in the Chicago area.

Irving Greenberg is former Chairman and Professor in the Department of Jewish Studies, City College, City University of New York and Director of the National Jewish Conference Center. He is an ordained rabbi, holds a Ph.D. from Harvard University and has taught at Brandeis University, Yeshiva University and Tel Aviv University. He has written extensively on various issues in Judaica, is an editor of two journals and is involved in many national Jewish community and academic organizations.

Rita M. Gross is Assistant Professor of Religious Studies at the University of Wisconsin in Eau Claire, where she teaches courses in Asian religions and women and religion. She received a Ph.D. in history of religions from the University of Chicago. She has published numerous essays, articles, and book reviews and is the editor of a book on women and religion to be published by Scholars Press. She has also traveled in India and lectures widely on the relevance of Indian concepts of female deities for the current revisions of patriarchal religion that are occurring in Judaism and Christianity.

Abraham J. Heschel, a descendent of several famous Hasidic rebbes, was a scholar and theologian. He is recognized as one of the most influential modern philosophers of religion in the United States. After coming to America, he taught at both the Hebrew Union College in Cincinnati and the Jewish Theological Seminary of America. His writings include: *Man Is Not Alone, God in Search of Man, Man's Quest for God, The Sabbath, The Prophets, Who Is Man?* and *Israel: An Echo of Eternity.*

Philip David Mandelkorn is a graduate of the Wharton School of Finance, University of Pennsylvania. He has served as a *Time* Magazine Correspondent and U.S. Navy Underwater Demolition Team

Platoon Commander. He studied under Rabbis Max Ticktin and Zalman Schachter. Currently, he is a freelance writer and yoga instructor and disciple of Swami Satchidananda, whose teachings he has edited for publication by Doubleday-Anchor Books.

Jerome R. Mintz is Professor of Anthropology at Indiana University, Bloomington, Indiana. He has done extensive research on the Brooklyn hasidic community. His publications include: *Legends of the Hasidim: An Introduction to Hasidic Culture and Oral Tradition in the New World* (University of Chicago Press, 1968; paperback edition, 1974) and *In Praise of the Baal Shem Tov: The Earliest Collection of Legends about the Founder of Hasidism,* with Dan Ben-Amos (Indiana University Press, 1970; paperback edition, 1972). His *Legends of the Hasidim* has been termed "the finest single source on American hasidism . . . " Professor Mintz received his BA and MA from Brooklyn College and his Ph.D. from Indiana University.

Richard L. Rubenstein is a Professor of Religion at Florida State University and Director of its Center for the Study of Southern Culture and Religion. He is the author of *The Cunning of History, Power Struggle, My Brother Paul, Morality and Eros, The Religious Imagination* and *After Auschwitz.* He spent the past year as a National Humanities Institute Fellow at Yale University. Recently, he was designated Distinguished Professor at Florida State University and was also named Winner of the "Portico d'Ottavia" literary prize for "the best book published in Italy in the past two years expressing the Hebraic spirit."

Zalman M. Schachter is an academic, Hasidic teacher and highly sought-after lecturer. Formerly a Professor of Religion and Head of the Department of Near Eastern and Judaic Studies at the University of Manitoba, he is now a Professor of Religion at Temple University where he teaches Jewish mysticism and psychology and religion. He is an ordained Lubavitch rabbi and holds a masters in the psychology of religion from Boston University and a doctorate from Hebrew Union College. He has written numerous scholarly theological papers, *The First Step* and most recently *Fragments of a Future Scroll: Hassidism for the Aquarian Age* (Germantown, Pennsylvania: Leaves of Grass Press, 1975).

David M. Szonyi is a doctoral candidate in modern Jewish and modern European history at Stanford University. He is with Lucy Y. Steinitz the co-editor of *Living After the Holocaust: Reflections of the Post-War Generation in America* and has written articles and reviews for *Sh'ma, Conservative Judaism, The Jewish Spector, Response* and *InterChange.* He is a member of havurah Derech Reut in New York, the West Side Minyan, the Domestic Affairs Committee of the Synagogue Council of America, the Executive Board of Breira and a former Director of Dorot.

Arthur I. Waskow is a Colleague in the Public Research Center, an independent research center in Washington, D.C. He is a member of the Executive Committee of Breira and also a member of Fabrengen, an alternative religous community and congregation in Washington. He received a Ph.D. in American history from the University of Wisconsin and is author of *The Freedom Seder,* "The Shalom Seder" (*Response,* Spring, 1977) and *The Bush Is Burning!* He is close to completing a new book *God Wrestling* to be published by Schocken Books.

Index